BRITANNIA'S DAUGHTERS

Women of the British Empire

JOANNA TROLLOPE

PIMLICO

For Gill

★

Published by Pimlico 2006

8 10 9 7

First published in Great Britain in 1983 by Hutchinson

First Pimlico edition 1994

Second Pimlico edition 2006

Pimlico
Random House, 20 Vauxhall Bridge Road,
London SW1V 2SA

www.randomhouse.co.uk

Addresses for companies within The Random House Group Limited
can be found at: www.randomhouse.co.uk

Random House UK Limited Reg. No. 954009

A CIP catalogue record for this book
is available from the British Library

ISBN 1845950186
ISBN 9781845950187 (from Jan 2007)

The Random House Group Limited supports the FSC Forest Stewardship
Council® certified paper. Our books carrying the FSC are printed on FSC certified paper.
FSC is the only forest certification scheme supported by the leading
environmental organisations, including Greenpeace. Our
environment

Printed and bound in the UK by CPI

INTRODUCTION TO THE PIMLICO EDITION

It astonishes me to realise it, but I wrote *Britannia's Daughters* almost twenty-five years ago. It was in the early nineteen eighties, I had just finished a historical novel set in nineteenth-century Burma called *A City of Gems*, and remember feeling impelled by a vague but powerful sense that if I was going to become a proper writer, I had to write something *serious*: i.e. non-fiction. I suppose the feeling is akin to that experienced by comedy actresses wondering if they really should try Cleopatra or Lady Macbeth and is liable to affect anyone growing up with England's ambivalent and nervous view of culture.

Anyway, I took my feeling to my then editor at Hutchinson, the wonderful Tony Whittome, and explained it. He listened with his usual sympathetic courtesy and then said gently, 'And on what topic?' I had no idea. I had read English at Oxford so flailed about for a while among biographical notions on little-known poets or early feminists or obscure diarists. All hopeless. Then Tony said, 'What about women and the British Empire?' I stared at him. 'What the British Empire', Tony said patiently, 'offered the women of Victorian England.' And *Britannia's Daughters* was born.

I have become, over the years, a diligent researcher, but always amateur. My sister, Victoria, however, is the real thing, a trained archivist. It was she who pointed me in the direction of the Fawcett Library, and she who did quantities of exhaustive academic research in places, and in a depth, for which I simply would never have had the patience or the application.

Even with her help, however, it was an enormous project. Quite apart from the time spent in the libraries of all the museums of the Commonwealth, there was South Africa House, the Natural History Museum and the Royal Commonwealth Institute, and I almost got to the point of asking for a camp bed in both the Fawcett and the London Libraries, I was spending so much time there. I only emphasise this point – a natural and inevitable point for all serious biographers – because I am *not* a natural non-fiction writer. I'm a novelist.

The subject matter, however, proved irresistible. I had written, among my early historical novels, one set in the Crimean War, called *Leaves from the Valley*, and in the course of researching that, had read an extraordinary paper called 'Cassandra', written by Florence Nightingale long before the hospital at Scutari turned her into an icon. In the paper, she described, with passion, the plight of delicately nurtured but clever Victorian girls imprisoned in the unbearable emptiness of respectable drawing rooms, like dolls waiting for men to come in and wind them up to a brief animation before leaving the room again and abandoning them to a desperate monotony. To be treated like this, Florence Nightingale wrote angrily, breeds agonising frustration and unhappiness and also, she said, darkly and honestly, 'dooms some minds to infantilism'.

Those able, thwarted girls and women became the seedbed of *Britannia's Daughters* because the irony is that the very Empire which seemed to dictate such stultifying repressiveness (as exemplified by the conduct of many memsahibs in India, for example) also offered extraordinary chances for freedom and self-fulfillment. A woman might not be able to qualify as a doctor in England – but she could in India. A woman might feel her life was over, in all senses, in England – but it wasn't in West Africa. Here is Mary Kingsley:

> When my Mother and Father died within six weeks of each other in '92, and my brother went off to the East, I went down to West Africa to die. West Africa amused me and was kind to me and scientifically interesting - and did not want to kill me just then.

Travellers, doctors, nurses, botanists, governesses, prostitutes, actresses, missionaries and pioneers – the British Empire offered these women of England opportunities they could only dream of at home. But, I soon discovered, it could deprive in just the same measure as it could give. The far-flung outposts of its immense influence – New Zealand, Australia, the remote parts of Canada –

never mind 'the high table lands of Central Asia', could also subject women to living and working conditions that are simply horrible to contemplate. For the convicted – the prostitutes and thieves – there were the prison quarters (the daily treadmill) of the transport ships and then the convict workhouses of newly settled Australia. For the free – the governesses, the wives of early pioneers – there was, too often, a life of terrifying isolation and alienness bedevilled by insects the size of saucers and Maori chieftans cheerfully trying to buy one's newborn baby for their own consumption. The stories of fortitude and gallantry and enterprise that emerged left me feeling, as a novelist, that I simply could not, with any credibility, have made them up.

It was the stories, in the end, that dictated the shape of the book. And the stories themselves naturally grouped themselves into three categories: those of working class women, educated middle and upper class women and a few – and, I often felt, peculiarly luckless – aristocrats like Mary Curzon, wife of the Viceroy of India, women who followed husbands who, in their turn, were following Kipling's 'ancient bride' of imperial duty.

And these stories, these categories, were bound together quite naturally by the continuing thread of Florence Nightingale's outburst against the Victorian view of women, a view that women had to be controlled, even confined, for their own good and, even more, for the good of men and society. I wrote the following in 1982. Re-reading it in 2006, I get hot under the collar about it all over again.

It all came back to the same theme that echoes dully and sickeningly, down the long Victorian years: that women, even pure women, are morally weak and that the impure are the invention of the devil. As an anonymous contributor to the *Cornhill Magazine* wrote in 1866: 'Again, it is notorious that a bad man – we mean one whose evil training had led him into crime – is not so vile as a bad woman. If we take a man and a woman guilty of the same offence in the eyes of the law, we shall invariably find that there is more hope of influencing the former than the latter. Equally criminal in one sense, in another sense there is a difference. The man's nature may be said to be hardened, the woman's destroyed.

So, there it was. Women were ripe for degradation, initially because of their appetites but later, and interestingly, because of the uncontrollable nature of their ambitions. How odd, how properly derisive, how delightful, then, that in so many cases, the British Empire proved the unlikely salvation of its feared and homegrown sisterhood.

May 2006

CONTENTS

ACKNOWLEDGEMENTS

I owe a very great deal to my sister, Victoria Moger, whose research for me on this book has been both diligent and imaginative, and also to Gabrielle Allen for great enthusiasm and enterprise in finding the illustrations. I would also like to thank David Doughan of the Fawcett Library for enormous assistance, the librarians in South Africa House, Australia House and New Zealand House, and the staff of the Royal Commonwealth Institute Library and the Botanical Library of the Natural History Museum for their help. And I am as usual indebted to Tony Whittome for his sympathetic and skilful editing.

J.T.

The author and publishers wish to thank the following for permission to reproduce photographs:

Between pages 64 and 65
Albany Museum, Grahamstown, page 4; Australian Consolidated Press, Tyrrell Collection, page 3 (*below*); BBC Hulton Picture Library, pages 1, 3 (*above*) and 16; Glenbow-Alberta Institute, page 12 (*above*); National Army Museum, London, pages 14–15; Dr Geoffrey Orbell and William Main, pages 10 and 11; Paul Popper, pages 8–9; Provincial Archives of Alberta, E. Brown Collection, page 7; Public Archives of Canada, pages 2, 5, 6 and 12 (*below*).

Between pages 128 and 129
Allport Library and Museum of Fine Art, Tasmania, page 16; Bridgeman Art Library, page 9; India Office Library, pages 1, 2–3 and 4 (*below*); Liverpool Public Libraries, page 10; National Army Museum, London, page 4 (*above*); Paul Popper, page 5; Public Records Office of Hong Kong, page 7; Royal Anthropological Institute, page 14; Royal Botanic Gardens, Kew, pages 8 and 12; *The Sunday Times*, page 13; Hilary Thomas, page 15.

Between pages 192 and 193
Albany Museum, Grahamstown, page 9 (*above*); Australian Consolidated Press, Tyrrell Collection, page 9 (*below*); BBC Hulton Picture Library, page 15; Ann Lady Belhaven and Stenton, page 13; Centre of South Asian Studies, Cambridge, pages 11 and 12; Church Missionary Society, pages 1, 3 (*below*), 4, 5 and 6–7; David Holloway, page 14; Kevin MacDonnell, page 8 (*above*); Mander and Mitchenson Theatre Collection, page 16; Paul Popper, page 8 (*below*); Royal Commonwealth Society, pages 2 (*above* and *below*) and 10.

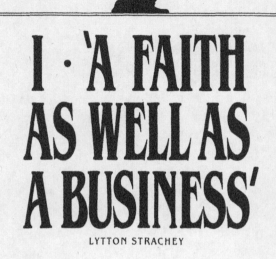

I · 'A FAITH AS WELL AS A BUSINESS'

LYTTON STRACHEY

I

'On Monday I go to Windsor to dine with the Empress of India,' Disraeli wrote to Lady Bradford on 28 December 1876. 'The Faery is so full of the great incident, and feels everything about it so keenly that she sent me a Xmas card and signed her good wishes Victoria Regina et Imperatrix.'

The dinner at Windsor that New Year's Day was worthy of the Imperatrix. While guests dined in a blaze of light – some of it no doubt reflected from the jewels worn by the Queen, given by Indian princes, of which Lord George Hamilton remarked ungallantly that 'they required a big and a dark woman to carry them effectively' – the Queen was declared Kaisar-i-Hind amidst great magnificence on the Plain of Delhi. When Prince Arthur had proposed her health, Disraeli asked her if she was wearing absolutely every one of the jewels that had been sent to her by the Indian princes. 'Oh no,' she replied with touching simplicity, 'If you like I will have the rest brought in after dinner for you to see.' As a crowning yet homely touch to an occasion of marvellous splendour, a procession of servants entered with 'a series of small portmanteaux', which the Queen opened to distribute the jewels of her Indian Empire for the admiration of her guests. Only one of them left a record of being unimpressed. It was 'a mass of oriental jewellery', Lord George Hamilton wrote disparagingly, 'mostly consisting of very large uncut stones and pearls, few of them perfect in shape or without some flaws in colour'.

The Queen's behaviour that night reflected most truly her view of her empire. It was not for her the mighty network of great highways along which British free trade and enterprise might reach the uttermost ends of the earth, but more a marvellous – if sometimes distressingly barbaric – possession which she saw with both a maternal and a romantic eye. Even that view was acquired over the years, for it was not until she had been on the throne for more than twenty years that she began to see the colonies as much more than a useful dustbin for irritating and unsatisfactory people. Even as late as 1872 she was suggesting that 'a post in the colonies' might be found for an official who had been 'rude and tactless'. The royal family network spread so absorbingly over the thrones of Europe that it was the chief topic of interest beyond Windsor and Balmoral and Osborne, but when the princes began to travel to Australia and Canada and South Africa, windows were opened for the Queen upon new worlds.

India, hardly surprisingly, caught fast upon her imagination. She confessed to Lord Derby, in 1858, 'all the romance she had felt since childhood for brown skins'. Travellers came back from India bringing stories of startling customs and the 'superior manners of the Indian lower orders compared with ours', and caskets of jewels as tributes from native princes. She herself even took to giving Kashmiri shawls as wedding presents and in a letter to Lord Northbrook, the Governor General of India, in 1875, regretted '. . . to hear that the trade in those unrivalled shawls is not at present progressing. The Queen will receive with much interest the new one which he mentions.'

News of the Indian Mutiny appalled her and caused her to second most energetically Palmerston's recommendation that more troops would be kept permanently in India.

'We are in a sad anxiety about India,' she wrote to her Uncle Leopold, King of the Belgians, after the massacre at Cawnpore in the summer of 1857, 'which engrosses all our attention. Troops cannot be raised fast or largely enough. And the horrors committed on the poor ladies – women and children – are unknown in these ages and make one's blood run cold. . . .'

The politics of the Indian situation, and of any other situation, she found frankly abhorrent. 'You know *how I* dislike political letters and politics in *general*,' she wrote to her daughter Vicky, the German Crown Princess, in June of 1875. But that did not prevent her from cherishing a powerful ambition as regards India. This ambition, to be officially proclaimed Empress of India by a Royal Titles Bill, had been in her mind since 1858 when the government of India had been transferred to the Crown; it gained impetus as her realization of being Queen of half the globe became vivid to her through her sons' travel. At Osborne in June 1873, she summoned

Colonel Ponsonby to her and made herself extremely plain.

'I am an Empress in common conversation and I am sometimes called Empress of India. Why have I never officially assumed this title? I feel I ought to do so and wish to have preliminary enquiries made.'

There was more to her request, however, than a desire to be more closely connected and identified with India, and that was a matter of European royal precedence. She was – through her daughter Vicky's marriage to Fritz (later Frederick III, Emperor of Germany and King of Prussia), and her son Alfred's marriage to Marie of Russia – connected to the 'world's haughtiest Imperial Highnesses'. Fritz, Vicky's husband, was even tactless enough to indicate that once he was Emperor as well as King, his son would take precedence over Victoria's own, his brothers-in-law. It was hardly amusing.

If these considerations were the spur, there did not seem any obstacles to the fulfilment of her wish to be declared Empress. She was known to have taken a keen interest in India since the Crown had taken over the government and she had sent a memorandum to the India Office that same year, 1858, requesting that:

All despatches, when received and perused by the Secretary of State, to be sent to the Queen. . . . No draft of instructions or orders to be sent out without having been previously submitted to the Queen . . . such drafts to be marked 'For Approval'. In cases of Civil appointments the Secretary of State will himself take the Queen's pleasure before communicating with the gentleman to be appointed. . . . The Secretary of State to obtain the Queen's sanction to important measures previously to his bringing them before the Council.

Letters from Lord Northbrook in the early 1870s, written from Government House in Calcutta, speak of 'devoted loyalty and humble gratitude for her deep sympathy' over the famines in Bengal and Bihar. He assured the Queen that her 'deep interest' has served '. . . to strengthen the bonds of sympathy not only between the people and her Government, but also between all classes of her subjects in India'.

The only sour note, and that was uttered in spirited self-defence, came from her daughter Vicky, smarting under an attack by her mother on Bismarck, whom Victoria considered 'overbearing and unprincipled'. No doubt impelled by the European precedence question, Victoria implied to her daughter that Vicky's father-in-law, Emperor or not, was no more than Bismarck's tool in the annexation of German princedoms in pursuit of unification. Vicky replied energetically that her father-in-law took no princely property that he did not handsomely pay for. In any case, she added crossly, the palaces that were taken in the process of unification 'we had as much right to inhabit as you to wear the Kohinoor or to place Indian arms in the Armoury at Windsor!' She went on to deplore the use of military strength as a way of solving things.

'God knows *I* am *not* one who admire "Conquest" but it has OFTEN been of the greatest use. England's Empire over the East is the best example of it and even *there* Englishmen have NOT always shown themselves as scrupulous, humane, civilized and enlightened as they *should* have done!'

Victoria was not to be deflected. She had, after all, hinted at the possibility of a change in her status in a letter to Palmerston as long before as December 1857:

As long as the government [of India] was that of the [East India] Company, the sovereign was generally left quite ignorant of decisions and despatches; now that the government is to be that of the Sovereign and the directions, she presumes, to be given in her name, a direct official responsibility to her will have to be established.

Disraeli, writing to her on the passing of the India Bill six months later, was clearly of the same opinion:

It is ... a wise and well digested measure, ripe with experience of the past five months' discussion, but it is only the ante-chamber of an Imperial Palace; and your Majesty would do well to deign to consider the steps which are now necessary to influence the opinions and affect the imaginations of the Indian populations. The name of your Majesty ought to be impressed upon their native life.

The Proclamation to be published to the Indian people in 1858 was written by Lord Derby in strict accordance with the Queen's wishes. It must, she said, 'breathe feelings of generosity, benevolence and religious feeling, pointing out the privileges which the Indians will receive in being placed on an equality with the subjects of the British Crown and the prosperity following in the train of civilization'. What was more, the Queen wished it to be made very plain that each Indian should continue to worship as he chose: 'Firmly relying ourselves on the truth of Christianity and acknowledging with gratitude the solace of religion, we disclaim alike the right and desire to impose our convictions on any of our subjects.'

When the Proclamation was finally drawn up to her satisfaction, she pronounced herself well pleased with both it and her new association with India. 'It is a source of great satisfaction and pride to her to feel herself in direct communication with that enormous Empire which is so bright a jewel of her Crown, and which she would wish to see happy, contented and peaceful. May the publication of her Proclamation be the beginning of a new era and may it draw a veil over the sad and bloody past.'

The 'new era' brought the Queen a great deal of information about India, a deluge of Oriental presents and considerable annoyance with the India Office, whose desire to do things their way rather than hers brought about a relationship she felt was 'unutterable and really too bad'. But it was not until 1875, after seventeen years of British government rule in India, that an official Royal visit was planned. Bertie, the Prince of Wales, thirty-three and with far too much time on his hands to spend losing money on horses, was delighted. The Queen was not. It was too 'long and distant a voyage' for the heir to the throne, he was still weak after 'his terrible illness of 1871' (four years previously), he was very careless about looking after his health, he was not a reliable model of exemplary behaviour. The family pleaded and at last she gave in, on condition that he followed the diet she prescribed for him, was always in bed by ten and behaved with pious and sober propriety on Sundays.

In October, burdened with maternal instructions and 'with a heavy heart', Bertie sailed for India. By the time he reached Suez his spirits were lifting and the Queen was perturbed to read reports in the newspapers of jolly practical jokes on board and insufficient royal dignity. He reached Bombay to a welcome by seventy princes and the celebration of his thirty-fourth birthday; he drove through crowded streets glittering with illuminated messages, one of which read, 'Tell Mama we're happy.' The visit was a success. Lord Northbrook wrote to reassure Queen Victoria that Bertie was wearing his pith helmet – 'a most necessary precaution against the Indian sun' – and Bertie, shocked at the 'rude and rough' manner of political officers towards native chiefs, wrote to his mother expressing his conviction that Indians of all classes would 'be more attached to us if treated with kindness and with firmness . . . but not with brutality or contempt'.

In Bertie's absence, the Queen applied herself to the business of being proclaimed Empress of India. Early in 1876, with Disraeli as her ally, she opened Parliament, announced her intention, and then took herself off at once upon a sentimental pilgrimage to her half-sister's grave in Baden-Baden. Disturbing telegrams followed her describing the reception of her declaration in Parliament. The Duke of Somerset had used language both 'ungentlemanlike and unusual' and had suggested that her wish to be Empress was no more than a ruse to give her children precedence over those at the German court. This 'falsehood' was 'really too bad' she confided indignantly to her journal, but in the end Disraeli's persistence won the day and the Royal Titles Bill was passed by the House of Lords, the Duke of Somerset notwithstanding, by a majority of 105.

'It is to be hoped,' she wrote in her journal in March 1876, 'that now no more stupid things will be said and that the matter will be dropped . . . all sensible people know that this Bill will make *no* difference here and that I am all for it as it is so important to India.'

Lord Lytton, now Viceroy of India, agreed with her. He wrote proposing a huge Durbar for the New Year of 1877 at which the princely guests should be presented with inscribed gold and silver guns and commemorative silken banners, and largesse 'and sweet-meats' distributed to the poor. The fact of her being made Empress needed to be 'judiciously stimulated into active expression' because, he explained laboriously, 'the Princes and people of India do not feel and reason like the vestrymen of Marylebone'.

That Durbar, in all its extraordinary splendour and imperial possessiveness, remains a powerful image of late Empire. It is an image that Kipling above all expressed to a nation hungry for the gratifying reflection of its glorious and worldwide influence.

In novels and short stories, but most eloquently in poetry, Rudyard Kipling elaborated the faith the Empire had become for the late Victorians. It was a faith embodied in the picture of the soldiers of the Queen marching abreast with God to break the bonds of tyranny, corruption and superstition that held the native peoples of the world wretched captives. There was no shadow of doubt in 1893 but that God was an Englishman:

Fair is our lot – O goodly is our heritage!
(Humble ye my people, and be fearful in your mirth!)
For the Lord our God Most High
He hath made the deep as dry
He hath smote for us a pathway to the ends of all the earth!

Between 1815 and 1889 that pathway, smitten by soldiers and sailors, administrators and emigrants, missionaries and convicts, had carried away twelve million British people to live and work in the colonies. By 1890 the Kiplingesque fervour of 'the faith the White Men hold', the belief in the creed

Freedom for ourselves, freedom for our sons
And failing freedom, War

had reach its passionate height.

It was not the view that the early or mid-Victorians had had of Empire, though it had grown from their beliefs, as Kipling himself recognized:

Once, two hundred years ago, the trader came,
   Meek and tame.
Where his timid foot first halted, there he stayed,
   Till mere trade
Grew to Empire, and he sent his armies forth
   South and North

Early Victorians would not have described the trade as mere. To them it was the foundation stone of the whole enterprise and only as the century wore on did the English desire and capacity to produce wealth become inseparable from their desire to improve the lot of those luckless enough to be born something other than English, the people, 'Celt and savage, buff and ochre, cream and yellow', of the races rich in desirable raw materials but poor in Western civilizing influences. Mid-Victorian Empire-building was intoxicating stuff, a compound of free trade, open minds and Christianity. The point of it all was, said Lord Palmerston in 1842, '. . . that commerce may go freely forth, leading civilization with one hand, and peace with the other, to render mankind happier, wiser, better'.

The English were, as all other nations were swift to point out, impossibly superior and self-righteous, but they were, too, bursting with excellent intention. Private enterprise, free enterprise, was to be encouraged at all costs, and in the process of expanding free trade across the globe, the English would raise up all those with whom they came in contact and take them along the path of progress that had made England great. Enterprise was everything, empire only the auxiliary that allowed it to flourish.

And if it was going to flourish, as Disraeli realized, it had to be safeguarded. 'There may be grave questions as to the best mode of obtaining wealth,' he wrote in 1863, '. . . but there can be no question . . . that the best mode of preserving wealth is power.' Palmerston had been of the same opinion over twenty years before: 'It is the business of government to open and secure the roads for the merchant.'

That, the mid-Victorians felt, was the business of colonial rule. It gave England, with her huge and growing demand for food and raw materials, opportunities to find the necessary trade outlets and subsequently to protect them for her own use. Annexation was not thought desirable unless it was the only way in which the ancient trade monopolies of the Far and Near Easts could be broken down; other methods were always declared preferable, such as the offer of a loan or persistent persuasion, or even threats. Of course the extension of power was difficult to resist. The middle years of the nineteenth century were so exuberant with energy and achievement that England was too small to contain such dynamism – expansion, by whatever name it was veiled, was inevitable.

The great markets of half the world – the white world – were gradually coloured pink. By the 1870s Canada was a confederate and the Cape, the West Indies, Australia and New Zealand – over whom sovereignty had been proclaimed as early as 1840 to put a stop to a rash of French annexations in the South Island – were all considered to be 'responsibly governed' under the umbrella of the British Empire. Ten years later, over half Britain's investment abroad went to pink places on the map, and two-thirds of her imports and exports were exchanged with the Empire. The enthusiastic desire to render mankind much improved, by English standards, took some punishment from reverses in attempts to subdue China and Africa to British values and trade requirements, but the business was successful enough to keep the trade alive. What has been called the 'gospel of restricted government and free trade' went on, to be sure, until the end of the century, but the cost of the whole enterprise tempered the ardour of the forties and fifties. It was to be fanned again, notably by Kipling, when the wars in India, Burma and South Africa threw up a new hero in Tommy Atkins, a barrackroom philosopher stoically cheerful in the face of the most taxing climates and conditions. But there was before that a period when business was emphasized strongly over faith.

The reason was that some of the natives had proved intractable. There was, from the earliest colonizing, a sense that the aboriginal races were different and should not be too much interfered with in matters of habits and conditions. Florence Nightingale, a pioneer in their protection, called for land to be provided for existing tribes in Australia and New Zealand and for the suppression of the liquor trade to save them from their own lack of 'civilization . . . and force of character'. But the indigenous peoples of India and Africa were another matter, not so 'innocent' in their ancient tribal behaviour. There was a strong feeling by the 1880s that the acquisition of India, though it could hardly be called a mistake since it took 19 per cent of British exports and had gobbled up £270 million in British investment, should never be repeated. As James Stephen of the Colonial Office replied late in the century when asked why England seemed so reluctant to commit herself in Africa, '. . . in Africa we cannot colonize at all without coming into contact with numerous warlike tribes and involving ourselves in their disputes, wars and relations with each other. If we could acquire the dominion of the whole of that continent,' he concluded firmly, 'it would be but a worthless possession.'

The mutiny in India had given everyone a bad fright, but India could not be abandoned. Apart from her trade value, she was a huge power base, a gigantic British barrack, from which troops went out to subdue Boers and Afghans, Burmans and Sudanese, Arabs and Chinese. But it was recognized that she was to be the exception to a new policy, a policy of trading with white areas, the places Europeans had been colonizing since the beginning of the century, the islands of Australasia and the West Indies. The pink expanses of the globe became not so much part of a traditional empire as of a huge commercial republic.

Even if she did not share her government's view of this, her most glamorous possession, the Queen had over twenty years, until her death, to enjoy being both Regina and Imperatrix. In those twenty years a spirit of pure imperialism was to rise, of which Kipling remains the most impassioned voice, a spirit which enabled him to write of South Africa – a country where, in the last thirty years of the century, hundreds of thousands of British soldiers were to die at the hands of Zulu or Boer, or from typhoid fever – as 'a woman wonderful', 'most perfect and adored' because she was 'bought by blood, and by blood restored'.

> On your feet and let them know
> This is why we love her!
> For she is South Africa –
> Is Our Own South Africa –
> Africa all over!

Not by any means all contemporary poets shared Kipling's view of Empire. Among the most celebrated to sound a chilling note among the patriotic cheers was Oscar Wilde, who in his 'Ave Imperatrix' describes England as climbing 'the steep road of wide empire' with 'bare and bloody feet'. There was romance and adventure in the business of empire to be sure:

> The brazen-throated clarion blows
> Across the Pathan's reedy fen,
> And the high steeps of Indian snows
> Shake to the tread of armed men.

But for all the glory and the sounding trumpets was there not too high a price to pay for such a thing as an empire?

> What profit now that we have bound
> The whole round world with nets of gold,
> If hidden in our hearts is found
> The care that never groweth old? . . .
>
> Where are the brave, the strong, the fleet?
> Where is our English chivalry?
> Wild grasses are their burial sheet,
> And sobbing waves their threnody.
>
> O loved ones lying far away,
> What word of love can dead lips send!
> O wasted dust! O senseless clay!
> Is this the end! Is this the end!

Hundreds of thousands of women in England between 1837 and the Great War would have agreed with him. The deprivation that Victorian women suffered on account of the Empire was not always as extreme as the 'anguished pain' of loss by death abroad, but it was very real. At its most basic level there was an enormous shortage of men at home because hundreds of thousands went off each year to serve or to colonize the empire. The result was, as the *Plymouth Times* reported in January 1848, 'forty single ladies for every single man in Weston-super-Mare', and presumably Weston-super-Mare was not alone. *Punch*, taking a deliberately alarmist view two years later, declared roundly:

If the surplus female population with which we are overrun increases much more, we shall be eaten up with women. What used to be our better self will become our worst nine-tenths; a numerical majority which it will be vain to contend with and which will reduce our free and glorious constitution to that most degrading of all despotisms, a petticoat government.

The facts were not to be avoided. By the middle of the century over 35 per cent of women between twenty and forty-four were single. But the Empire was only partly to blame for that; certainly it demanded a huge manpower to forge new links around the world, and subsequently to maintain them, but men were leaving England throughout the century for reasons much less positive than that of serving the Empire; they were abandoning it too for escape. What they sought to escape was marriage, not for any reasons of misogyny, but because of the demands made upon a married couple by middle-class Victorian society, that class that provided such a huge amount of the enterprise and creative energy that fired the last seventy years of the century. To get married it was necessary to set up an establishment and the rules for that were so exacting and expensive that ducking the issue altogether was understandably common. In Mrs Gaskell's *Cousin Phillis*, Mr Holdsworth falls very much in love with Cousin Phillis but goes off to Canada without saying a word because he is not in a financial position to offer marriage. It was possible to live with great modesty upon £300 a year, but it was not thought prudent. In the early fifties, in a 'lonely hearts' column of the *London Journal* a man who described himself as 'gentlemanly' and who hopefully sought a wife on 24 shillings a week (the wage of the average coalminer) was told sternly by the editor that such an income was insufficient for marriage. In Anthony Trollope's *The Small House at Allington*, published in 1862, Adolphus Crosbie complains that in the first London house he occupies after his marriage, he has to use a cupboard under a staircase as a dressing room. His wealthy and titled mother-in-law has scant sympathy. 'But if you have no private fortune of your own,' she says tartly, 'you cannot have everything.' For most middle-class men with insufficient income, the reasons for remaining single were lucidly expressed in Eliza Cook's poem:

> Sweet girl! You know three hundred pounds
> Would prove a slender axis
> For household wheels to run their rounds
> In yearly rents and taxes.
> You see dear, that our home *must* be
> Out West, about the squares,
> With good reception rooms, full three
> And servants' flights of stairs.
> . . .
> I've asked my uncle for his aid;
> Of course, he won't accord it;
> And so our bliss must be delayed
> For means, love, won't afford it.
> A housemaid, cook and liveried boy
> We must, at once, engage;
> One of the two we must employ –
> A footman or a page.
> . . .
> I must keep up my name at 'White's'
> Despite all uncle says;
> You still must have your opera nights,
> And show on Chiswick days.
> Now, if I had three thousand, dear,
> You know I would not hoard it;
> But on three hundred pounds a year!
> I really can't afford it!

A job in the Empire saved both money and face, but it hardly helped the plight of young Victorian women brought up to regard marriage and the maintaining of an establishment as the highest female ambition. Florence Nightingale, who wrote copiously on women and vocation for forty-five years, felt God had a hand in it. 'I think He has as clearly marked out some to be single women as He has others to be wives.' Victorian society at large would not have agreed with her. It was not simply the administrative aspect of running a house that was held up to them as so covetable, but, even more powerfully, the moral one, the chance to be 'the angel in the home'. Ruskin described that home in *Sesame and Lilies* as 'the place of Peace, the shelter, not only from all injury, but from all terror, doubt and division'. Frances Power Cobbe called the 'making of a true home', in her *Duties of Women* of 1881, 'our peculiar and inalienable right'. She too was not thinking so much of actual housework – after all, general servants could be had for between six and ten pounds a year – as of the preservation of the standards and values of the family. In an article that appeared in the *Saturday Review* in August 1870, Elizabeth Lynn Linton described the woman at home as the 'careful worker-out of minute details and the upholder of a sublime idealism', her maternal influence being 'the real bond of family life'.

There were good reasons for such attitudes, quite apart from the stifling Victorian protectiveness of females (middle-class, that is; working-class women were another and more expedient matter altogether). Outside the solid comforts of home was a great deal of beastliness, appalling poverty, brutality and crime on the streets, filth and squalor and smells. For men quite as much as women it was desirable to shut such things out. To make the home, and the woman in it, into some sort of moral haven presided over by a spirit of purity and sweetness justified shutting the door on what it was preferable not to see. Frances Power Cobbe tried to see home-making, the provision for women of something *womanly* to do, as an assertion of female independence. But *Punch* for one refused to see marriage and all that went with it as any more than the only thing you could do with an abundance of daughters. In its issue of 20 February 1875 there appears a cartoon, set in a drawing room, in the background of which is an Indian nabob with drooping moustaches surrounded by eager ladies. In the foreground is a large mother, a small father and two identically matched brace of daughters. The caption reads:

Mother: 'My dear, *do* get Mrs Lyon Hunter to introduce you to His Highness. You might then ask him to call, you know.'
Papa dear: 'What for?'
Mother: 'Well, my love, you know the custom of his country! He might take a fancy to several of the girls at once!'

Thomas Carlyle would have sympathized with *Punch*'s mockery, since he declared that it was largely the fault of contemporary fiction which 'made love and marriage seem the main business of life'. Henry Traill, giving a Toynbee Lecture in 1888, quoted Anthony Trollope as being firmly of the opinion that young people were more influenced by novels than anything else, and if he was right, then so to some degree was Thomas Carlyle, particularly with reference to early and mid-Victorian novels. The aim of all the heroines of the Brontës, Jane Austen, Mrs Gaskell and, to some extent, those of George Eliot, was marriage. Even a man as enlightened as Henry Fawcett (Gladstone's postmaster general and husband of that pioneer of women's rights, Dame Millicent Fawcett) saw marriage as the aim of even an educated woman:

I venture to assert, with no little confidence, that the more a woman's mind is trained, the more her reasoning faculties are developed, the more certainly does she become a suitable companion for her husband; she is better able to manage his house with tact and skill and to obtain the best, the most tender and the most enduring influence over her children.

As *Punch* said of those remarks, 'Isn't that *nice* of him?' And Florence Nightingale would have told him bluntly that he was, like most men, only pleasing himself by holding such opinions:

The family uses people *not* for what they are, nor for what they are intended to be, but for what it wants them for. . . . It thinks of them not as what God has made them for, but as something that it has arranged that they shall be. If it wants someone to sit in the drawing room, that someone is supplied by the family, though that member may be destined for science, or for education or for active superintendence by God i.e. by the gifts within. This system dooms some minds to incurable infancy, others to silent misery.

She found this attitude to Victorian women far worse than the lack of husbands or the oppressive ethical demands of home-making, if you found a home. Angelica in Sarah Grand's *The Heavenly Twins* cries in despair, 'I had none of the domestic virtues and yet they would insist on domesticating me. . . .' On the whole, there was precious little insistence on educating instead of domesticating because there was, after all, so little you could do with an education, as a girl, once you had it. More dangerously, an education might blight the chance of marriage:

> Sally was a pretty girl
> Fanny was her sister;
> Sally read all night and day,
> Fanny sighed and kissed her.
>
> Sally won some school degree;
> Fanny won a lover,
> Sally soundly rated her
> And thought herself above her.
>
> Fanny had a happy home,
> And urged that plea only;
> Sally she was learned – and
> Also she was lonely.

Still, Sally was lucky, since *Punch* describes her as being clever *and* pretty, a combination not considered generally possible. A bemused government circular of 1855 complained that because teachers selected for government schools of art were constantly getting married, 'to avoid these losses plainer candidates were selected for training but they too have obtained preference as wives to a perplexing degree'. Looks entirely apart, there was a distinct feeling that educating girls was a waste of time. This opinion is expressed by Mr Tulliver in *The Mill on the Floss*, about his daughter Maggie, whom he loved dearly. She was, he said, 'Too 'cute for a woman' and 'an over 'cute woman's no better nor a long-tailed sheep – she'll fetch none the bigger price for that!' Mr Helstone, in Charlotte Brontë's *Shirley*, was of the same opinion:

At heart, he could not abide sense in women; he liked to see them as silly, as light-hearted, as vain, as open to ridicule as possible; because they were then in reality what he held them to be and wished them to be – inferior, toys to play with, to amuse a vacant hour and to be thrown away.

One night a little later in the century, Sir Henry de la Beche, the pioneer of the Geological Map of England, and Warrenton Smyth were placed either side of Florence Nightingale at dinner in her father's house. Everything went swimmingly at first as Florence charmed Sir Henry by drawing him out on the subject of geology. Then she proceeded to discourse on Latin and Greek and left Sir Henry floundering. Turning to Warrenton Smyth she began to talk to him about the inscriptions she had just seen in Egypt, a subject in which he could hold his own, but then she plunged into quotations from Lepsius which she had studied in the original, and dumbfounded him. 'A capital young woman that,' Sir Henry confided to Smyth as the ladies left the room, 'if only she hadn't floored me with her Latin and Greek.'

As the century wore on, there was plenty of rebellion – indeed, as early as 1847 Jane Eyre had cried 'women feel just as men feel' and another Brontë heroine, Shirley, had declared that, 'Men, I believe, fancy women's minds something like those of children. Now that,' she added darkly, 'is a mistake.' There were certainly more educational opportunities for women – Bedford College, London opened in 1849 – but the climate of opinion was still hardly helpful. *Punch* suggested in November 1873, when Girton College Cambridge was founded, that the winter lectures should include courses in 'Patchwork', 'Winter fashions' and 'Washing at home'. No wonder, given the prevalence of such ideas, that Rachel, the heroine of Charlotte Yonge's *The Clever Woman of the Family*, published in 1865, declaims on her twenty-fifth birthday, 'Here am I, able and willing, only longing to task myself to the uttermost, yet tethered down to the merest mockery of usefulness by conventionalities. I am a young lady, forsooth! – I must not be out late; I must not choose my acquaintance; I must be a mere helpless useless being.'

In its edition of 15 November 1872, *Punch* provided a cartoon in which a heavily moustached Colonel and a very young man are seated together on an ottoman regarding two earnest young women talking to a distinguished-looking man.

Colonel: 'As for what they call intellect and that sort of thing, why, what I say is, the less of it in a woman, the better my boy!'

Little Tomkyns, 'My sentiments to a T, sir! Intellect indeed! As for me, I've always looked upon woman as a mere toy!'

Whoever comes out worse in this exchange, the opinion persisted. Even as late as April 1902, an article entitled 'The New Woman' was nagging on at the question. The new woman, the author wrote, 'must bear in mind that in becoming a brilliant mathematician, a sharp critic, a faultless grammarian, she may do so at the expense of that ready sympathy, modesty, noble self-control, gentleness, personal tact and temper, so essential for the best type of womanhood and the most exalted standards of female excellence'.

'Men of England!' Caroline Helstone cries in *Shirley*. 'Look at your poor girls. . . . Fathers! Cannot you alter these things?' Eliza Warren, in her highly successful *A Young Wife's Perplexities*, written in 1886, had no doubts. 'Talk about girl graduates and having successfully passed a Cambridge examination. What for – I should like to know? . . . I would have girls educated sufficiently to be companiable; and to earn their bread if need be; but either first or last, they should be well grounded in the duties belonging to wifehood and motherhood.'

None of these opinions would have excited any comment if there had been any other occupation possible for a middle-class Victorian girl, educated or not, apart from wifehood and motherhood or the 'penance and mortification' of being a governess. Education was not an unqualified advantage in itself since it gave an experience to girls which they could then put to little or no use, unless they remained in the academic world and provided Tennyson's 'Prudes for Proctors, Dowagers for Dons and Sweet Girl Graduates'. Indeed public opinion went further than that and looked upon wage-earning, for those who did not need it, as uncharitable at best, since it took bread – in the shape of jobs – out of the mouths of the hungry. Women did not in any case have the capacity, it was thought, to do more than sew or teach. When it came to women's rights, Queen Victoria, who apparently saw nothing 'unwomanly' in the conspicuousness of her position as both monarch and Empress, was emphatic in her disapproval. She wrote to Sir Theodore Martin in May 1870, professing herself

. . . most anxious to enlist anyone who can speak and write . . . [against] this *mad, wicked folly* of 'women's rights' with *all* the attendant horrors on which her poor feeble sex seems bent, viz. in forgetting every sense of womanly feeling and propriety. . . . It is a subject which makes the queen so furious that she cannot contain herself. God created man and woman different and let each remain in their position. . . . Woman would become the most hateful, heartless – and disgusting – of human beings were she allowed to unsex herself! Where would be the protection which man was intended to give the weaker sex? Pray try and get some good writing against it. *The Times* has written extremely well about it. . . .

Queen Victoria was, after all, as fully occupied as she wished to be. But there were thousands for whom occupation was a financial necessity – and the opportunities few and intensely unattractive – and thousands more who cried with Angelica of *The Heavenly Twins*, 'I wanted to *do* as well as to *be*!' Florence Nightingale must be the most celebrated example of that desire and she would without question have strongly seconded Sarah Grand's heroine when she claimed that ' . . . it is dangerous to leave an energetic woman without a single strong interest or object in life . . .'. For far too many such women, life at home in Victorian England was doomed to be just as unsatisfactory as Florence Nightingale found it as a young woman or as penurious and humiliating as it was for a large proportion of governesses. It is small wonder that Miss Nightingale became such a heroine, an idol to whom the wealthy and good-looking young woman Agnes Jones could write when at last she entered the Nightingale Training School to nurse: 'In the winter of 1854 when I had those *first longings for work* and had for months so little to satisfy them, how I wished I were competent to join the Nightingale band when they started for the Crimea! I listened to the animadversions of many but I almost worshipped her who braved them all.'

For a remarkable minority there was an escape. The Empire which claimed such huge numbers of Englishmen was seen by a significant number of middle-class women, whether out of enterprise or of desperation, to offer a chance of self-esteem and achievement that could not be obtained at home. There were many who felt, like Florence Nightingale, a sense of self in the 'consciousness of power . . . satisfaction in its exercise . . . devotion to [a] cause', however small and humble both power and cause might be. Some left England quite frankly in pursuit of a husband, some to earn a living or a status denied them at home, some – more as time went on – to accompany and support men in the lonely, difficult and responsible business of setting up and maintaining colonial rule; some went because missionary zeal was so much part of the Victorian religious attitude and found themselves nursing and teaching with equipment and in conditions that would not be contemplated today; and some, commonly those with private means, went out to explore the world quite literally, travelling astounding distances and bringing back with them anthropological information and botanical specimens which contributed significantly to the scientific research of the day. The Empire may have initially taken from Englishwomen their men, but it compensated for that subsequently by holding out a hand offering adventure and self-fulfilment for those enterprising enough to grasp it.

If straitened financial circumstances meant that there was often very little choice of a future for an educated middle-class girl without private means, there was often no choice at all for her working-class counterpart. A middle-class wage was counted in pounds a year but a working-class family thought in terms of shillings a week, every one of which was precious. Victorian society, particularly in the cities, was harsh in its dealings with the poor and it took so little – an accident at work, illness, a strike – to plunge a family from poverty to the utter poverty from which there was little hope of recovering. The only insurance policy against this disastrous possibility was to spread the burden of wage earning around as many members of the family as possible; and of course the women of the family were included in the total. Many Victorian philanthropists deplored this, seeing what hideous deprivation a working mother caused her home and family. Lord Shaftesbury called their need to work an 'evil' which is 'desolating like a torrent the peace, economy and the virtue of the mighty masses of the manufacturing districts'.

He had reason to sound so impassioned. Working-class women were driven to the mills by sheer grinding need and the consequences were horrible. Drawings of the dwellings of Manchester cotton operatives in the 1860s show a pitiful bareness, often they are without one single stick of furniture, with water pitchers and food dishes on the floor lying beside sleeping forms under heaps of rags, tattered garments hung on lines across the ceilings, empty grates, childminders of eight or nine squatting listlessly by the babies in their charge. And of course these drawings cannot convey the dirt or the damp or the smell.

To these bleak and insanitary dwellings a woman would return from a factory after sixteen hours' work – reduced after 1847 by the Ten Hours Act – a day that had been gruelling and health-destroying and for which she received perhaps 12s. 6d. a week. As society required household duties to be performed solely by women, the days of drudgery in mills, workshops and factories ended in the domestic round of dealing with children (invariably too many), preparing food (frequently scarce and of monotonously poor quality), and cleaning and washing. The latter was in itself an enormous problem. In the cities, standpipes in the courts and alleys were turned on irregularly and infrequently by the private water companies that owned them. The water which emerged from the pipes was stale and discoloured and then had to be hauled up tenements in buckets and tubs; because it was so difficult and exhausting to obtain, the same water had to be used for cooking, cleaning and washing. When it came to drinking the disgusting stuff, it is hardly to be wondered at that many of the working classes infinitely preferred gin.

Unlike middle-class women, a working-class woman had no difficulty in finding work. The mid-nineteenth century radical view that women should be protected like children because they were, like children, restricted in capability, meant that women were cheap labour. They often, in fact, undercut the men because they were not organized to demand more money. Even towards the end of the century, shop assistants and waitresses earned only between 5 and 8 shillings a week and the plight of the seamstresses stitching for unconscionably long hours for the reward of a few pence is legendary. No wonder so many took to prostitution, where earnings might be reckoned in pounds rather than shillings, nor that *Punch* should suggest in January 1850, in the 'Needlewoman's Farewell', that emigration to the Empire could offer an alternative to walking the streets as an escape from poverty:

> Now speed thee, good ship, over sea,
> and bear us far away,
> Where food to eat and friends to greet
> and work to do await us –
> Where against hunger's tempting, we
> shall not need to pray –
> Where in wedlock's tie, not harlotry,
> we shall find men to mate us.

It was not only the poverty but the fagging toil that led to prostitution. Victorian moralists believed that drudgery would redeem the soul of the whore, but Esther, the prostitute aunt of the heroine of Mrs Gaskell's *Mary Barton*, saw that it was the other way about: 'I found out that Mary went to learn dressmaking and I began to be frightened for her; for it's a bad life for a girl to be out late at night in the streets and after many an hour of weary work, they're ready to follow after any novelty that makes a little change.'

Some women took to prostitution only temporarily to get themselves out of debt, though it was essential always to avoid police arrest and inspection under the detested Contagious Diseases Act. Those women found infected were placed – for the good of society, declared the instigators – in the notorious 'lock hospitals' of which Beth, the heroine of Sarah Grand's *The Beth Book* (1897), says with uncharacteristic primness, 'The principles of the medical profession with regard to sanitation when women are in question seem to be peculiar.' It was not uncommon for a proportion of the inmates of the hospitals, especially those suspected of even the least misdemeanour, to be sent to the colonies, rather in the manner of Queen Victoria suggesting them as convenient places to dispose of someone disturbing.

Prostitutes, it would seem, had emigration thrust upon them rather than them choosing it, but for hundreds and thousands of working-class women it was a choice. Given the conditions of most of their lives, it can hardly have been a difficult one to make. Harriet Fletcher left Lancashire (for New Zealand in 1849) with her cotton-spinning family. She remembered her father shaking his fist at the smoking mill stacks of his birthplace and vowing never to return. The Government, eager to see settlements, particularly in Canada, Australia and New Zealand, set up a scheme offering free passages and assisted passages to encourage working-class emigration and notably, as time went on, emigration of women. Some went with their families, some on their own in search of jobs as domestic servants and some, like the wives of the thousands and thousands of soldiers who left England between the start of the Crimean War in 1854 and the end of the Boer War in 1902, because they had, quite simply, nowhere else to go. As the Irish had long known, tearing up roots in search of even mere survival was often the only solution. Thomas Carlyle, in the second edition of his *Chartism*, published in 1840, went so far as to declare the matter to be one of the two burning issues of the day:

'Two things, great things, dwell, for the last ten years, in all thinking heads in England; and are hovering, of late, even on the tongues of not a few. . . . Universal Education is the first . . . general Emigration is the second.'

II · 'PIONEERS! OH, PIONEERS!'

WALT WHITMAN

II

'On the day of Henry's birth,' wrote Marianne Williams of Paihia, the New Zealand mission station on the shores of the Bay of Islands, 'I drank tea with the family, and with great difficulty washed my children and put them to bed, after which I walked out in the moonlight with Henry – and soon retired to my room. Henry summoned the family to prayers, before the close of which Mr Marsden arrived in the company of Captain Moore, in the boat of the latter. While Henry was getting tea for them, and giving grog to the boat's crew, Mrs Fairburn was at the other end of the house putting her children to bed and attending to her baby. I, left entirely to myself, did feel more justly my only aid to come from God, and did cling more closely to the only source of strength. As soon as the children had played themselves to sleep I made my preparations and went to bed. I gladly heard Captain Moore depart; and a short time afterwards, Mrs Fairburn arrived to my assistance just as the dear little one began to cry. I never felt so much joy before. Henry wrapped himself in his boat cloak to watch through the night. The children awoke and were shown the baby; it seemed like a dream.'

To many of the thousands of pioneer wives the experience of emigration must have seemed like a dream, to some wonderful and invigorating, to others a nightmare. The endurance, resourcefulness and achievement of these women are perfectly remarkable, from little Kate Bee of the Mohaka River who in 1869 armed herself with a broken bottle tied to a stick to defend her family from the huge tattooed Maori warriors of the rebelling chieftain, Te Kooti, to Catherine Parr Traill, given an island in Stony Lake by the Canadian Government in 1893 as 'but the smallest acknowledgement which is due to you for your life long devotion to Canada'.

In character and social class the pioneer women differed widely. At one end of the spectrum was Sarah Ann Cripps, who arrived in 1852 to desperately hard beginnings in the Auckland Islands, and who died forty years later, successful postmistress and local mid-wife and lamented as 'the best loved woman from Wellington to Ahuri'. At the other was Charlotte Godley, who went out to supervise the establishment of the Canterbury Settlement in 1849 with her husband, and whose sisters urged her not to go for fear of 'spoiling her hands'. She took heed of their anxiety and sailed with her lady's maid Powles. Her grand-daughter remembered her possessing 'all the grace, gentleness and dignity of the Victorian ideal'. Mrs Godley, whose sitting room at Dunedin contained 'a grand pianoforte, a brass inlaid clock, red twill curtains and at least a dozen pictures in large gilt frames', would have been appalled at the living conditions which Elizabeth Hamlin, wife of a missionary, had to endure. Twenty-two when she arrived in New Zealand, she bore twelve children, miscarried between live births, confronted savage Maoris alone, was frequently servantless, often hungry, cold and wet, and performed the miracle of survival in a series of crude and leaking cabins, floored in mud and roofed in fern.

The contrasts are endless. Young Catherine Maclean, married in the Hebrides in 1860, arrived in Port Chalmers able only to speak Gaelic. One cannot help setting her inevitable difficulties alongside those very different ones of the Strickland sisters, gently reared and highly literate, writing down eagerly every step of their progress across the Canadian backwoods. If there is more quotation from the women of the middle classes, it is only because they, as inveterate Victorian diary-keepers, recorded their lives and their impressions of the curious worlds to which their husbands took them. Of the rest, those matchlessly resourceful women who raised families, kept house, planted orchards, harvested crops and ran small businesses, one must rely on infrequent letters and reports of their achievements written by others. They themselves were simply too busy to write.

The colonization of New Zealand by pioneer families – probably the most striking example of such achievement – began in 1838, the year after Queen Victoria's accession to the throne. There was a high moral tone about the whole process, but in fact the purchase of land by the New Zealand Company from the Maoris round Port Nicholson (now Wellington) was effected to protect England's material interests and to keep out the French, who had begun a series of annexations in the South Island. Within two years, after the

Treaty of Waitangi signed with Maori chiefs, British sovereignty had been proclaimed, and after that the pioneer flood began.

Some of it, particularly the large Scottish element, came out of sheer necessity. John Anderson, an unemployed Caithness shepherd, came to Dunedin with his wife Helen in 1848 on a free passage that they were thankful to obtain. There is no record of what became of them subsequently but no doubt, arriving with nothing but the clothes that they stood up in, they shared the fate of Ann Finlayson who lived for two years in three tents (one for herself and her husband, one for the children and a separate kitchen tent) while her husband worked to make enough money to build them a house. There was money to be made in New Zealand but necessities were costly. An emigrant with a wife and two children arrived in Dunedin from Dalkeith in 1847 with thirty shillings and sixpence in his pocket. Eighteen months later he owned a cottage, a potato garden and was owed £100 for work done in the colony. The Maoris would build a house for ten shillings and a blanket, but they wanted four shillings a day for wages as servants (this was in the 1850s); bread was ninepence for a four-pound loaf, butter was two shillings a pound. And 'such washing bills!' Charlotte Godley exclaimed, 'about three shillings a dozen for everything!'

Land, on the other hand, was cheap and plentiful. In 1855 an old Maori chief at Pourerere offered Elizabeth Crosse a thousand acres of land in exchange for her new baby, then about five months old, because he said that it was when they were cutting their teeth that they tasted sweetest. She seemed entirely undismayed by this bizarre suggestion and went on to farm in the outback for ten years without the sight of another white woman and to grow to love the Maoris dearly.

She was not alone. Unlike the letters of the governesses and the superior domestic servants, most of the journals of the pioneer women in New Zealand show nothing but affection for the Maoris, a state of affairs which reflects excellently on the Maoris as well as the settlers. The first pioneers to come had taken Mairo mistresses – a situation described by the Secretary of State with reference to West Africa as 'a state of concubinage with native women' – both for personal and practical reasons. There is an attractive story of a Maori girl persuading an English settler, George Willsher, of how invaluable she would be to him:

By and by you go to Otago, to Waihora, to Toutu. You stay three weeks – you stay five weeks – you stay two moons. You come back, you say Hullo where's the cow? Gone! Where's the bull? Gone. Where's the goatee? Gone. Where the chickeni? Gone! Where the stockeni gone all all gone. You get the Maori woman. By and by you go to Otago, to Waikawa, to Tourere – you stay three weeks, you stay five weeks, you stay two moons, you come back, you say Hullo where's the cow? Me say all right. You say where the bull, the chickeni? Me say all right. You say where the goatee? Me say all right, blankety all right, stockeni all right, all, all right. Are very good the Maori woman.

Not surprisingly, she convinced him and lived for some years as his common-law wife. But then, sadly, he tired of her and his isolation, and went home to marry one of his own kind leaving her, one hopes, with at least the goatee and the chickeni and blankety for some small consolation.

The coming of white women changed such associations – as it did inevitably in India and Canada as well – but the friendliness of the Maoris remained, on the whole, constant. In 1856, James Wilson brought his two young daughters, Charlotte and Ruth, then aged nine and ten, to Dunedin. Within weeks a flood had swept away their fern-and-wattle cottage entirely, taking all the possessions as remained to remind them of their dead mother. Immediately Maoris came to their rescue with presents of potatoes and smoked eels and helped to build a new house. James Wilson was clearly an admirable father. He made his daughters help in the planting of trees after school – the establishment of an orchard was a priority in New Zealand – but then, when they were old enough, sent them off to school in Sydney, enabling Charlotte to become a teacher and Ruth a nurse. Ruth was only fifteen when she delivered her first baby, assisted throughout by helpful troops of Maoris bringing herbs, roots and leaves and urging the process on with loud and rhythmic chanting.

Childbirth looms large in all the journals of the pioneer women. Harriet Fletcher – whose father had shaken his fist at leaving the mill stacks of Lancashire – was married off at seventeen, then departed from Napier to her bridal home two weeks' journey into the back of nowhere. In the slab hut she found there, she gave birth to seven children in nine years. Catherine Dahm bore nine, Mrs Haldane of Dunedin six (the two eldest had hidden under her crinoline at the first sight of Maori warriors) and several accounts speak of babies delivered by husbands in remote places because no midwife was to be had. The alarms and dangers of confinement – borne, it must be remembered, by women whose life was physically and emotionally extremely taxing – made sometimes for a perfectly understandable tension between husband and wife. Emily Eaton, married to a scholarly carpenter, a man well versed in Latin and Greek, wrote tellingly in her diary one day in 1854, 'One of the most miserable days with Edward I ever spent. Never spent one like it with him before. Hope I never spend another like it.'

She bore him ten children and her journal is full of miseries – 'Very uncomfortable', 'Our things have not come', 'The house is unfinished'. It was not uncommon for that to be the case. In photographs, settlers' houses in the 1860s look cosy enough, often verandahed, set in marvellous landscapes (though spectacularly empty ones) and neatly fenced garden plots. The interiors of the most comfortable had slate-floored dairies, fireplaces built of clay dug from the roadsides, iron-lidded camp ovens and cradles carved from hollow logs. At their best, they inspired a powerful nostalgia, as expressed by Ada Cambridge, writing of the early pioneer houses in the country towns near Victoria in Australia:

Ah those dear Bush houses – so homely, so cosy, so hospitable, so picturesque – and now so rare! In the humblest of them the bed stood always ready for the casual guest, a clean brush and comb on the dressing table and easy house slippers under it. And then the paper covered canvas walls used to belly in and out with the wind that puffed behind them; opossums used to get in under the roof and run over the canvas ceilings which sagged under their weight, showing the impression of their little feet and the round of their bodies where they sat down.'

But these houses were not achieved in a moment and many were never achieved at all. Huge numbers of pioneer women made bread and soap and candles and clothing in leaking huts built of fern logs and running with water. Water was always a problem – either there was not enough or far too much; sudden storms and floods caused devastation. Generally, however, washing was not the greatest difficulty. Most households had a huge galvanized tub which could be used for washing clothes as well as people, and when it came to washing blankets, the children of the family were dumped on top to tread the blankets and their feet clean in the same operation.

Perhaps it is not so surprising that those who could survive the journey out to New Zealand could then make something of the country when they reached it. The accommodation in emigrant ships was in open berths, two deep, and the staple diet of bad bully beef and good preserved potatoes was taken in a mess between the berths. The rules were rigid and the complaining vociferous – notably from Protestant girls from the north of England and Scotland over light-fingered Catholic girls from Ireland and from *all* girls about being forcibly segregated from the men. Eighty-three days was not considered a long voyage but it was possible to be becalmed for several weeks in the tropics, when the pitch sealing the decks melted and dripped blazing drops down into the confined spaces below, and bored boys were beaten for climbing the rigging. There was always two hours of larking about while crossing the line, with King Neptune and riotous beard-shaving, but there were frequent sweeping epidemics of measles. As many babies born at sea died as struggled to make their destination – it was very common in the last half of the century to have 'born at sea' inscribed on one's birth certificate.

For the more prosperous the journey was quite pleasurable. Charlotte Godley wrote of flying fish landing on deck and being served to her small son Arthur 'to his great delight'.

'We are not to consider it hot until the seams on deck begin to melt,' she wrote to her sister. 'We wake each morning before six with the pump for washing the decks and then the gentlemen all go up on deck to have buckets of water thrown over them. . . . We must make up our minds to nothing but sea, sea and always sea. . . .'

When she arrived, however, it was all worth it. 'We ran up the coast at a great pace and such a mountain range as the sea view I never saw. . . . It made me think of Wales. . . . It is *so* beautiful.'

Even poor Emily Eaton could not help but notice the beauty, and nor could Marianne Williams, though both women had enough on their hands to be reasonably excused from ever finding time to look out of the window. The sheer burden of things to be done must have kept them all from feeling their isolation too keenly. Many of them spoke of it – Mrs Charleston of Mason Bay had so little society that she was forced, for her own sartorial satisfaction, to dress up in all her finery and parade in solitude up and down the beach – but few actually complained. On the contrary, a few such as Sarah Midgley, eldest daughter of a Yorkshire farmer who had arrived in Koroit,

Australia, with her family in 1851, grew positively to resent the encroachment of civilization upon the isolation of their early years. On 14 May 1859 she wrote in her diary:

This is the anniversary of our arrival at Yangery Grange, seven years have transpired since we came to what was then a desolate spot surrounded with dense scrub, stringy bark and gum trees with an occasional Blackwood interspersed and not a single house within a mile, where all was solitary and still except the singing or screeching of the different birds . . . then we might be for weeks and not see a visitor, but now how changed the scene! We are surrounded with habitations and Yangery Creek is now almost like a village, the Bullock whip and the screams of naughty children resound rather harshly to the sensitive ear. The forests are rapidly giving way before the hand of Man.

Jessie Kid – later, as Jessie King, the first woman Justice of the Peace in Southland, New Zealand – had plenty to complain of in the matter of loneliness, but she never did. Her widowed mother bought a piece of land by deferred payment on condition that the land was lived on. There was no one to live there but adolescent Jessie who appears to have made no objection to doing so, even though she was a day's ride from home (astride in the open country, sidesaddle if there was a chance of meeting anyone).

Harriet Fletcher lived even further from the nearest human contact and her path was obstructed by the bridgeless and frequently dangerous Waipawa River. She writes of it as a nuisance and no more. For some, the isolation was only a spur to their resourcefulness. Catherine Dahm, the wife of a sheep farmer, took to the way of life like a duck to water. Each week she made 54 pounds of flour into bread, subsequently using the flour bags to make pinafores, tablecloths and linings for the boys' shorts. She bore nine children of whom only the last, in 1907, was born in a nursing home, and instructed all of them on a meticulously regular basis. All her cooking was done on camp ovens, yet she kept up her garden and found time later on to run a store and a post office. She was also an excellent friend of the Maoris. A similar spirit existed in Elizabeth Daniel of Jacobs River, the whaling township, who wrote a recipe book in 1867 which included instructions on 'How to Use Pig's Ears'. The Maoris considered her advocacy of salads quite extraordinary, describing raw vegetables as *he kai mate kau* – food fit for cows not humans, and not much good to cows at that.

43

Food, on the whole, was remarkably like home. Diaries are sprinkled with mention of rabbit pie, fruit saved up for Christmas puddings, bacon sides hanging to cure from rafters, porridge pots that were such a chore to scrub out each morning. Apples turn up constantly in New Zealand, the fruit of all those orchards planted as the pioneer's first stake in his new country. Mrs McGaw of Southland, recalling a childhood in the nineties, wrote of the daily school lunch prepared by her mother: '. . . jam sandwiches usually with the addition of a currant bun, a piece of apple turnover and *always* an apple. The apple was the staple fruit of which our extensive orchard seemed to provide an endless supply.'

There were, as the century wore on, towns to exploit as well as the tussocky wastes of the backblocks. Dunedin was founded in 1848, Otago even earlier as the result of sizeable Presbyterian settlement there in the 1840s. By the 1880s Invercargill could boast such an asset as Mrs Pettingall's Academy for Young Ladies. By 1850, Wellington could be described as 'uncommonly pretty and with very good comfortable houses though no fine buildings' and it offered a considerable social life with calls and dinners and occasionally even a ball. By 1900, photographs of Riverton – a place whose female inhabitants had been derided forty years before for bringing out ancient Regency leghorns for parties and wearing shillings and sixpences as earrings – show groups of boys wearing Norfolk jackets, caps, Eton collars and, pleasingly, bare feet.

There were difficulties and advantages for the pioneer women in these new townships. For some, like the redoubtable Mary Ann Bibby of Hawkes Bay, they offered the chance to set up a highly successful shop; Bibby's Store became something of a landmark and ran a flourishing mail-order business. For others they meant the increasing social stratification which had been such a tyranny of life at home. Equality might have been a word with no meaning – everyone did what had to be done – but propriety was all-important. There was a great dearth of parsons which made weddings difficult but it was socially absolutely essential that marital status be officially established, even in a slab hut fifty miles from anyone among the red tussock grass. Inevitably the position of the half-caste was uncomfortable and there is sadly no record of the white pioneer women looking with much compassion or friendliness upon their sisters of mixed blood. There is the unhappy case of pretty little Caroline Brown of Riverton, the daughter of an English-man and a Maori woman. She complicated her position by marry-ing a European who had previously had a Maori wife, and found herself no longer able to associate with the Maoris and frightened to death of the English.

The only places where these awkward distinctions were ignored were in the sealing townships of the Roaring Forties and the mining centres – such as the one at Preservation Inlet where dances were held three nights a week in the nineties, the miners having to dance with each other as there were never enough girls to go round. There were always, of course, the other kind of girls. Miss Turner of Round Hill remembers trainloads of prostitutes arriving for the Chinese New Year celebrations at the Round Hill gold diggings, which were worked mainly by the Chinese. Their 'generous appli-cation of paint, the incredible hair and jangling bracelets . . . differed greatly from [our] soberly clad respectable mothers and aunts'.

Occasionally a white woman got drunk – Mrs Turnbull of Riverton is solely remembered for her insobriety – and even more occasionally took to crime. Minnie Dean strikes a black note in the shining rollcall of female pioneer achievement. She was well edu-cated and well respected and it was only after the bankruptcy of her shiftless husband that she took to the doubtful occupation of placing illegitimate babies for adoption. In fact, no child that passed through her hands was ever adopted; all ended their days, after a heavy dose of laudanum, in a grave in Minnie's back garden. She is the only woman to have been sentenced to hang in New Zealand and her life, even if despicable and hideous towards the end, shows a versatility and tenacity that is the stamp of the pioneer. 'She lay in bed,' said a son of his mother, old Mrs MacMillan of Southland, in the early years of this century, in admiration, 'She lay there and she *wouldn't* die!'

For the middle-class educated pioneer wife, unused to the back-breaking toil of running a nineteenth-century house, life in the colonies was often a nightmare rather than a challenge. In no way were they prepared to let standards drop, however remote their lives, and as they were frequently servantless, this pride necessitated ingenuity as well as courage and astonishingly hard work. Reverend Wollaston from Perth in Australia described the hospitality offered

45

to him in 1848 by Georgiana Molloy, whose husband was resident magistrate at Augusta, two hundred miles south of Fremantle:

The Molloys are at present without servant of any kind, and if it had not been for the loan of the steward of one of the ships in the bay and the Governor's servant, they must have done everything for us themselves. As it was, Mrs Molloy, assisted by her little girl, only nine years old, attended to everything in the cooking way. Although the dining room has a clay floor and opens into the dairy, the thatch appears overhead and there is not a single pane of glass on the premises (the windows being merely square frames with shutters), yet our entertainment, the style of manners of our host and hostess, their dress and conversation all conspired to show that genuine good breeding and gentlemanly deportment are not always lost sight of among English emigrants.

Mrs Molloy wrote to friends describing her life and it is plain from her letters that though she would do what had to be done, she was worn out by the effort of it all:

I need not blush to tell you I am, of necessity my own nurserymaid....

I have had seven letters of Molloy's relating to business to answer besides my own correspondence, to weigh out rations, attend to baby and, although needle-work of every kind both for her, Molloy, myself and servant is required, I have not touched a needle for this week. I am now exhausted and the day uncommonly hot....

My head aches, I have all the clothes to put away from wash; baby to put to bed; make tea and drink it without milk as they shot our cow for a trespass; read prayers and go to bed besides sending off this tableful of letters. I wish I had you here to help me. What golden dreams we used to have about your coming to stay with me! How would you like to be three years in a place without a female of your own rank to speak to or to be with you whatever happened?

In Australia the fatigue of heavy housework – sodden bedclothes to wring by hand, filthy fuel stoves needing constant filling and cleaning, carpets to be heaved onto clothes lines and beaten free of dust – was compounded by the climate. The heat and the dust and the insects seem to have loomed large in everyone's consciousness. Mary Thomas, wife of the printer of the *South Australian Register*, gave this description in 1839:

I cannot say that I much relish working so hard as I do now at my time of life, especially as I see little prospect at present of its being otherwise, for the climate is such that cleanliness and comfort, according to English ideas, are entirely out of the question and incompatible with the country altogether. For I cannot call any place comfortable where the clouds of dust cover all your furniture three or four times a day, driving through every crevice; where you are incessantly hunting fleas and bugs and are overrun with ants, spiders of an enormous size, and flies or some other teasing insect, and where the water, which in England is generally plentiful and delicious to drink, is here both scarce, comparatively speaking, and never palatable as a beverage without an infusion of some kind. In short, I am determined, if ever I have it in my power, to quit this country and return to my native land....

For Louisa Meredith, society – or rather the lack of it – was more oppressive than the spiders and the dust. In *My Home in Tasmania* she wrote of the crudeness of social life in Hobart, where the girls only wanted to gallop about dancing at evening soirées and talked freely on most curious topics:

I was sometimes rather startled by the very *veterinary* character of the conversation prevalent among some few young and (otherwise) lady-like women of our acquaintance. Good and fearless horse-women themselves, their whole delight seemed to be in the discussion of matters pertaining to the stable; and when meeting any young lady friend from a distance, the first questions were not enquiries after parents, sisters, brothers, or friends: no, nor even the lady-beloved talk of weddings and dress; but the discourse almost invariably took a 'turfy' turn, that was, to say the least, unfeminine in the extreme.

She would have found something of an ally in Susanna Moodie, the elder of the Strickland sisters, who even after a lifetime in Canada and some small literary success there, could never reconcile herself to the rigours of colonial life. She and her sister Catherine Parr Traill represent the two basic attitudes of the educated pioneer woman and both, after a cultured and comfortable childhood at Reydon Hall in Suffolk, where they were taught by their parents, wrote most copiously and eloquently of their reactions to life in mid-century Canada.

Neither, at first glance, seems a suitable candidate for pioneering. Both wrote elegantly and in great quantity – Catherine had had nine books for children published before she came to Canada – but a well-to-do and intellectual Suffolk childhood hardly seems fitting preparation for what lay ahead. Indeed Catherine's in-laws, the Traills, lamented that she was 'truly a lovely bright sunny thing to take out to the untracked wilds of a colony'. From the beginning, the sisters showed their differences. Both married officers discharged on half-pay from the Royal Scottish Fusiliers who wished to take up the grants offered as inducements to gentlemen emigrants to Canada; from the beginning Catherine was eager to go and Susanna deeply reluctant. It was not the physical hardship she feared – though she resented it later – but more the 'loss of the society in which I had moved, the want of congenial pursuits'. She knew, however, that going was inevitable since her husband James Moodie, whom she described as 'a lover of ease' could not support her and their baby in England. 'The half pay of a subaltern officer, managed with the most rigid economy, is too small to supply the wants of a family, and if of good family, not enough to maintain his original standing in society.'

For Catherine, to be free of the shackles of social pretension was a delight, even if she did have to sink her pride and lend a hand in field labour. 'We are totally without the fear of Mr and Mrs Grundy; and having shaken off the trammels of Grundyism we laugh at the absurdity of those who voluntarily forge afresh and hug their chains.'

She and her husband, after an initial stay with her younger brother at Peterborough, pioneered for seven years in the Otonabee District – near the modern Lakefield, Ontario – and she drew on those experiences to write the book that became the pioneer wife's bible. Her aim, she declared, was to write an accurate account of what the pioneering life was like and to dispel the romantic image of it that the land companies suggested in their selling campaigns. *The Female Emigrant's Guide*, published in 1854, is exactly what its title suggests and an awe-inspiring example of what a cheerful and industrious approach could achieve. Describing herself as one of 'we bush ladies [who] have a wholesome disregard of what Mr and Mrs So-and-so thinks or says', she gave recipes for making candles, soft soap and vinegar, notes on servant-handling, general instructions for running a house and small farm in primitive circumstances and advice on how to cook the plants and animals of Canada. She was not only informative but gave an idea of the pleasures to be had, if one was prepared to suspend the judgements of upper-class England: 'The work went merrily on,' she wrote of the logging 'bee' which provided the materials for their first home, 'with the help of plenty of Canadian nectar [whiskey] . . . our bee being considered so very well conducted in spite of the difference of rank among those that assisted that the greatest harmony prevailed.'

Susanna Moodie, unhappily settled at Coburg, described a similar occasion in much greater detail and with an air of profound distaste. Bees, she said, were 'noisy riotous drunken meetings [which] often terminate in violent quarrels, sometimes even in bloodshed'. Her first house, a shack on a farm, appalled her. 'I could only stare at the place with my eyes swimming with tears . . . a room with but one window – the rain poured in at the open door . . . and dropped upon our heads from holes in the roof . . . nothing could exceed the uncomfortableness of our situation.'

To compound her unhappiness, her husband – who had had visions of living the life of an English country gentleman in Canada – was not at all successful and her life was lonely and grindingly hard. There was however a silver lining in that her misery unleashed her creative powers and the conventional and sentimental stuff she had produced as a girl in Suffolk gave way to writing that was much more powerful and unorthodox. *Roughing it in the Bush* appeared in 1852 and was immediately regarded as a classic. It made no bones about its aim:

If these sketches should prove the means of deterring one family from sinking their property and shipwrecking all their hopes by going to reside in the backwoods of Canada, I shall consider myself amply repaid for revealing the secrets of the prison house and feel that I have not toiled and suffered in the wilderness in vain.

Life in the backwoods at Ashburnham near Peterborough took a toll of her body and social self-confidence:

For seven years I lived out of the world entirely; my person had been rendered coarse by hard work and exposure to the weather and I looked double the age I really was and my hair was already thickly sprinkled with grey. I clung to my solitude.

But it poured a wonderful energy into her mind. At first impeded from getting anything published by her inability to afford either paper or postage, she was rescued in 1838 by James Lovell of Montreal who was starting a periodical called the *Literary Garland* and offered her $5 a page. 'I actually shed tears of joy over the first twenty dollar bill,' she wrote, and went on to be a steady contributor for the thirteen years of the magazine's life. Some years she earned as much as £40 and found enough encouragement to start her own literary periodical – which only survived a year – and to write three novels, which were a success commercially even if they lacked the realism and comic sense of her pioneering master-piece.

Catherine was not to be outdone. By the time she died in 1899 she had become an acknowledged authority on Canadian natural history, so much so that she was emboldened, on account of this and her pioneering fame, to apply to Queen Victoria for a 'reward' for all she had done for the colony. She might have declared how delightful it was to be free of Grundyism, but, as Desmond Pacey the literary historian observed, 'The sisters made no attempt to disguise their sense of social superiority to the impoverished Yankee and British settlers who surrounded them, and though we may deplore their snobbery, we must admire their frankness.'

Whether Catherine was also impelled by the fact of having nine children to support is uncertain, but she wrote to the Queen from Rice Lake Plains claiming that she had 'reaped to herself and her family no reward beyond a literary reputation' from the land she had 'so materially served'. It was assumed in the Colonial Office that Mrs Traill was asking for land; the Queen, while remarking that she hoped something could be done, expressed 'no positive desire' and the matter fell into the tangles of bureaucracy. Free grants of land were governed by the Colonial Enactment and could not be made from London. 'It is therefore not in the power of the Crown to comply with the application which you have preferred,' wrote Arthur Blackwood, chief clerk in charge of the North American Department.

It was discouraging to ask for a reward and to receive in reply a letter about land regulations in Canada. But Catherine was a tenacious creature and if the government of her country of birth would refuse her request, that of her country of adoption might not. Almost forty years later, after a life of great hardship as well as achievement, Catherine asked for a small island in Stony Lake which was to be sold at a public auction. What Windsor and Whitehall had refused, Ottawa granted.

'It has been a great pleasure to everyone here, from the highest to the lowest official, to do everything in their power to do you honourable service and to gratify your every wish – every one of them feeling that the most any of them can do is but the smallest acknowledgement which is due to you for your life-long devotion to Canada.'

Canada illustrates another facet of the pioneer woman's life. Since its foundation in the late seventeenth century, the fur trade had imposed a virtual ban on the presence of white women in its settlements but, as Victoria's reign began, the Chief Traders and Factors of the Hudson Bay Company began to go on furlough to Great Britain in search of something other than a breath of civilized air. 'There is a strange revolution in the manners of the country,' wrote James Douglas, an employee of the company. 'Indian wives were at one time the vogue, the half breed supplanted these and now we have the lovely, tender exotic fern from its parent bed to pine and languish in the desert.'

The exotic fern had not been unknown but she had been very rare. There had been the extraordinary Isobel Gunn from Orkney who had arrived at Moose Factory in the early years of the century in pursuit of her lover. She had disguised herself as a boy and, under her male name of John Fubbister, worked so well that her sex remained undetected until she had been forced to beg for help in the delivery of a baby son, ripping open her jacket to convince those from whom she sought assistance – and to reveal beautiful breasts – that she was indeed a woman. For most of the fur traders there was a much more available alternative than battling over the odd Isobel Gunn; *mariage à la façon du pays* had grown up in Rupert's Land, complete with European and Indian marriage customs, and become a central and recognized social aspect of a fur trader's life.

In those tightly knit trading communities of Western Canada the Indian 'country' wives helped to create and advance trade relations with other tribes, quite apart from relieving the monotony of isolated life. Rupert's Land – the hinterland of Hudson Bay – was an inhospitable place with a climate of 'merciless cold or insect-ridden heat' and therefore highly unsuitable for a white woman, but an Indian bride, 'cleansed and scoured' and put into some sort of European garment as well as the native blanket and leggings to which she clung, would do very well there. As long as they remained around the Bay and worked, settling not being permitted, all was well. But problems arose if the officer of the Company wished to go home on furlough or to retire to Eastern Canada. In both places his 'bit of brown' was forbidden. It was a bitter decision to have to take, to leave behind the partner of many years – and the mother of many mixed-blood children – and the practice arose of paying another officer remaining at the trading settlement to take on the Indian family.

By the early nineteenth century, things were changing. When the Red River Colony in Rupert's Land began, traders and their 'swarthy idols' were actually permitted to settle there, and with the settlement grew an addiction to things European. Company officers tried to wean their Indian wives away from their own native habits and induce them to accept European ways, quite oblivious, it seems, that the very qualities of refined gentleness and delicacy which they most extolled were the least suitable attributes for a life in a fur-trading settlement. The mixed-blood women embraced European fashions and manners with all the enthusiasm their menfolk, and the pure-blood Indian men, showed for the vast quantities of imported liquor, but Indian wives were reluctant to relinquish either their moccasins or their tobacco. Many of the Company officers were genuinely fond of their country wives – as shown by Charles Ross's description of his Ojibwa wife, Isabella:

I have yet said nothing about my wife, whence you will probably infer that I am rather ashamed of her. In this, however, you would be wrong. She is not exactly fitted to shine at the head of a nobleman's table, but she suits the sphere she has to move in better than any such toy. . . . As to beauty, she is quite as comely as her husband.

They were not only fond but felt themselves, as Daniel Harmon put it, 'under a moral obligation not to dissolve the connection if she is willing to continue it'. Quite apart from the emotional ties between European man and Indian woman, families of twelve and thirteen children were not uncommon. For all that, and even after the Hudson Bay Company lifted its ban on bringing Indian wives to Britain in 1821 – an offer few took advantage of – a creeping dissatisfaction with the brown women was setting in. They had been referred to as 'my guid wife' and 'the mother of my children' and now were insultingly hailed as 'squaw' and 'brown jug'. The growing numbers of mixed-bloods were making racial feeling a real threat and causing the image of the white woman to be increasingly admired. The assumption was that sexual abstinence was impossible for a man and therefore a little indulgence in the charms of 'a dark-eyed beauty' was only natural, but when it came to marriage, the fur trader began to dream of a woman '. . . capable of adorning his station in life and if possible with the connections to advance his career. She would be of spotless character. . . .'

The fur traders' eyes turned homeward. They might not be able to offer a life of polish but they could offer status in a small community and undoubted economic security. Lord Selkirk, founder of the Red River Colony, was strongly advised to encourage the bringing out to Canada of white wives – not least as an inducement to gentleman emigrants – and then Governor George Simpson, one of the most influential figures of the nineteenth-century fur trade, went home on furlough and returned with his lovely eighteen-year-old cousin Frances. He was the first important man to bring out a white bride, but he is even more remarkable for the singular callousness with which he cast aside all his previous Indian mistresses once he was possessed of something more desirable. And desirable she was, with her pretty face and 'fascinating accomplishments', as she toured through Rupert's Land. But unwittingly she brought with her the beginnings of what has been called, with reference to India, the 'memsahib syndrome', the disdaining and displacement of native dark women by imported white girls.

Soon she was not alone. The desire to have an elegant and ladylike bride was highly infectious. Catherine MacTavish, Eleanor MacMillan, Laetitia Hargrave and Isobel Finlayson were only a few of the delicately nurtured girls who came – some feeling a 'moment of bitter sorrow' – to the alarming ruggedness of Western Canada in the first decade of Victoria's reign. They had hardly arrived before problems of race arose – distressing problems of which they can have had no suspicion at all and which only widened the gulf between brown and white. Laetitia Hargrave described the meeting in 1840 between Catherine MacTavish and her husband's thirteen-year-old mixed-blood daughter Mary:

[MacTavish] rose and took her up to his wife who got stupid but shook hands with the Miss who was very pretty and mighty impudent. . . . [Mrs MacTavish] got white and red and at last rose and left the room, all the party looking very uncomfortable except her husband and the girl. [Mrs Simpson] followed and found her in a violent fit of crying. She said she knew the child was to have been at home that night but thought she would have been spared such a public intro-duction.

MacTavish, clearly as unfeeling as his colleague George Simpson, omitted the pretty and impudent Miss entirely from his will in 1860.

Racial distinctions led to exclusiveness on the part of white couples, which in turn meant an awful loneliness for the wives, prevented by their status from occupying their time like other pioneer women and without the companionship they or their husbands would have considered suitable. Governor Simpson, anxiously watching the pretty Frances languish at Red River, wrote to John MacTavish at Moose Factory:

I am most heartily tired of Red River . . . and should be delighted to join you at Moose next fall, indeed my better half is constantly entreating me to take her there so that she may enjoy the society of her friend. Here she has formed no intimacies. McKenzie's wife is a silly ignorant thing . . . Mrs Jones is a good unmeaning woman and Mrs Cockrane . . . shines only when talking of elbow grease and the shining of pots and pans.

A Chief Factor who brought his 'bit of circulating copper' to introduce her to the Simpson and MacTavish ladies, was told it was the height of impertinence. Hardly surprisingly, neither lady lasted long in Canada. 'No society, no relative, no friend' and failing health in a harsh climate drove both of them home – Frances after only three years.

A few – a very few – were tougher and even outlasted the 'novelty of getting Hudson Bay stocked with European Ladys'. When Lae-titia Hargrave consented to share her husband's bleak lot at York Factory (a place notorious for its Indian prostitutes) his friend James Douglas wrote in reverent rapture, 'What a debt of gratitude you incur, through such heroic devotion, which a lifetime of the tenderest attentions can hardly repay.'

She endured over ten years at York Factory and in 1851 was rewarded by her husband ordering her to command herself a gown 'worthy of being worn by such a wife as you are to me'. She clearly had great strength of mind, since the first sight of York Factory had made her turn her 'back on the company and cry myself sick'. Her friend Isobel Finlayson, wife of the Red River Settlement's Chief

Factor, although 'little and ladylike' and frail physically, kept a remarkably resilient diary account of her journey out to the colony in 1840. She did, it is true, have every known comfort (such as a travelling case containing a cruet and 'Chrystal flaggons for wine and other liquids') but she was wet right through most of the time.

When it is time to encamp for the night, your tent may have to be pitched in the long wet grass, or worse than all on the wet sand; your bedding perhaps has got damp in the boat, and wet as it is there is no alternative but to spread it on the damp ground and every thing is cold and comfortless about you, and owing to the wood being wet, the fire will not even blaze to cheer you in your miserable condition. The situation of the poor men is worse than your own, for they must still be exposed to the heavy rain, performing the various duties of the evening. After a comfortless night you rise in the morning to resume the wet cloaks you have thrown off the previous day, with but little prospect of being able to better your condition the following night.

But her spirits remained dry enough to appreciate the scenery and the romance of the great forests; however poor her health she had to walk at times, once 'above half a mile through a swamp of moss', when she was 'so much amused' at the soggy tumbles her companions took that she was quite 'disposed to laugh'. She admired the Indians' teeth and dandified attention to their beaded finery but deplored their low foreheads and 'dark, piercing and restless eye . . . continually wandering around as if in search or fear of treachery'.

This apparent furtiveness might have contributed to the suspicion with which female white viewed female brown. Most of the health problems of the white women arose during pregnancy and childbirth but nothing on earth would have persuaded them to listen to Indian advice and have their children delivered while they squatted, native fashion, by their beds. Indian medicines and ways of keeping warm were similarly spurned and although Laetitia Hargrave allowed curious native women to see her 'very fat, very white' firstborn, she was appalled by the New Year's Eve party given by the clerks at York Factory:

I went and sat for a little in a room off that in which they were dancing. It was a humbling affair. Forty squaws, old and young with their hair plaited in long tails, nothing on their heads but their everlasting blankets smelling of smoke and everything obnoxious. Babies almost newly born and in their cradles were with their mothers and all nursing them in front of everyone. I was glad to come home.

Her husband put his finger on the result of the arrival of the lovely tender exotics. The Indians themselves had not changed, it was rather, he said, that 'this influx of white faces has cast a still deeper shade over the faces of our Brunettes in the eyes of many'. Only recently has the pendulum even begun to swing back. As late as 1923 a book was published entitled *Women of the Red River*. Many of the women interviewed were descendants of the old Hudson Bay Company pioneer families and while making virtually no mention at all of their Indian ancestry, took much pride in revealing the purity of their connections with English and Scottish blood.

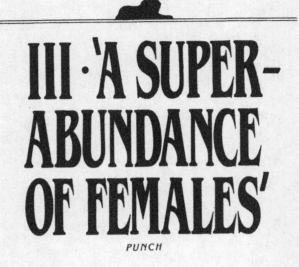

III · 'A SUPER-ABUNDANCE OF FEMALES'

PUNCH

III

The daughters of England are too numerous,' *Punch* stated robustly in January of 1850. 'And if the Mother cannot otherwise get them off her hands, she must send them abroad into the world. . . . It is lamentable that thousands of poor girls should starve here upon slops, working for slop-sellers and not only dying old maids but dying young when stalwart mates and solid meals might be found for all in Australia.'

This was a simple and positive notion but it stirred not a step from the belief that marriage was the only proper sphere for a woman, a belief entirely unshaken by the consequence that the men who remained in England had such an array of girls to choose from and were so petted that they could, to a large extent, have their cake and eat it. In 1861 seven mothers wrote to *The Times* complaining that young men were perfectly happy to sponge off a girl's family for entertainment, but had no intention of doing the decent thing and marrying their host's daughters since it was far more amusing to live with 'the pretty horsebreakers' of Rotten Row. This letter brought a reasonable reply from a man who said it was respectable families themselves who drove prospective sons-in-law into the arms of a mistress. 'Girls are now so thoughtlessly brought up, are led to expect so lavish an outlay on the part of the husband that, unless his means are unlimited, he must, to comply with the wishes of a modern wife, soon bring himself to beggary. . . . Respectability may be too dearly purchased.'

Education, the early feminists saw, was also a long-term answer to the surplus of women in Britain. But women found they had to climb a long and stony track before they could win social acceptance as professionaly qualified workers. The law, as a profession, was to remain closed to women until 1919 and in 1876 the examiners of the Royal College of Surgeons resigned to a man rather than examine three women for diplomas in midwifery. In the

1870s a stipendiary magistrate, Mr Llenfer Thomas, pleaded in an article in *Prevention*, the organ of the National Council for Public Morals, for a little female help in the police force:

Has the policewoman no place in our national life? Is it not desirable that the Home Office should permit and even encourage the appointment of a limited number of high-minded specially trained policewomen for such special duty in some of our larger towns? Such an innovation would inevitably tend towards the introduction of more humane methods into police operations. . . .

Humane such an idea might be, enlightened, imaginative and sensible it certainly was, but it fell short of satisfying the great god Propriety. Where people nowadays speak of values and the quality of life, the Victorians spoke of propriety. 'To be considered unlady-like,' says Duncan Craw in *The Victorian Woman*, 'was to court the outer darkness and often reach it.' Sport was taboo on these grounds, even painting out-of-doors might be if it involved wearing thick shoes. When a group of pioneers at Girton College, Cambridge, acted some scenes from Shakespeare for the college staff in 1871 wearing men's clothes, the audience was frozen with horror and outrage. Earning money, and even worse (indeed the most unthinkably improper activity of all) any association at all with the suffrage cause meant an ostracism that only the rich and therefore independent could afford. And they were rare and lucky in the extreme.

For the majority of those thousands of unfortunate women for whom marriage and its consequent dependence was not to be, life cannot have looked a very tempting business. True, some of the doll-Madonnas of the drawing rooms were well content with their enforced idleness – Mrs Kirkpatrick in Mrs Gaskell's *Wives and Daughters* reflects with intense relief on the prospect of protected inactivity that lies before her after Dr Gibson's proposal – but there were plenty who felt with Florence Nightingale when she cried out in 'Cassandra', the conclusion to her unpublished book, *Suggestions for Thought to Searchers after Religious Truth*:

Women are never supposed to have any occupation of sufficient importance *not* to be interrupted, except 'suckling their fools' and women themselves have accepted this, have written books to support it, and have trained themselves so as to consider whatever they do as *not* of such value to the world or to others but that they can throw it up at the first 'claim of social life'.

Pitiful the Dora Copperfields may look in retrospect, but to another group, their social equals often, but single and with no private means, they must have been objects of the purest envy. For such women, gently born and reared to the exacting standards of Victorian propriety but finding themselves, through bereavement or ill health or luck, without the means of maintaining a ladylike way of life, the drawing room surely assumed the desirability of paradise. To be poor in Victorian England was a solemn matter, to be hungry, common – Josephine Kamm reports on girl students who, having spent their pittance on books rather than bread, wore tight fabric bands around their waists at night to stifle gnawings of hunger – but to be considered respectable at all costs was essential. There was only one profession not overshadowed by the frown of public disapproval, only one way to earn bread and keep society's stringent rules, and that was to teach: not in schools, until later in the century, but in schoolrooms, to be one of over 21,000 governesses in employment in 1850.

It is difficult to find anyone with a good word to say for the position of governess in Victorian England. For the most part, in novels and memoirs and letters, the opinion of enlightened people was that expressed so forcibly by Mrs Jameson in her *Memoirs and Essays*:

What is the point to fit a woman for a private governess? You must not only cram her with languages and dates and all the technicalities of teaching but educate her in the seclusion of a nunnery and inure her to privation, discipline and drudgery and above all, cruelty – yes, that is the word – the cruelty of giving her ideas, nay feelings, aspirations which might render the slavery of her future more dreadful than of necessity it must be.

It was necessity that drove them to it. To be a woman, to be middle-class, perhaps educated, and to be without either a husband or money was to be in a position for which society had no pity. Early in the century, Jane Austen wrote candidly of this plight, 'A single woman with a narrow income must be a ridiculous old maid, the proper sport of boys and girls; but a single woman of good fortune is always respectable and may be as sensible and pleasant as anybody else.' Fifty years later, in all seriousness, the *Saturday Review* echoed her: 'Married life is women's profession and to this life, her training, that of dependence, is modelled. Of course by not getting a husband or losing him she may find that she is without resources. All that can be said of her is, she has failed in her business and no social reform can prevent such failures.'

Such a woman not only carried a social stigma, she carried the immensely arduous burden of providing for herself in an age when legally it was extraordinarily difficult for a woman to make or retain any money of her own. It must be remembered that divorce was not possible until 1857, that any money a woman possessed could, with the law's full consent, be used or abused by her husband until 1882, and that, for a further nine years after that, a husband could by right imprison his wife in her own house if he so chose. Morally and financially it was a case of 'My wife and I are one and I am he.' Single women might have escaped such tyranny, but they did not escape the very real threat of destitution. For most of them, the only means of warding it off was to teach in the schoolrooms of middle- and upper-class households, an outcast from life both below and above stairs.

It was a depressing prospect and, in *The Poor Teacher* (1845), Richard Redgrave describes the governess as looking as downcast as her hopes. She wears, he wrote, 'an all eclipsing cottage bonnet, drab all enveloping merino shawl; threadbare gloves, neatly furled umbrella and carpet bag.'

No wonder. The very best, the most highly qualified among the 25,000 employed in the 1850s, might hope for £100 a year; the great majority received only £30 or £40, and this at a time when an adult daughter living at home was estimated to cost her father at least £100 each year and the minimum income required to support a woman in any kind of genteel style was estimated at £150 to £200. Barbara Bodichon, the great champion of women's rights, was given £300 a year by her enlightened father when she came of age; as she said herself, the income gave her freedom and dignity. He was a rare father indeed; most Victorian fathers were of the type described by Madame Mohl, the great friend and correspondent of Florence Nightingale:

[A] father spends more every year on his dog kennels than he will give to [his daughter]. Daughters are his playthings but as to thinking of their future well-being, he never does. . . . He thinks they are to make his tea and nurse him when he is old and gouty — and that is what they were born for.

They certainly were not born for education if a governess could be had for something between one and two pounds a week, and then be discarded upon charity when she was too old or sick to be of further use, having, on such an income, been unable to save for her old age. On top of her financial distress – and as keen a pain – was the ambiguousness of her social position in the family, a misery described by Elizabeth Eastlake in 1848, a year in which a hundred governesses a day advertised for positions in *The Times*:

She is a bore to almost any gentleman, as a tabooed woman, to whom he is interdicted from granting the usual privileges of the sex, and yet who is perpetually crossing his path. She is a bore to most ladies by the same rule and a reproach too, for her dull fagging bread and water life is perpetually putting their pampered listlessness to shame.

'You should hear Mama on the chapter of governesses,' Blanche Ingram exclaims loudly in Jane's hearing in *Jane Eyre*. 'Mary and I have had, I should think, a dozen at least in our day; half of them detestable and the rest ridiculous. . . . I have just one word to say of the whole tribe; they are a nuisance.'

They were not only a nuisance because they did not fit in but also because they were an embarrassing, separate race that *could* not fit in. As late as June 1890, the *Daily News* carried the report of a court case in which the governess had clearly been treated as neither fish nor fowl nor good red herring:

Miss Harker took day service as a governess in a family at Stockton at a salary of 25 shillings a month, coupled with the privilege of dining in the house. She found herself under the necessity of taking a lodging, the rent for which more than absorbed her modest stipend. She taught three children English and Music. Afterwards a couple of infants were placed in her charge. Nor was that all, for when the servants left, the new governess had to cook the dinner, wash the dishes and clean the knives. After this she asked for a holiday the result being that she was shown the door.

That was their position at worst; at best it was a 'life of genteel obscurity'. Yet 'the pathetic governess', as Charlotte Yonge described her, was not without her champions or, for the enterprising, her means of escape. John Ruskin made a public appeal in Manchester in 1864 which was to become a milestone in the reformation of attitudes to governesses:

What teachers do you give your girls? And what reverence do you choose to show the teachers you have chosen? Is a girl likely to think her own account or her own intellect of much importance when you trust the entire formation of her character . . . to a person whom you let your servants treat with less respect than they do your housekeeper?

Ruskin might deplore the situation as it was but Miss Maria Rye at the Social Science Congress in 1861 could offer a practical solution. Miss Rye ran a highly successful law-copying office for women clerks in Lincoln's Inn Fields, and because she was besieged by the demands of educated women for work, she had cast about her for alternative and suitable occupation and had come up with the idea of emigration. There was a rising demand in Australia, New Zealand and Natal for superior servants and for governesses and Miss Rye felt that the women who begged her for employment would be ideally suited, not least because of 'an elevation of morals being the inevitable result of the mere presence in the colony of a number of high class women'.

Bessie Parkes had expressed the same opinion only months before. She was most distressed at the impossibility of introducing large numbers of educated women into the 'fields of competitive employment' and longed 'to see the immense surplus of the sex in England lightened by judicious, well-conducted and morally guarded emigration to the colonies where the disproportion is equally enormous and where they are wanted in every social capacity'. It was plainly not only a salary that the colonies could provide but also, and equally important, a social and intellectual status which the great preponderance of women, and opinion in general, denied women at home.

Miss Rye took the practical step of founding, in 1862, the Female Middle Class Emigration Society. The Society caused an outcry. It was, said Lord Osborne, a masquerade for a degrading form of husband-hunting. So what? said *The Times* sharply in reply; so, if one was honest, was an archery meeting and the lady emigrants were at least as liable to benefit the colonies they went to as to gain a husband from them. The society lasted for twenty-three years, in which time it settled over three hundred women in the colonies – not a vast achievement in relation to the thousands of Britons who were emigrating at the time, but it was carefully organized and provided valuable experience for later migration societies. 'It seems as though

The leaving of Liverpool. An emigrant family
bound for Australia, 1913

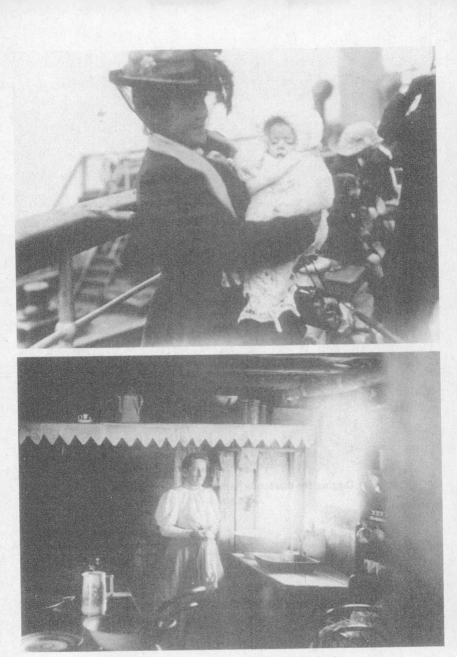

A new life for a new life. Aboard the *Zealandic* on
the voyage to Australia, 1913

Recreating home. An early pioneer kitchen in Australia

LEFT: Skipping to Canada on the *Empress of Britain*, 1910

Digging for diamonds. A hopeful early family at
Kimberley

To sew a fine seam. A domestic training class in
London, Ontario

Mrs Brown boiling the spuds. Photographed by
her husband in Alberta, Canada

LEFT: The promised land? The interior of a Canadian
immigrant's home, c. 1905

PREVIOUS PAGE: Leaking roofs and starched pinafores.
An old pioneer bark hut in Gippsland, Victoria,
in the 1840s

Coming through the Rye, and The Monthly
Shearing: two snapshots from Jessie Buckland's
New Zealand scrapbook

'Come out here and take your chance.' Domestic
servants newly arrived in Quebec, 1911

'It is the Mecca of teachers, or should be.' Anglican mission
school, Blackfoot reserve, Southern Alberta 1900

Florence Nightingale in old age, photographed by
Emery Walter

'Give me the ladies. Every time. Give me the
ladies.' Nurses at the Johannesburg Hospital, 1905

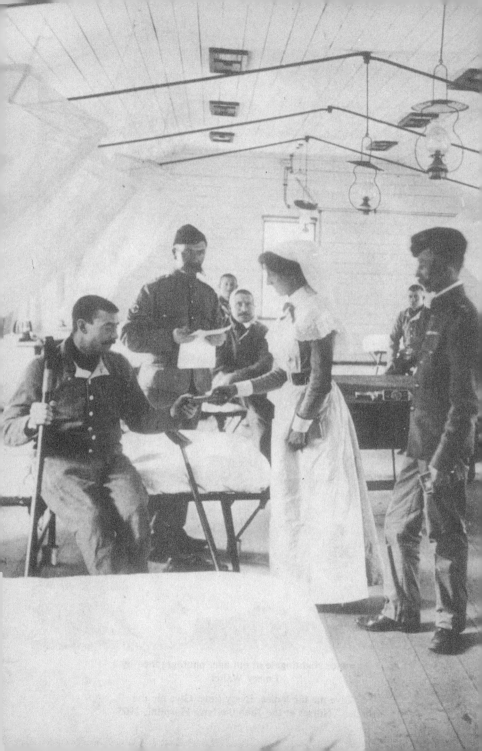

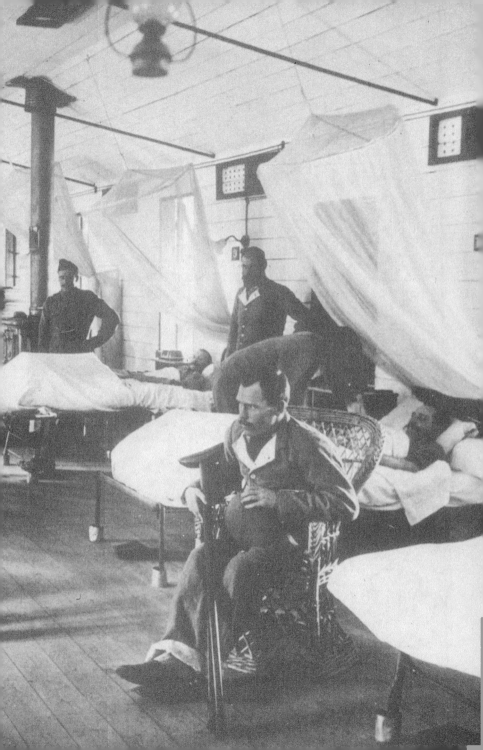

Harriet Georgiana Blackwood, later the 1st Marchioness of
Dufferin and Ava, Vicereine of India in the late 1870s

PREVIOUS PAGE: Nine nurses to care for six hundred men.
Wynberg Hospital during the Boer War

the dark cloud which has hung over my life is fast disappearing,' one woman who benefited wrote from Natal in 1866, and a Melbourne teacher explained in raptures, 'We were and are now quite sure that if the people of England had any idea of it, they would want to come out in a body.'

No less than seven similar societies sprang up in Miss Rye's wake in the following sixty years, including the Women's Migration and Overseas Appointments Society, which still exists. Both Miss Rye and her educated emigrants had a lot to learn from the colonies themselves and benefited from such advice as that given by a former resident of Australia at the Social Science Congress in 1862, who recommended that intending emigrants should undergo 'a short training on the theory at all events of household work and duties and needlework of the most useful kinds and in medicine so far as to treat ordinary diseases'. The Society's representative in Hawke's Bay, New Zealand, wrote warning of the roughness of colonial life where 'there are fewer servants – sometimes the family is left for weeks without any – and a governess who stood on her dignity and refused to help would do a foolish thing'.

Most of them, though initially startled at the vigour of colonial life and its lack of 'intellectual refinement', were prepared to make considerable efforts. One teacher wrote to Miss Rye from New South Wales, 'People are wanted here, but not people of any sort. People who come here should be intelligent.' She herself had enormous admiration for what the Australians had achieved with their country but she saw it as very unlike home:

Australian ladies are very different to English and they dislike as they term it our particular ways. . . . Children are very much indulged and have no energy nor application, do not like the least trouble. All Australians ride like Arabs, love luxury and money. They live very much out of doors and eat great quantities of fruit. Beef and mutton are very cheap here. Rice is eaten as a vegetable and tea is very much taken.

Annie Davies, also writing from Australia, in 1863 wrote in answer to Lord Osborne's anxieties about indelicate husband-hunting, 'I am aware there is an idea in England that young and accomplished governesses soon marry in this land. That is a mistake, at least nowadays; in the early years of the Colony it did so happen for educated women were very rare then.'

She was writing of Sydney, but another governess writing from upcountry in Queensland twenty years later declared, 'Australian men seem to have quite a fancy for marrying governesses.' Upcountry had other charms than the prospect of a husband since the more remote the place, the higher the salary. Annie Davies took the chance of £100 a year with an outback family but found their being *nouveau riche* too much for her sensibilities; she retired thankfully back to Sydney to £80 and a 'refined, educated' post.

It must have been a relief, after the unrelenting social codes of England, not only to be able to pick and choose, but also to feel oneself in a position of equality and sometimes even of superiority. Louisa Geoghegan, while doubtful about Australia, found the absence of class differences there welcome indeed. 'I am very glad I came to Australia,' she wrote from Victoria in 1867. 'But I cannot say I like it very much. It is such an out of the world place and so monotonous, but as far as treatment goes I could not meet with nor desire kinder. With no one in this neighbourhood have I seen the social distinction made with governesses that there is at home.'

It seems the distinction made was so very little that if there was any disdaining to be done, the governesses could outshine their employers at it. A few years later Miss Geoghegan could write of the existence of two distinct social sets, one composed of gentlemen, the other of social climbers whom she coyly refers to as mushrooms:

For one gentleman there are six mushrooms, I suppose you would call them. The former, I have heard say, would like thoroughly good lady Governesses from home if they had anyone there conscientiously to select them. The mushroom class pay largely but expect rather queer things, viz. that the Governess should light the schoolroom fire – and similar things. . . . In my short experience I have known of two cases where *ladies* got with these people and very soon had to separate. It is a totally different life from what it is at home. In *nearly* every instance you are looked on as the Intellectual Member of the Establishment. You are the constant companion and associate of the Lady, considered – I might say indulged – in every way, and your only difficulty is to civilize the children, which you are supposed to do through example, as they are uncontrolled to a degree, and the parents object to anything else. . . . I think with you that capable women have a better chance here than at home, but I think a few of a good class not *long* accustomed to home scrubbing and drudgery would be a better importation than a large number of the common run of Governesses.

In some cases, the governess carried such an air of superiority that she almost cost herself employment. One wrote from New Zealand in 1870 describing the effect she had produced on her would-be employers:

Two or three ladies called upon me in the first instance who wanted helpers but who said when they saw me that they could not think of asking me to perform many of the duties which they should require. I got quite into a fright and had some thoughts of dressing myself as a *servant* and calling myself one.

Colonial families were not slow to observe such trends and a Dr Spratt, writing to Miss Rye from New Zealand in 1863, made it very clear that he wanted no one to educate his daughters who suffered from delusions of superiority. He wanted, he said,

... a middle-aged lady to educate my four girls, of whom the eldest is eighteen, the youngest eight. The accomplishments are simply plain English, plain sewing with a little piano and singing. Of course, when I offer fifty pounds a year, which is certainly much higher than many obtain here, I fully trust you will make a careful selection, for I hope to get one gentle and ladylike in her manners and accustomed to teach. She will have no household work of a menial kind, but I wish my daughters to have no companion who thinks it derogatory to be domesticated.

Luckily Miss Rye excelled herself and produced the paragon Dr Spratt had in mind, who was herself more than contented with her position:

Of this family I cannot speak too highly. Dr Spratt is a Gentleman, a term in my idea which comprises a great deal out here. He is clever and agreeable and most anxious to see me happy and comfortable. My pupils are amiable, well-behaved girls and I like them very much. We are all very fond of music so can spend a few hours very pleasantly at the piano, Dr Spratt and I being the performers.

When she wanted, in the course of time, to leave the Spratts and open a school, she was twice persuaded to stay on even though, as the custom was, her salary was reduced as each child grew up and left the schoolroom. Another New Zealand governess, signing herself 'Augusta' in her letters back to the FMCES, was not so lucky. In her first post she was required to 'slave' sixteen hours a day and sit up constantly with sick children, and when she abandoned this drudgery for a job in the backblocks, she found herself jolting over treeless wastes for two days to a house which was a 'small, miserable broken-down looking thing situated on the riverbed of the Waimakariri; everything about the house and its environs was wretched and comfortless to a degree'. She had six pupils to teach and a daily round that must have made her long for England once more, status or not status:

I was only engaged to teach 5 hours a day, but I found I was expected to teach for 8 hours and a half, and although there were 6 daughters above 12 years of age I was expected to clean out the school hut, also to fetch sticks and light the fire, etc. I had to scrub floors, wipe up dishes and do all kinds of menial work, and after all I was accused of not doing enough and not sewing sufficiently for the family, although I had been allowed by my engagement to have every evening to myself, and although every evening was spent in playing the piano from half past six till half past nine for the amusement of the children or Mr K., and every moment stolen from that time was spent in fancy work for Mrs K.

She would no doubt have agreed with another governess who wrote from a sheep station outside Canterbury, 'My ideal of New Zealand life has been spoiled: and although it is undoubtedly the paradise of servants, I am afraid the paradise of governesses has yet to be discovered.' But then, as Mrs Blanchard, an ardent supporter and helpmeet of Miss Rye's, would have observed, a colonial paradise was very much what each emigrant made of it. This governess, writing from Dunedin in 1869, would undoubtedly have made a success of a challenging life anywhere:

I must thank you on behalf of my sister and also for myself for the kind interest you manifested in us, and assure you that we have never for one moment had cause to regret having left our native land. For those who are ready to work there is abundant scope out here, and what is better still, they get paid for what they do. True it is rougher, and there are things to be done one could not and would not do at home, but where everyone works there is no occasion for pride, and I think it no disgrace to be able to help oneself. I am charmed with Colonial life, and the more refinement one can bring into the everyday occupation the more it raises the work, I think. Good, sensible, well educated governesses are appreciated here, I am certain, and they can always command salaries varying from £30 to £60, but for those who object to be on an equality with the family and are afraid to render assistance when required, I do not think there is such good promise.

Another in the same mould, who had been delighted to discover that she was worth above twice her annual £20 English salary to a family in New South Wales, wrote ruefully that there was no point in trying to make ordered English children out of little Australians:

Australian children are just like the vegetation here, for neither appear to submit to much control. Pineapples, peaches and the finest fruit grow in open air without care and the children are equally wild and impetuous. You meet with very few quiet girls here, they like no trouble nor will they take any about anything. The floor is the place for everything, and it is no use making yourself unhappy because they will not acquire English manners, for they do not like them. . . .'

Even though Australian and New Zealand children feature quite largely in the letters, there is a surprising dearth of comment on the presence of Maoris or Aborigines. Only the writers from South Africa mention the natives, one to say that she did 'not think Natal is the most desirable place for [governesses] – the almost entire want of white servants being a drawback', and another emphasizing how important it is to learn to speak Kaffir. If black servants were considered a disadvantage on account of colour, their presence was an undeniable asset in other ways since some of these writers complain of the necessity of performing household chores, as was often the case in Australasia. Letters from Port Natal in 1865 speak of the 'charming climate' and 'the eternal sunshine', warning of the advisability of bringing out from home as high a standard of dress as could be managed since the place as 'as fashionable as possible, there being three or four mails a month and constant immigrations from England and the Continent'.

It is of course always impossible to please everyone. Even in South Africa, with its beautiful climate and abundance of servants, there was discontent. A Miss Jackson, writing from Verulam – 'a nice little colonial village' twenty miles from Durban – in the 1860s, had a poor opinion of most things. She had been engaged to teach the children of the resident magistrate, but considered her salary too small – they mostly were in South Africa – the low canvas-roofed houses too flimsy, the staple vegetable, boiled pumpkin, tasteless to a degree and the few English servants uppity and obsessed with the idea of marriage. To crown it all, she felt herself wasted in South Africa. 'They need maidservants,' she wrote firmly, 'not governesses.'

Perhaps she was soured by failing to receive a proposal, unlike one governess who wrote excitedly to Miss Rye in 1862 from Natal,

'I have done one *very* foolish thing which I did not *mean* to do. However, I am not going to do anything rash and shan't marry just yet. I am going to wait a little while first and see how the Gentleman gets on.' Lord Osborne would have felt his worst fears quite justified.

South Africa might not have paid as handsomely as the other colonies but the demand for governesses endured there far longer than elsewhere, well into the 1880s and 1890s. At first in Australia and New Zealand, some sixty frantic ladies might beseech each new arrival from England to teach her children, but demand waned after 1860, partly as economic depressions hit the colonies and partly as governesses left their families and set up schools, creating securer employment for themselves but fewer jobs for their fellows.

By this point, the status of the governess abroad was to be envied, that of the mistress of a school even more so. No doubt the image had derived much burnishing from a few legendary governesses, notably Miss Emmeline Lott, engaged to teach the infant Pasha in Egypt in 1862, and of course Anna Leonowens, who in the same year accepted King Mongkut of Siam's offer to instruct the twenty-five princes and princesses of the blood royal. Even without the subsequent Hollywood glamorizing, her story is remarkable enough. She had attracted the King's notice by opening a school for officers' children in India after her husband's death and was to spend five years in Siam with impressive effect. The influence of her enlightened Western views on slavery and on the gallant treatment of women made her chief pupil, then the heir apparent, a very different ruler to his tyrannical if engaging father. She taught her lessons in a temple, whose only concession to being a schoolroom was a map of the world bearing a large red and a small green patch. The large red patch was Siam, the little green one was Burma, clasped in the arms of an Englishman – Lord Clive – wearing a cocked hat with red feathers. When this small oversimplification of the globe had been put right, and Anna had wrung from the King the right to teach his concubines as well as promises that he would in future moderate his despotism, she prepared to leave Bangkok a very different place than she had found it. The King, despite daily wrangling with her, is reputed to have made a most touching farewell speech:

Mem, everyone is in affliction of your departure. Even that opium-eating secretary is very low down in his heart because you *will* go. It shall be because you must be a good and true lady. I am often angry on you and lose my temper, though I have a large respect for you. But nevertheless, you ought to know you are a difficult woman and more difficult than generally. But you will forget, and come back to my service, for I have more confidence on you every day. Goodbye.

Whether inspired by Mrs Leonowens and Miss Lott or, no less deservingly, by the more ordinary Misses Jones and Smith of Dunedin and Melbourne, Delibes put an English governess into an opera: *Lakmé*, produced at the Opéra Comique in Paris in 1883. In it Miss Bentson – always addressed as 'venerable' by the rest of the cast – sings regretfully as she contemplates the abominations of India, 'When I think how comfortable we might now be in London, in Hyde Park, inhaling that delightful fog which gives us our clear complexions.' She is, of course, a contralto.

As governesses grew thinner on the ground, schools grew thicker. There were excellent state schools in Australia but a large proportion of colonial families wished to see their children privately educated, which could be done, in the early stages at least, at modest cost. A Miss Barlow, after losing her position in England when she had to have time off to nurse a sick mother, emigrated to Australia and set up an infant day school of twelve children, each one paying a shilling a week. They were all, she said with emphasis, *'respectable* children'. Later she progressed to a township outside Melbourne and wrote enthusiastically of her success:

My school has prospered beyond my expectations, though I have had many expenses and my remuneration is very small, the fees low even for England; however, it is a much more independent life than that of a governess, and I like it. . . . I have out 18 day pupils, 2 boarders and 5 private music pupils, so that I have plenty of teaching; and as I have no servant the care of my house absorbs all the leisure time I might otherwise have. I shall indeed be glad when Mamma comes to render me some assistance in that respect. I like Bush life very much. I have only twice been into Melbourne since I came, and the blacksmith and a storekeeper who is a very intelligent man are my nearest neighbours, the latter and his wife have been truly kind to me. . . . It is now the depths of winter, a delightful change after the hot winds. My household scrubbing and rubbing used to be rather trying at those times; I am getting quite a Colonial woman, and fear I should not easily fit into English ideas again, can scrub a floor with anyone, and bake my own bread and many other things an English Governess and Schoolmistress especially would be horrified at.

71

From New Zealand came similar reports – though shot through with frightened hints at the Maori wars – of the popularity of schools run by English governesses. Miss C. wrote from Dunedin in 1864 frankly acknowledging her own talents. 'I was at once offered the charge of a Ladies' School. I came for the first month on trial and from having an attractive manner of teaching the schools soon became so large they had to move into a larger house.'

It was pride that came before a fall. Less than a year later trade crashed in Dunedin and Miss C. had to retreat to Wanganui and, with the help of friends, try again. But the school was not a success:

Believe me, it is a hard struggle for a lady to succeed in this country. . . . It is no use for a well educated lady over 30 years of age to come out. What the settlers like is a young, strong, middle-class sort of person that can be helpful to them and teach their children to read and write. . . . I may do better in time, but I do not expect it for no person could work harder. . . . I keep no servant. I do all my own teaching. Believe me, it is a great mistake to fancy that an unprotected woman can made money in a Colony. Men can do it, they know how to rough it, and it is land that turns in the money.

Miss C. would presumably not have cared for the South African camp schools, set up by several hundred enterprising teachers towards the end of the Boer War. Some of these schools, such as the one at Kabusie, were 'beautifully situated' and the teachers were given their own accommodation and servants. Others were altogether more primitive:

We started a school of 140 pupils. My class met at first on the veldt, sitting around the edge of a hole which was left from making bricks for the school building. I sat in the centre on an empty box. It wasn't easy to keep out of mischief sixty children – children who couldn't speak any English. Teaching here consists of talking, talking, talking from 8.30 till 1, till the throat is parched and aching, while the infants sagely answer 'yes' or 'no'. . . . We went to a picnic out at McMillan's farm, where General Snyman had his headquarters during the siege of Mafeking. It was so odd to go to a picnic beside a river with no water in it, where there were no trees to sit under. They had an improvised fence of canvas stretched between two transport wagons to keep the sun off. Of the hundred people there, only four men were not in khaki.

From these camp schools in the Transvaal and Natal, teachers filtered down to Cape Province to staff the growing educational service, and to be joined by other women sent out from England to

72

be trained at the Grahamstown Training College. Their numbers were swelled by Canadians, surprisingly because Canada itself was in need of teachers, particularly out in the prairie.

Prairie schools, it seemed, demanded initiative and forward planning as this letter, written from Lloydminster, in 1911, shows:

'... about 10 pupils in a dear little schoolhouse right on the prairie. ... It is the Mecca of teachers, or should be. If you are interested in your work and the children, you can do anything you like. ... Perhaps you may find this hint useful to give girls coming out to the prairie; bring all the clothes and *books* and sewing material you can lay hands on – never mind the excess luggage, it is worth it fifty times over. ... Have your skirts bound with a deep band of leather. The rose bushes, 6″ to 30″ high, tear all skirts to ribbons, and these roses are all over the prairie.

It is the most glorious country one can imagine. Now I am here I cannot think how anyone ever stays at home in the old country. Any girl with a mother ... may, everyone here says, safely bring her out, as schools are in such abundance and one's salary would more than cover two. The only difficulty would be in Boarding. The shacks are very small, and the settlers' wives are so hard worked. The best way would be to bring a tent (they, too, are at famine prices here), and sleep out ... until something could be arranged.

Canada, the writer said, 'was clamouring for teachers'. It was also, as Australia, New Zealand and South Africa had made plain for fifty years, crying out for good domestic servants, the working-class girls and women for whom the government-assisted schemes had been devised. The following extract includes about one-tenth of such advertisements placed in the *Sydney Morning Herald* on one day in March 1868 alone:

WANTED, a respectable NURSEGIRL, who can use her needle. Apply Mrs G. Law, Glebe Road.

WANTED, clean active GIRL, 12 or 14, to mind a baby and be useful. Mrs Jordan 104, King Street.

WANTED, HOUSE and PARLOUR MAID, and HOUSE and NEEDLE WOMAN (Protestants), good references indispensable. Apply between 9 and 11 o'clock, on Wednesday and Thursday, to Mrs M. C. Machardy, Edgecliffe Road, Double Bay.

WANTED, a GOVERNESS, for a family living in a retired place on the sea coast, in the Hunter River district. Applications, stating salary required, to be addressed to Mr J. S. Paine, bookseller, Newcastle.

WETNURSE wanted in a family, must be young, healthy, and strong. Apply 283 Castlereagh Street, near Park Street, between 11 and 1.

Although the colonies had from the beginning made it plain that they did not want England's orphans, destitutes and problem cases, the notorious 'bounty system' begun in the 1850s was operated by agents who were interested only in filling the emigrant ships and who rounded up women of dubious repute from the slums of England's cities. The ships destined for Australia had more than the usual proportion of prostitutes and paupers because not only was North America most emigrants' first choice but Australia's image was tarnished with the stigma of the convict ships which had first arrived there in 1788. Many of the women, though potentially good workers, were morally and physically broken by the voyage on the ships. 'A distressing promiscuity prevails from the moment of embarkation. ... Men, women, children, sailors, stokers, coal trimmers live and take their meals in common without the slightest supervision ... there is no division in the lavatories.' Fifty years later, in 1909, an American lady noted that the lot of female steerage passengers had not improved. 'The behaviour of the crew towards girls travelling alone was most improper. Sailors and stewards used brutal language and took all sorts of liberties; the head steward of steerage, even, did not shrink from shaking, pinching and pulling girls, while they were in bed.'

Until the end of the century a steerage passage to Australia cost about £3 with £2 more for extras. The ships were damp and infections rife, particularly those of the lungs and bowels, to which the women and children seemed particularly susceptible; food was reasonably plentiful but not really nutritious, particularly for the babies with which all ships seem to have abounded. The journey endured and over, however, prospects brightened considerably, with eager Australian mistresses offering up to fifteen shillings a week – over double what one might expect in England – and in the main an attitude towards servants not to be encountered readily at home. In 1904 the widow of a bishop explained the behaviour that had prevailed among Canadian employers for the last twenty years of the nineteenth century:

In engaging a servant or lady-help, I used to say that I would never ask any work of her that I had not undertaken myself, but that I could think of no work which at one time or another I had not had to do. In going out to British Columbia a girl ... must be prepared to do the best she can under the circumstances. If saucepans are few and far between, let her take an old lard-can, or even an old tomato-can. If she needs a pail, an old oil-can, with a piece of telegraph wire for a handle, makes an excellent one. Old flour-sacks can be used as dish towels, and the most unlikely things utilized.

Enterprise and industry were necessary, but they were rewarded. A letter from Quebec in 1891, written by a young woman who had been despatched to Canada to remove her from bad company at home, speaks of her growing accomplishments and responsibilities, and of the kindness of her employers:

My master brought us all home a present from England. He brought the dear baby a cloak and a bonnet; he brought the mistress a darning machine and other things and the two boys some tops, and he brought himself home safe; and he brought me two embroidery afternoon aprons, and very large, too. I thanked him very much for them, for a great many masters would not think of the servants, but he would. We was all so very pleased when he arrived. I never forget my prayers night and morning. I go to Church every Sunday morning when fine and all well.

Emigration had proved her salvation, as it had for a pauper child from the workhouse at Shipston-on-Stour. She had found a job even though only in her early teens and was earning enough to think of paying for her little brother to come out and join her:

Madam, I am now writing to tell you how I am getting on. I am very happy and comfortable, but I am always fretting for my little brother. I do wish he was out here. If you would see him on a good ship and see he came safe to Morden, I would send the money for him to come out. I think my mistress would have him with me. My brother is in the Workhouse Union at Shipston-on-Stour near Honnington, he is such a good little boy. I like Canada better now; I shan't want to come back again if my brother comes out – it is him I am thinking of so much. I am sure Mrs Townsend would help to get him out, for she did not like to see us in the workhouse.

There were, of course, pitfalls. Money in Australia might be good but character-destroying temptations were not. Early female emigrants of good character had been appalled at their reception by hordes of men who would congregate on the beaches when a ship arrived to bellow welcoming obscenities and, quite literally, attempt to take their pick. The mid-century emigration societies made huge efforts to prevent these unprotected arrivals but even if a girl was safely landed and placed in her first post, the dangers were not over. The Whitechapel branch of the Metropolitan Association for Befriending Young Servants warned not only of the risk women ran in associating with sailors on the voyage, which could jeopardize the chance of a good situation once it was over, but advised also that all girls should studiously avoid the goldfields. 'If possible, do not go to the goldfields,' a servant wrote from Fremantle in 1894 to prospective emigrants. 'Several of us thought it very hard because we could not go near them but we think differently now. It is true you receive higher wages but you lose your character as so many poor girls fall. One has to be very careful indeed of one's character as it is soon lost.'

Mrs Chisholm, who started the Family Colonization Loan Society in the 1850s, aimed to send out girls who were a cut above the women of the government and bounty schemes. Her emigrants were more educated mothers' helps and as such found great favour, with their ability and willingness 'to make beds, sew, push the perambulator, cook, wash the children's clothes, do the elementary teaching . . . and . . . scrub the floors'. It was not simply the money that was an allure – a girl used to earning £4 on a Derbyshire farm found herself offered £12 and £17 in Canada – but the attitude, yet again, of colonial employers:

In Canada, where men are too scarce to be employed in domestic service, and where the women-servants are as modest and dignified in all moral matters as their mistresses, the discomfort of associating with persons of low habits, vulgar speech and coarse manners would not exist. If more ladies would go to Canada with the determination to take a situation, even as what is called a general servant (but how different to the same class here only those who have lived in Canada can form any idea), they would lead not unpleasant lives at starting, and speedily rise to better things. The Canadian ladies themselves do much of the work of the houses; very few keep more than two servants; there is little or no scrubbing, all the wood being varnished, etc., and the number and uses of labour-saving machines are so great and varied, that the duties of a general servant in Hamilton, London, Toronto and other towns, would be so easy as to be quite within the scope and powers of the lady who is the general servant as well as of the lady who is the mistress.

Even among the dissatisfied – their voices fewer and fainter than those of the fulfilled – there is hardly ever a note of despair. You had to be resilient for the colonies, but if you were, it was difficult to go under completely. Emigration was not a step to be taken lightly, certainly not if there was the smallest chance of a desirable alternative offering itself at home, as *Punch* pointed out in June 1850.

'According to the latest intelligence from California, there are scarcely any ladies there. Probably lovely women will never emigrate to California for gold so long as there is enough of the precious metal at home to make a little hoop that will just go round the fourth finger of the left hand.'

But given the prospect of a ringless finger coupled with a life of penury or grinding hardship and labour at home, thousands of women evidently agreed with Annie Davies when she wrote from Sydney:

Were I in the position of a third or fourth rate governess (I was going to say second) in England I would unhesitatingly become a domestic servant in Australia in preference. . . . It would require some humility and common sense for such a governess to become a servant, but she would be better off – servants are more considered, there is more freedom and independence here than at home. . . . Be sensible, undergo a little domestic change and come out here and take your chance with others with a certainty of succeeding withal.

IV · 'EVERY WOMAN IS A NURSE'

FLORENCE NIGHTINGALE

IV

When the Nightingale School of Nursing was set up, Lord Granville, referring to Lady Palmerston's opinion of it, wrote, 'Lady Pam thinks the Nightingale Fund great humbug. The nurses are very good now. Perhaps they do drink a little but ... poor people, it must be very tiresome sitting up all night ...'

That was in 1860, by which time anaesthetics were being introduced, Pasteur had discovered germs in his experiments with the fermentation of wine, Lord Lister was teaching the use of antiseptics in surgery and Koch had isolated the tuberculosis bacillus. Fifteen years earlier the picture had been very different and if, in retrospect, Mr and Mrs Nightingale were parents of astonishingly little imagination, let alone vision, one cannot entirely blame them for seeking to shelter Florence. It is difficult to believe how appalling conditions were in the hospitals of the mid-nineteenth century, nor how zealously they and their inmates were avoided by all women of the middle and upper classes.

A Victorian hospital was no place, in any way whatsoever, for a respectable woman. The buildings were poorly designed, dirty, ill lit and ventilated, and invariably insanitary to a degree. Without anaesthetics or antiseptics, any treatment, whether medical or surgical, was agonizingly painful and doubtful of success. Since the well-to-do were always nursed at home, the inmates of hospitals were of the poorer classes and were nursed by their own kind, who apparently felt little vocational spirit for a life of such long hours and low pay. They had not the education to appreciate the aims of medical science and suffered the debilitating effects of drudgery and scant leisure that affected most of their class.

They also suffered notoriously from drink. Alcohol flowed freely in Victorian hospitals with the full sanction of medical authority. Journals and textbooks of the time repeatedly advocate stimulants—chiefly whisky—in the treatment of feverish or low conditions, with doses of up to a quart a day of whisky not being uncommon. A nurse would have had to have been a pillar of moral rectitude to have withstood the river of spirits that washed past her in her dirty and wearying life. There was little incentive to avoid becoming a Sairey Gamp.

The chief sufferers in this situation, the patients, showed an understandably powerful reluctance to come into hospital. On the Continent, Roman Catholic sisterhoods were nursing the sick in their own homes or running hospitals, but in England the only option was your own bed and family until you were desperate and then the insanitary and alarming discomforts of a public ward in the care of ignorant and careless women. A change in attitudes to the sick themselves, as well as to nursing as a profession, was acutely needed, as Elizabeth Fry and Florence Nightingale saw. Curiously enough it was the Empire and her armies that were largely to bring about such a change and to give thousands of women a chance to use their talents and capabilities. When Florence Nightingale said with some asperity that it was commonly supposed that nurses worked by instinct, she was not denigrating the female capacity for caring for the vulnerable, but merely underlining the need for professional training.

'When did you first determine on sending nurses to Scutari?' the Duke of Newcastle, Secretary of State for War, was asked at the Crimean War Commission in 1855. He had wanted, he said, to send them at once, but the idea 'was not liked by the military authorities':

It had been tried on former occasions. The class of women employed as nurses had been very much addicted to drinking, and were found even more callous to the sufferings of soldiers in hospitals than men would have been. Subsequently, in consequence of letters in the public press, and of recommendations made by gentlemen who had returned to this country from Scutari, we began to consider the subject of employing nurses. The difficulty was to get a lady to take in hand the charge of superintending and directing a body of nurses. After having seen one or two, I almost despaired of the practicability of the matter until Mr Sidney Herbert suggested Miss Nightingale, with whom he had been previously acquainted, for the work, and that lady eventually undertook it.

The letters to the press that he refers to had expressed the national outrage felt after the battle of the Alma, where the wounded and dying either lay neglected on the battlefield or found themselves shipped in terrible pain to Scutari and the nightmare of the Barrack Hospital there. William Howard Russell, the celebrated war correspondent of *The Times*, had demanded that the 'daughters of England' should volunteer to be 'by the bedsides of the wounded and dying, giving what woman's hand alone can give of comfort and relief'. If nursing as a profession had had anything but the most tainted of reputations, the response would have been enormous – as the Boer War was later to prove – and it is yet further evidence, if such evidence were needed, of the extraordinary determination of Miss Nightingale that she should seek to change social opinion so radically, as well as challenge orthodox military medical procedure.

How she ever had time to write her copious letters and journals is a matter for awe, but luckily she did, and even four days after her arrival in Scutari was writing at length to her friend Dr Bowman, the ophthalmic surgeon:

On Thursday last (November 8th), we had 1715 sick and wounded in the Hospital (among whom 120 cholera patients), and 650 severely wounded in the other building called the General Hospital, of which we also have charge, when a message came to me to prepare for 510 wounded on our side of the Hospital, who were arriving from Balaclava.... I always expected to end my days as a Hospital Matron, but I never expected to be a Barrack Mistress. We had but half an hour's notice before they began landing the wounded. Between 1 and 9 o'clock we had mattresses stuffed, sewn up, laid down, alas! only upon matting on the floor.... We have had such a sea in the Bosphorus, and the Turks, the very men for whom we are fighting, carry in our wounded so cruelly, that they arrive in a state of agony. ... Twenty-four cases died on the day of landing.... We have now four miles of beds, and not eighteen inches apart.... The wounded are now lying up to our very doors, and we are landing 540 more from the Andes.... In all our corridor I think we have not an average of three limbs per man. And there are two more ships 'loading' at the Crimea with wounded. ... I am getting a screen now for the amputations, for when one poor fellow, who is to be amputated to-morrow, sees his comrade to-day die under the knife, it makes impression and diminishes his chance.... We have erysipelas, fever and gangrene, and the Russian wounded are the worst.... If ever you see Mr Whitfield, the House Apothecary of St Thomas's, will you tell him that the nurse he sent me, Mrs Roberts, is worth her weight in gold ... Mrs Drake is a treasure.... The other four are not fit to take care of themselves, but they may do better bye and bye if I can convince them of the absolute necessity for discipline.

Her nurses were a problem; she was the only educated one amongst them even if they had had some nursing experience. Fired by her example, several middle-class girls set off for Scutari in her wake, filled with romantic notions of laying a cool (and well-manicured), white hand upon the fevered and respectfully grateful brow of the common soldier. Such girls were a great trial to Miss Nightingale – a greater trial even than the idle tipplers – since they had no training, no stamina and no stomach for what she required of them. Only a few, such as Lady Alicia Blackwood, stayed the course. Lady Alicia was given the disagreeable task of dealing with the cellars beneath the hospital into which not only did the sewers drain but also the discarded wives and children of the army had crept to live in appalling squalor. The filth was compounded by degradation since the women had found *arrak* an acceptable alternative to gin and prostitution the only means of obtaining it. Emaciated children scampered like rats in the shadows and women in labour lay on piles of rags, rotten with damp and dirt. The stench was indescribable. There was even, Lady Alicia discovered, a dead baby wedged in a pipe to halt the flow of effluent from above. White-handed or no, she dealt with the problem as best she could, as requested by Miss Nightingale.

If hygiene was extraordinarily difficult, so was food. The soldiers' diet had been their daily allotted ration of meat boiled, in the lump, in a cloth they could identify as their own, in giant cauldrons with hundreds of others. And this for men weak from cholera, fever and gangrene. As there were four miles of corridor, it took four hours for the patients to receive this unappetizing nourishment. And there was nothing for them between meals. It was one of Florence Nightingale's greatest innovations to point out that whisky and salt pork is no diet upon which to recover and she installed boilers all over the building to make arrowroot that might reach the men not only before it was cold but also more often than once a day.

Florence Nightingale is invariably associated with the Crimea, but although her work during that war set many wheels in motion, the rest of her life was to achieve immeasurably more – and in quite another part of the Empire. A letter written to her on New Year's Day 1879 shows that her contemporaries saw her just as posterity has come to do – as the Lady with the Lamp and little more:

There was a great deal of romantic feeling about you 23 years ago when you came home from the Crimea (I really believe that you might have been a Duchess if you had played your cards better!). And now you work on in silence and nobody knows how many lives are saved by your nurses in hospital . . . how many thousands of soldiers who would have fallen victim to bad air, bad water, bad drainage and ventilation, are now alive owing to your forethought and diligence, how many natives of India (they might be counted probably in hundreds of thousands) in this generation and in generations to come have been preserved from famine and oppression by [your] energy. . . . You are a myth in your own life time. . . .

Her work for India was enormous. She never visited it, but laboured on in the curtainless flower-filled bedroom she scarcely left after her return from Scutari. Her great ally was Sir Bartle Frere, ex-governor of the presidency of Bombay, who had a seat on the India Council and who worked with Miss Nightingale on the Royal Commission on the Sanitary Reform of India. She was also much aided by the Governor General, Sir John Lawrence; in fact new Governors General and later Viceroys, with the exception of Lord Northbrook (an omission which 'troubled' her), took to visiting her for advice on Indian sanitary matters before they took up their posts. From her bedroom she had unhealthy swamplands drained, irrigation channels dug, airy, properly run and hygienic barrack hospitals built, sanitary regulations imposed in gaols, asylums and at fairs and on pilgrimages, sewage tanks installed in rural areas and pure water supplies piped to cities, including Calcutta. In 1868 Mr Jowett hailed her as the 'Governess of the Governor of India'.

Despite her relentless efforts – she wrote five hundred letters to Sir Bartle Frere alone in five years – there were periods of enormous depression. To be sure, the mortality rate of the British soldier in India dropped from sixty-nine men in every thousand in the early years of the century to only five in every thousand by 1913, but things in the India Office moved too slowly for her and the officials were always advancing lack of money as a reason for not making sanitary improvements a priority, however persistently she hounded them.

'She is worse than a Royal Commission to answer,' Colonel Yule complained during her later years, 'and in the most gracious, charming manner possible, immediately finds out all I don't know.'

It was not only in matters of health that she worked so indefatigably from her South Street bedroom. Bills on Indian local self-government, educational reforms and new regulations on land tenure all brought forth reams of letters to those in positions of influence. Her last years were crowned with triumph. In the Jubilee year, 1885, Lord Roberts, then Commander-in-Chief in India, wrote to inform her that the Indian Government had sanctioned the employment of female nurses in military hospitals – a mere twenty-two years after she had first suggested the scheme. In 1888 the Government of India bowed to her pressure and set up a sanitary board in every province (not that such a step saved it from a continuing deluge of instructions from South Street), and in 1907 she became the first woman to receive the Order of Merit.

She remained unquenchable of spirit to the end and although frail, with failing sight and coordination, must have been exasperating to nurse. In a biography written in 1913, E. T. Cook describes her reaction to being looked after: 'She did not take kindly to the introduction of a nurse. The ruling passion of her life was strong, and when the nurse tucked her up for the night, she would often reverse the parts, get out of bed and go into the adjoining room to tuck up the nurse.'

There was one acute inadequacy in Indian medical care of which Miss Nightingale makes no mention – she scarcely had time, after all, with everything else that preoccupied her – and that was the huge problem of childbirth and of all female diseases. It was a particularly intense area of distress in India but the hazards were the same all over the Empire, with the possible exception of Australia which possessed, by 1870, more doctors per head of population than in England and also was a pioneering country in the teaching of obstetrics. The University of Melbourne's medical school, founded in 1865, was the first to teach gynaecology and obstetrics and it was followed by similar schools in Adelaide and Melbourne. Yet though the skill was there, it was not to be had cheaply. A straightforward confinement cost three guineas but a delivery by Caesarian section could be as much as a hundred.

The menace of puerperal fever was ever-present, even in progressive Australia. It stalked most nineteenth-century childbeds and was rife in India. It is a form of septic poisoning which sets in when the wound caused by the separation of the placenta is infected, usually in the simplest way by the doctor or midwife who is delivering the baby failing to wash their hands or change their clothing between deliveries. The eighteenth-century medical men knew that the fever was rampantly contagious and how it could easily be avoided; nineteenth-century medical men persisted in ignoring such knowledge.

In India the problem of puerperal fever was worse than in any other part of the Empire and the evil was compounded by the purdah system, one of the recognized principles of Indian life since the Mohammedan invasion of the eleventh century. The restrictions the purdah system imposed upon women are scarcely credible. It did not simply mean that a woman might see no man except her husband – or in some cases her nearest relations – but more brutally that she spent her life in a room, or series of rooms, often windowless, sometimes with windows too high to see out of, the doorways screened with grass, in a most unhappy confinement. There was no air, no exercise, no occupation. Education was impossible as getting girl children to school inevitably exposed them to men's eyes, with the result that in the major cities of India around 200 women in every 1000 were literate as late as the First World War; in the rural areas the literacy rate was only two or three per 1000. The female mind was supposed to dwell on the family and religion and the female hands to lie idle altogether unless engaged in the simplest household tasks.

Confined in their dim cells or labyrinths of cells, ill health was frequent among the women of the zenana. In the middle of the nineteenth century, an Indian woman who fell ill was likely to have her symptoms described to a doctor by her husband who then attempted to carry out the suggested treatment himself. Particularly enlightened husbands permitted a male doctor to sit behind a screen and feel a proferred female pulse; one surgeon was even allowed to go so far as to remove a cataract through a hole cut in a sheet.

But when it came to childbirth, the full horror of the purdah system was revealed. Women brought up to believe that to show themselves to a man not their husband was the most degrading shame upon earth, would frequently die undelivered of a baby rather than summon male medical help. Conservative mothers-in-law frequently strengthened this tragic resolve and sent for a *dai*, a native midwife, who in her ignorance could inflict such horrifying injuries as actually pulling off the limb of a half-born baby in her efforts to induce it to emerge. Even if a baby arrived safely and the dreaded puerperal fever was avoided, the delivered woman was considered unclean for forty days afterwards and was left unwashed, unchanged and generally neglected in the meanest room of the zenana. And the zenana, it must be remembered, was largely unventilated, shuttered from sunlight but not from flies, and situated alongside narrow lanes down which ran open drains choked to overflowing.

For the young brides of the Indian system, the whole grisly process often broke them down entirely. Hindus were accustomed to marry teenage girls to men old enough to be their grandfathers and great-grandfathers; even if they survived childbirth, such women would inevitably spend most of their lives as harshly treated and shameful widows. Girl babies were unwelcome because the dowry involved in marrying them off was such a huge financial burden on all but the richest families; in the rural areas particularly, female infanticide was so common that frequently there were no daughters to be married for years at a time.

Into this nightmare twilight of ignorance, fear, dirt and entrenched superstition came some of the remarkable medical women of the nineteenth century. One of the first was Miss Hewlett, of the Church of England Zenana Missionary Society in Amritsar, who perceived that the most acceptable form of constructive help would be to train the *dais*, who were not only a separate hereditary class in India but also much trusted by the poor prisoners of purdah. The Amritsar Dais School had opened as early as 1866 but had suffered enormous difficulties – chiefly because the *dais* themselves were incensed at being retaught their age-old skills – but under Miss Hewlett in the eighties is became accepted and successful.

Miss Hewlett was, like many zenana missionaries, untrained when she first came to India. Whatever notions these early pioneers had had that nursing was an instinct fell away before the awful facts of ill health and childbearing in the zenana. They set to with their medical chests; when on leave, they haunted hospitals in England in search of information and returned to India laden with supplies and medical books. Their knowledge was hard-earned as medicine was still a closed profession to women, but the need in India was too great to allow themselves to be deterred.

The medical women who came out to India after the opening of the London School of Medicine and the Royal Free Hospital in 1877 were hardly in a better position than the enterprising missionaries. Wherever she ended up, a woman was invariably alone since there were no Indian nurses and an English one – even if she could be persuaded to come to India – had to be paid from the woman doctor's own pocket. All the doctor's work had to be carried out in some Indian house, frequently possessing all the insanitary disadvantages of the zenana, and she had to be her own anaesthetist and dispenser and fund-raiser. Worst of all, the patients had to be cajoled with gentle persistence to come to her, and the smallest of mishaps could destroy a reputation built with agonizing patience over months. Dr Ellen Farrer, writing from Bhiwani in 1891, gives some idea of the resolute self-sufficiency of each day:

Dispensary as usual today . . . old woman with ear trouble returned for more medicine. . . . Sterilized instruments (where *are* the supplies from Bombay?). . . . Opened nasty abscess on groin under chloroform and scraped it. . . . Black ants everywhere just now. . . . Woman with dropsy arrived from Dadri on a camel. Cut orange peel for marmalade. . . . Went to see the postmaster's daughter, she has hysterics. . . . Thirty five patients at Dispensary. . . . Snake killed in Annie's bedroom.

Fanny Butler was the first doctor to arrive in 1880. She only survived nine years but in that time set up practices in both Jubbulpore and Bhagalpur and then went on to Kashmir, where she successfully established a hospital and dispensary at Srinigar. Before her was not only Miss Hewlett, but Rose Greenfield, a promoter of the Society of Female Education in the East, who had set up a hospital in Ludhiana in the Punjab and was to be most influential in organizing a Woman's Medical School in the city. She had come to India in 1875 and was to spend almost fifty years there, retiring with a Kaisar-i-Hind medal of the first class.

Elizabeth Bielby also arrived in 1875. Although she was eventually to go home to qualify as a doctor, she still, in old age, paid tribute to the work the missionaries had done:

It is very difficult to describe the real state of things I found in Lucknow and how hopeless everything seemed to be . . . the people were far more ignorant, superstitious and prejudiced than they are now. Female education was nil except what the zenana missionaries gave. It ought never to be forgotten that it was these ladies who first brought education to the purdah women of India.

Miss Bielby opened a dispensary in Lucknow and subsequently a small hospital. Then, frustrated by her own lack of knowledge, she decided that she must go home to qualify as a doctor. She went, taking with her a touching message:

In the year 1881 it became known to the Maharajah of Punna that Miss Bielby was carrying on her work as a Zenana Medical Missionary in the city of Lucknow. He asked her to visit his wife and she at once undertook the journey. Happily her medical knowledge, skilfully applied, effected a complete recovery. Miss Bielby, having resolved to return to England to take a degree in a regular college, went on the morning of her departure to say farewell to the Maharani. 'You are going to England;' said the royal lady, 'I want you to tell the Queen and the Prince and Princess of Wales, the men and women of England, what the women of India suffer when they are sick.' She then gave charge that Miss Bielby herself was to convey the message to the Queen. She asked her to write it down. 'Write it small, Doctor Miss Sahib,' she said, 'for I want you to put it into a locket, and you are to wear this locket round your neck till you see our Great Queen and give it to her yourself. You are not to send it through another.' Miss Bielby duly reached England when the Queen, hearing of the message, sent for her and graciously admitted her to a personal interview. To what Miss Bielby said of the condition of suffering Indian women Her Majesty listened with much interest, asking many questions, and showing the deepest sympathy. The locket with its writing was given to the Queen, and Her Majesty entrusted Miss Bielby with a kind and suitable reply, adding, 'We had no idea it was as bad as this. Something must be done for the poor creatures. We wish it generally known that we sympathize with every effort made to relieve the suffering of the women of India.'

Once qualified Miss Bielby returned to India in 1885, intent upon setting up a women's hospital in Lahore. The Municipal Committee of the city offered her a row of still-occupied cowsheds for the purpose; these she understandably declined in favour of a tiny mud-floored house off the Anarkali bazaar. From these small beginnings grew the Lady Aitchison Hospital, which the Countess of Dufferin opened in 1888 and which Dr Bielby ran for fifteen years.

The early medical pioneers had a great champion in George Kittredge, an American businessman living in Bombay who not only believed that 'women must be recognized as the equals of men in the medical care of their own sex' but did something about it by organizing, with some wealthy and enlightened Indian gentlemen, a 'Medical Women for India Fund'. Attracted by this idea, a Mr Pestorijee Hormusjee Cama offered one lakh and 65,000 rupees to the Government of Bombay to build a hospital on condition that it should provide a site, maintain the hospital and leave it solely in the charge of women doctors whom it was intended should be recruited from England. Site and maintenance, the government replied, were no problem, but women in ultimate authority was another matter. However, it would '. . . willingly agree to utilize the services of competent medical women acting under the instruction and guidance of the male superior staff'.

Mr Kittredge, a man of tenacity, argued his point and then set off to England to find staff, of a calibre no government could baulk at for the Cama Hospital. He returned with a prize in the form of Dr Edith Pechey, who had started to study medicine at Edinburgh with the celebrated Sophia Jex Blake but who had found the opposition to her sex too intolerable to bear and had completed her training in Switzerland and Ireland. For 500 rupees a month, accommodation and a first-class return ticket, Dr Pechey set out for Bombay and a dramatic career. She was not only an excellent doctor but participated in Bombay's social life and was an eloquent public speaker. She had an excellent sense of her own value and insisted that her services were worth exactly the same as those of her male colleagues, and also that women should accustom themselves to visiting her in the hospital, where she had all resources available. As a result, the Cama Hospital was a byword for high standards throughout India. Drawn by its reputation, more distinguished women doctors began to look eastwards for the fulfilment of their talents, so Dr Pechey was emboldened to ask Bombay University to admit women to medical classes. As with most things, it seems, she got her way. The doors to a degree in medicine were opened for women in 1883, so that Indian women might learn to care for their own countrywomen for the first time in history.

Things were less progressive in Madras. Mary Scharlieb, who had gone out to India with her barrister husband in 1866 and been appalled at the suffering of Indian women, had managed to batter her way into the Madras Medical College and gain the reluctant instruction of Surgeon Branfoot. Branfoot told her it was both mad and wrong to educate women as doctors, that she might walk the wards with him but he would teach her nothing. So she walked silently beside him and listened and inevitably he relented and helped her to pass her examinations – his bark, she observed, being considerably worse than his bite – so that she could return to England and complete her qualification in London. Like Dr Bielby she was received by the Queen, who was deeply disturbed – 'How *can* they tell me there is not need for medical women in India?' She returned to Madras to set up her own hospital, the Queen Victoria Caste and Gosha Hospital.

Back in London the Queen did not forget. In 1883, a year after her visit from Mary Scharlieb, Lord Dufferin was appointed Viceroy of India and Lady Dufferin was summoned to Windsor and informed of the royal concern over her female Indian subjects. Victoria had chosen the right person. Lady Dufferin wrote to all women of influence with any Indian connection whatsoever, proposing the setting up of a fund to provide medical relief for women in India, particularly those in purdah. There was a certain amount of huffing and puffing – Indian women did not want medical help and never had, so to provide it was a waste of time and money – but two years later, in 1885, the fund was born, the National Association for Supplying Female Medical Aid to the Women of India. Its Patron was the Queen–Empress, the Viceroy was Patron in India and his wife the President; it spread out in a proliferation of augustly chaired committees over all the provinces of India and was perhaps one of the most star-studded organizations of the Empire. Under its influence, the lives of medical women, both English and Indian, blossomed; hospitals were built – the Dufferin Victoria Hospital in Calcutta treated 20,000 women each year as out-patients alone; training schemes were funded, passages from England paid for and, perhaps the greatest achievement of all for the future, the foundation was laid for the first training school for Indian women to be run entirely by women – the Lady Hardinge Medical College for Women in Delhi.

The committees of the Countess of Dufferin's fund, liberally sprinkled with Governors General, were a far cry from nursing in the other wild places of the Empire. Long before the pioneer doctors of India, long even before Florence Nightingale was treading the wards of Scutari, the early pioneers in Australasia had taken to nursing since there was, quite simply, no alternative. Some of the early missionaries had brought out rudimentary medical skills, learned at such establishments as the St Luke's Hospital in Old Street, which gave a very basic instruction in maternity nursing. But most of the women who came to be relied upon for their nursing skill were those who had brought out with them to their new lives their mother's herbal recipes. These tonics and medicines, amplified and refined by the knowledge of herbs that the Maoris, in particular, and the Aborigines, were possessed of, constituted the backbone of outback medical care. The name of the game was self-help. Even Charlotte Godley, for all her comfortable conditions in Dunedin, wrote home in 1850, 'You know the evil dispositions of my teeth and all that Rogers did for me at starting and more too, left me before I had been two months in *Lady Nugent* [her ship] and so I must turn dentist myself and scrape sixpences, in the way he describes to you, for home made amalgam.'

Remedies for tooth cavities pale into insignificance beside some of the home cures used for tropical diseases such as infestation by the guinea worm, prevalent in West Africa. This waterborne parasite much afflicted the administrators and their wives around the end of the nineteenth century. The eggs would hatch inside the victim's body and then the worm would meander about until it found an extremity to lodge in, such as a leg, which swelled monstrously. Eventually the worm would break the skin. The nineteenth-century remedy was to seize the projecting tail, nip it firmly in a piece of straw and, day by day, bit by bit, wind it out. Even more grotesque was the method for removing filaria flies, which travelled about the body in huge numbers causing swellings like oranges. A fly could only be caught at the moment when it moved across the eyeball – the victim could tell by a sudden onset of double vision – and had to be neatly speared with a needle.

If the early home remedies were colourful, so were some of the people involved. There was Nurse Gallie of the Waihi mining township in New Zealand – who weighed 20 stone and had no patience with any man who squandered his money or abused his family – and Mrs Burke, the local midwife, whose donkey thrust his head into each confinement chamber and brayed triumphantly at every safe new arrival. There was – perhaps the most peculiar and dramatic of all – Dr James Miranda Barry, a woman who passed herself off as a man for the whole of her life. She was always controversial and mostly a figure of fun, a tiny dandified figure with flaming red hair and a temper to match. She took an excellent degree from Edinburgh and carried it to Cape Town where she became a skilled surgeon with powerful views on diet, rising in her profession to be appointed Inspector General of Hospitals in Upper and Lower Canada in 1857. No one quite knew what to make of her and she had one or two accomplishments which set her ever further apart from the coarse world of the army surgeon which she inhabited. Lord Albemarle remarked, after sitting next to her at dinner in Cape Town and being much puzzled by the ambivalence of her appearance and behaviour, ' . . . his style of conversation was greatly superior to that one usually heard at a mess table in those days of *non*-competitive examination'.

Medical matters in New Zealand, as in Australia, were advanced in comparison with Mother England; like everywhere else in the Empire, this progress was mostly the result of a military presence. The Maori wars brought imperial troops and they in their turn brought a handful of nurses – wives of soldiers – and created the need for hospitals. The first group of these, opened in the 1840s, were unsophisticated affairs. Forty years later, the Inspector of Hospitals in Wellington complained that medicines were still being kept under beds beside chamber pots and that the old habit of cutting up new blankets to patch old ones was as exasperating as it had ever been. Irritating it undoubtedly was, but the hospitals of which he was writing and others all over both islands were beginning to attract qualified nurses from England. The Dee Street Hospital in Invercargill was even able to charge nurses in training for the privilege of scrubbing floors and wards, on the doubtful principle that every chore taught a girl something and therefore constituted instruction. Girls from England and Scotland, seemingly undaunted by the prospect of a twelve-hour day, a mattress in any old corner and a diet largely composed of bread and jam, came out to Australia in the eighties and nineties in considerable numbers, and stayed. Operations were performed in lavatories, the wards and clinics were lit by candles, and hospital life was bedevilled by half-trained diehard old eccentrics – such as old Dr Brown of Dunedin who kept all the teeth he pulled in dozens of old kerosene tins and flew into a rage if anyone so much as commented upon this strange habit. Yet the young nurses stayed on in much the same spirit as had encouraged the pioneer women of forty and fifty years earlier. Out of their determination grew, in New Zealand in particular, a proliferation of old people's homes, orphanages, hospitals and training schools, in addition to the splendid Backblocks Nursing Service. This began in 1909 and sent girls out in all weathers and over all terrains to the empty spaces of the islands with their widely scattered inhabitants. There were similar intrepid schemes in Australia and Canada, where girls found themselves in mining and logging camps or acting as midwife and mother's help to a family of twelve in a wooden hut with three beds among the dozen of them. 'The Pioneer spirit is absolutely essential if you want to hold your own,' one wrote from a tiny hospital in Alberta in 1913, adding robustly, 'Don't think that I regret coming, for I don't.' Another woman, Mary Lyons, the first matron of Masterton Hospital, had been a Nightingale Nurse – and evidently a good one – and the letter Miss Nightingale wrote to her on her departure gives some idea of the strength of mind that drew the early nurses away from England to the Empire:

MY DEAR NURSE LYONS,

I feel very much interested in your going to New Zealand, very sorry that you have determined on leaving England, but sympathizing in your desire to go to the new country and hoping and trusting that you will, in God's strength, humbly and steadfastly turn them to account.

Remember what Bunyan says: 'Captain Experience' was a man very successful in his undertakings. May God Almighty, the Father of good nursing as of all good works, be with us all. . . .

Tell me if there is any Medical or Surgical book that you would like and I would gladly send it to you before you leave. My note is short but my wishes and prayers for you are not short. I have been thinking of you all night, but I have so many cares and overworking cares just now that I cannot write more except to say,

God bless you, dear Nurse Lyons,
FLORENCE NIGHTINGALE

By the turn of the century, the acceptability of nursing had increased so greatly that the rush of volunteers at the start of the Boer War quite overwhelmed the system.

'What can I do for you, my poor man?' a lady visitor inquired of a sick soldier at a base hospital in 1899. 'Shall I wash your face?'

The soldier was acutely embarrassed. 'Thank you kindly, ma'am, but I've already had to promise fourteen ladies that they shall wash my face!'

Army nurses were by now nothing new. Several had already been awarded the Royal Red Cross by the Queen for their work during the Egyptian and Sudan campaigns and their sweeping grey-clad figures, although not universally familiar, were no longer a rarity in military hospitals. They were, however, too scarce during the Boer War and through no fault of their own.

The Army Medical Corps in 1890 had been understaffed for years and was therefore not abreast of the newest medical developments. There is no doubt, however, that it knew full well the problems of hot days and cold nights on the veld, and that typhoid was prevalent in South Africa, particularly after the first rains of summer and in any township or native kraal. The corps might have been short of men but it remained prejudiced against the use of women in any military situation, maintaining stoutly that all soldiers infinitely preferred to be nursed by an orderly. Sir Frederick Treves, the distinguished civilian surgeon who served during the war, thought otherwise. He wrote of the women nurses at Chieveley after the battles around Colenso that, 'They brought to many of the wounded and the dying that comfort which men are little able to evolve, or are uncouth in bestowing, and which belongs especially to the tender, undefined and undefinable ministrations of women.'

Those ministrations the Army Medical Corps thought the soldiers could do without. In 1899 about eight hundred women nurses of the Army Nursing Service Reserve were grudgingly sent out, a ratio of about 2 per cent to the fighting men they were to nurse. The reserve, which had been set up in 1897 on the initiative of Princess Christian of Schleswig-Holstein, demanded the same qualifications for enrolment as the Army Nursing Service itself. The problems to be confronted in South Africa were simply enormous. Some were administrative, for example all medical supplies were controlled by fighting officers (one soldier exclaimed, 'Anything more ridiculous or absurd than going to an artillery officer to get pills and powders I cannot imagine'). Others were the result of the South African climate and age-old military habit.

The standard of hygiene was appallingly low. Most camps had open latrines, there was a general refusal to boil water and a lackadaisical approach to the preparation of food which enabled flies to breed excessively fast. 'We were very much troubled with flies,' Sister Barnwell of the nursing reserve wrote from Bloemfontein. 'We had a few strips of mosquito netting to lay over the face of

the patient but still one had to clear flies out of the patient's mouth.
. . . In drinking you would have to cover your hand over the cup and
when eating you would have to put your hand over the food. . . .'

Such conditions only gave the Army Medical Corps more
ammunition; when the special war correspondent Burdett Coutts
asked why there were not more female nurses, he was told that army
camps were not fit places for women, that (horrors) flirtations might
occur and that the presence of women would cramp the freedom of
convalescents to lounge and smoke at will. The Field Service
Manual allowed for one superintendent nursing sister and eight
nurses for each hospital of over 500 beds, but they were only
supposed to supervise the male orderlies and were not permitted
actually to nurse. Inevitably, as the war wore on, the number of
nurses in each hospital rose to twenty and they were finally allowed
to nurse. Even so, a hospital such as Wynberg, which sprawled over
a quarter of a mile, had only nine nurses to supervise and care for
600 men.

The same hospital boasted three bedpans for every 250 patients, a
lack aggravated by the cross-infection spread by the staff. The
doctors and orderlies were dressed in heavy khaki serge which could
not be laundered and the nurses, glamorously enough attired in
long, soft grey dresses (with matching parasols for out-of-doors),
contributed to the spread of infection with skirts that swept the
often otherwise unswept floors. Typhoid was the great menace of
the war and the British method of treating it was to starve a man on
water for seven days. Where this procedure was ignored – as in the
Volks Hospital in Bloemfontein or in Kimberley – the results were
enormously improved.

Most hospitals were an overcrowded, unhygienic, understaffed
muddle. Sister X wrote down her impressions of them in *The
Tragedy and Comedy of War Hospitals* after a war that took her
from Pietermaritzburg to the Mooi River, and then to Ladysmith,
where she laboured in Number 11 Field Hospital in the Tin Camp
where thousands of men lay sick with enteric fever during the siege.
She was welcomed there by an army surgeon who almost wept with
relief at the sight of her, as he and his colleagues had been 'nearly off
their heads' with overwork. There was no question but that there
was a job for her to do:

But for the previous experiences and the lessons I had learnt thereby, I think we should have been absolutely dismayed at everything . . . no linen of any sort . . . no pillows except flat straw bolsters . . . awful mattresses just off the floor. . . . Most distressing of all was the condition of the men themselves. Rows of white and yellow boned, hollow-eyed men were lying or sitting up in their beds and a few were crawling about with their clothes literally hanging on bones waiting on one another. The orderlies on our approach had hastily entered their wards concealing their pipes, smoking as usual. The heat was intense and those with fever were lying panting and saturated with perspiration, their poor mouths all clogged together and the flies swarming round them in thousands with their horrid buzzing noise. . . . Truly it was a sight to haunt one all one's days.

There was no soap, no methylated spirit, no linen, no fresh milk and the orderlies were bored with the whole affair and skulked, smoking, in corners. So much alcohol was prescribed that Sister X was taken for a barmaid on account of her skill at opening endless champagne bottles. When she pointed out to the surgeon that many of the men 'trembled like aspen leaves' with delirium tremens he said, 'There is nothing else to give them.' Resolutely she battled on, scrubbing and dosing and consoling, frustrated at every turn but maintaining a sufficient level of satisfaction in what she achieved to comment regretfully, when safely stowed away on a transport ship at the end of the war, 'I felt quite sorry I was on my way home to quiet, conventional, narrow little England.'

By 1900, after the great battles of Magersfontein and Colenso and Spion Kop, after the sieges of Kimberley and Mafeking and Ladysmith, there were thousands rather than hundreds like Sister X. Many of them had to wait in frustration in Cape Town since the army could not find sufficient accommodation for them upcountry. But gradually, as typhoid cut swathes through the fighting forces, the nurses were filtered north to cope. Of those who have left records, most speak of situations such as Sister X found, wretched men in filthy clothing, unspeakable smells, no sheets, no water (though plenty of brandy), few bedpans or commodes and everybody crawling with lice. Almost none of them gave in and went home and their letters and journals show a quiet pride in the compliments that began to trickle their way. Even an officer of the Army Medical Corps, Major Westcott, was moved to admire. 'The Nursing Sisters and Nurses were probably never called upon in any campaign to endure such hardships and to exhibit such devotion to their duty.'

It could not be denied that where there were female nurses, the standards of nursing shot up. The Volks Hospital in Bloemfontein, under its matron Miss Maud Young, 'stood out like an oasis in the desert of this ghastly mortality'. As Sir Frederick Treves had said in the early days of the war, 'They did a service during those distressful days which none but nurses could have rendered and they set to all an example of unselfishness, self-sacrifice and indefatigable devotion to duty.'

Even when the hyperbole had died down, huge numbers of women were left nursing the armed forces. The Queen, 'who took such a deep personal interest in the welfare of her soldiers', wished to see the Army Nursing Service reorganized. Although she did not live to see her wishes realized, Edward VII announced in March 1902 the setting up of Queen Alexandra's Imperial Military Nursing Service.

The seal of high social approval rested firmly upon the profession at last. The Queen was president of the nursing board, there were to be three grades of nurse, from matrons at £300 a year to staff nurses and sisters at £50 per annum, all applicants were to be British and to have received three full years' training. As well as serving in hospitals at home, the nurses went out to Egypt, Gibraltar, South Africa, Malta, Bermuda, Canada, Ceylon, Hong Kong and Singapore in their grey and scarlet uniforms. They were equipped with such status that they were soon giving lectures and practical demonstrations to the untrained men of the Army Medical Corps. By 1906 it was necessary to sit an examination to be a matron and in the same year a nurses' home was built for the QAs on Millbank. When the Boer War began there were eighty-seven army nursing sisters; four years after the founding of the QAs there were over 400.

It was not only the women themselves who benefited, nor simply the soldiers they nursed, but eventually the sailors of the Royal Navy too. There had been certain rumblings among sailors when the army had seemed to capture 'all the ladies in sickbay' but the main problem for the navy was the type of woman traditionally associated with sailors. Any attempt to induce a respectable woman to work at the naval hospitals was hopeless, and during the nineteenth century all women were gradually eliminated from the hospitals, leaving sick sailors in the hands of naval pensioners, who proved remarkably capable. The gradual emergence of the army sisters induced the navy to try again, with such success that Queen Alexandra founded a branch of her service for naval sisters at the same time as the military one.

A few months after the inauguration of the service, a kindly visitor paused before an old sailor in a ward at the Royal Naval Hospital, Haslar. She indicated the nurses moving down the ward and said archly to him, 'And do you like the change? Or do you prefer to be just men together?'

He surveyed the tattoo on his wrist for a long time and then he said, in a voice of deepest satisfaction, 'Oh, give me the ladies. Every time. Give me the ladies.'

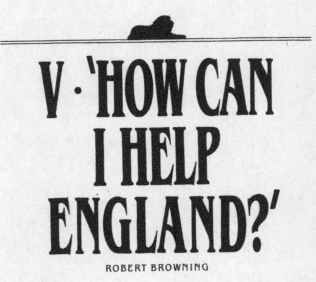

V · 'HOW CAN I HELP ENGLAND?'

ROBERT BROWNING

V

'Some day though,' Mary Curzon wrote in 1903, about the time of the great Delhi Durbar, 'the bell will go and I shall not appear as India, I know, slowly but surely murders women. But I suppose many humble and inconsequent lives must always go into the foundations of all great works and great buildings and great achievements.'

It was most fortunate for George Curzon that Mary Leiter, the daughter of a Chicago millionaire, should regard his life as one of great work and achievement. It was perhaps a prerequisite of marrying him since he regarded his own life in just such a light. They met at the Duchess of Westminster's Ball on 17 July 1890. She was twenty and for her it was love at first sight. For him it was an enormous attraction which had to be tempered by the programme he had laid out for himself for the following five years. He proposed to her in Paris in 1893, even then taking care to explain that their relationship must bow to his ambition, as his description of their meeting in the Hotel Vendôme makes plain:

I had entered the hotel without the slightest anticipation that this would be the issue. She told me her story; how she had waited for nearly three years since the time we had first met, rejecting countless suitors and always waiting for me. I told her that while I felt from the very beginning that we were destined for each other, I had not dared to speak and had even run the risk of losing her because there was certain work in my scheme for Asiatic travel which I had resolved to do and which I would not ask any married woman to allow her husband to carry out. Some of it, notably the journey to the Pamirs and Afghanistan, still remained undone: and even now when we became secretly engaged it was on the understanding that I should be at liberty to complete my task before we took the final step.

The task he had set himself was in the great imperialist mould. The summit of his ambition (next to being prime minister) was to be Viceroy of India. When he achieved it in 1898, now three years married, he took with him to Calcutta his lovely American wife who was to support and assist him unflaggingly in the most arduous role of any woman in the Empire. She can have been in no doubt as to the kind of man she was marrying, a man who believed deeply in the need for a Conservative government, since it was in Conservative hands 'that the interests of this country are safer . . . [as they] regard the British Empire as a majestic responsibility rather than . . . an irksome burden'. He echoed the early imperialists of the century who had seen the Empire as the guardian of British free trade as well as the harbinger of order. While Undersecretary for Foreign Affairs he had championed the completion of the important Uganda Railway because it 'will carry with it not merely commerce and civilization but peace'.

In all this, Mary Curzon supported and applauded him. It was to be her great service to the Empire. She made a splendid and impressive Vicereine whom diamonds and peacock feathers became admirably, and she took a suitable interest in the medical projects set up by Lady Dufferin and in the plight of the poor, as well as urging Curzon to preserve such Indian glories as the Taj Mahal and Fatehpur Sikri. But she never breathed a breath of criticism over Curzon's brilliant but often high-handed and inflexible behaviour. In fact she held her tongue to such a degree that her friend Consuelo Vanderbilt, the American-born Duchess of Marlborough, expressed her incredulity at such 'powers of self-abnegation', particularly in an American woman. However deep her devotion to Curzon, it must have required great self-control, particularly as he liked to take the decisions in all things; he even chose colours for the walls in their London house and engaged all the domestic staff, down to a nurse for his children. (This nurse startled him by asking if she might take a bicycle with her to India. Curzon – no supporter of female emancipation – eventually agreed provided the roads permitted, saying graciously that 'there would be no objection to her taking her exercise in that way'.)

Whatever Mary Curzon thought of his behaviour, she gave no sign in her diaries. Even the glories he brought to her, such as her title, she writes of with a breath of amusement. 'Oh the Ladyships! – I feel like a ship in full sail on the high seas of dignity.' The same wry delight fills her letter to Curzon on her first sight of Viceregal Lodge in Simla, where she withdrew after three months in Calcutta to escape the 'fierce heat with which spring notified its arrival in Bengal':

> The first view of Simla amused me so – the houses slipping off the hills and clinging like barnacles to hill tops – and then our house! I kept trying not to be disappointed! . . . A Minneapolis millionaire would revel in this and we shall love it and make up our minds not to be too fastidious. . . . The fireplaces, corner cabinets, papers, curtains and furniture reek of Maples but a look out of the window makes up for it all and I can live on views for five years.

For the Viceroy's workroom being next door to her sitting room, she wrote, 'I thank God and the architect.' But she hated to be away from him ('My heart never stops aching. . . . I miss you every second') and revelled in his letters and his praise. 'You made me so happy by telling me you thought I had made a good start the first two months in India. Anything I do seems so minute beside all I want to do to help. . . . Oh! I miss you and miss you and have to keep on the jump not to cry.'

She worried constantly about his incurable tendency to overwork ('your life and your strength are so precious'), particularly in temperatures that she herself found scarcely bearable. 'Oh the heat! The heat! I am getting more used to it, but dressing in it is simply awful and with broad, swift rivers running down all over you, it is hard to appear dry and smiling at a daily dinner party.'

Despite the exhausting climate, and a constitution weakened by a severe miscarriage, Mary went on an eight-week tour of India with Curzon, of which she kept a detailed diary. It was two months of overwhelming ceremony, every last moment being attended by splendour and formality and a positive herd of painted elephants. The trains by which they travelled were 'the most uninviting form of locomotion in the world' and the heat and dust made the formality a terrible strain. None the less, there were light moments outside Agra:

> Her sedan-chair was brought in, and the Rani popped into the drawing-room, wearing huge Turkish trousers of bright pink, a white jacket, and at least 60 yards of bright blue gauze wound about and dragging behind her. On her hair was a very quaint silver ornament, four arms of a Dutch windmill 8 inches across fastened on her forehead, and two wreaths of silver flowers forming a kind of hat. Her hair was parted up the back, and bunched amidst the silver roses on the top of her head. She spoke a little English and she explained that her health was poor. Lady McDonnell

asked her from what she was suffering. She replied: 'Me inside out.' The trial of looking grave was terrific, and as soon as she had gone I laughed till I cried. I forgot to say that she had white gloves on, with rings on each finger over the glove.

There were other delights. At a dinner party – mercifully short – at Hyderabad, each guest was presented with a pie containing a live bird; this flew out when the lid was cut to alight on her tiara and then 'comfortably on George's head'. Such moments were necessary relief from the strain and the climate, which told terribly upon her. She wrote of it constantly, particularly when near the coasts of the peninsula where she was enervated almost to extinction: 'The heat has been fearful and the sea like molten lead without a ripple and if it were not for electric fans in my cabin, I should dissolve entirely.'

For Curzon she went on, and yet when, on account of her failing health, she went home to England in the summer of 1901, she took a certain degree of her own loyalty to India with her. It angered and depressed her that India should be so little understood in England, and if her indignation chiefly arose because such ignorance meant her beloved George was not recognized as the greatest Viceroy of all time, there was in addition a sense that the average stay-at-home Englishman did India an injustice. 'India is the great unknown,' she wrote to Curzon in May 1901. 'The moon seems nearer to the majority and India isn't more than a huge troublesome name that spells famine and plague. . . . [Sir Alfred Lyall] made my heart leap to hear him talk about India with a depth of feeling, imagination and knowledge that came like a burst of radiance after all the clouds of ignorance I have been enveloped in.'

If she hated every second of their separation, so did he. 'You don't *know*,' he wrote that same summer, 'what my isolation has been this summer. I am crying now so that I can scarcely see the page.'

Her reply was representative of the ideal of womanhood of her time:

I do feel in my heart that in our life there is a sense of comradeship almost as great as love. A man can know a woman well because her life – consequently the interests which mould her life and conceive her thoughts – are more or less simple. A man's life is so complex and much of it lies outside the woman's sphere. . . . But what is within her grasp has the power of making her truly happy – but take her away from it all and give her a blank six months in search of health and she must feel she has nearly lost her anchorage.

Her health was scarcely improved by six months in a gentle climate but the Empire had not finished with her yet. Curzon – the possessor by his own admission of a 'grim personality' lightened only by his sense of duty and his love for Mary – accepted a second term of office. She had suffered a serious illness at Walmer Castle in Kent in 1904 and dreaded returning to the merciless climate of India. But the Empire, in the form of the Viceroy, was not to be failed and even though she felt 'every bit of my vitality has gone and I am iller than I have ever been', she agreed to follow him. It was not only their huge need to be together – who could resist, after all, a man who wrote, 'I have not dared to go into your room for fear that I should burst out crying' – that drove her but the storm clouds that were looming over his relations with Lord Kitchener and which preoccupied him deeply. As well they might, since they resulted in a bitter wrangle over the military and civil administration of India that led to Curzon's resignation as Viceroy in August 1905. Without Mary's support Curzon would probably not have been able to bear such a blow. He did know what she was to him and left an extraordinarily (even for Curzon) emotional and overwritten poem pinned to her pillow in Simla:

'I would have torn the stars from the Heavens for your necklace,
I would have stripped the rose-leaves for your couch from all the trees,
I would have spoiled the East of its spices for your perfume,
The West of all its wonders to endower you with these.

'I would have drained the ocean, to find its rarest pearldrops,
And melt them for your lightest thirst in ruby draughts of wine;
I would have dug for gold till the earth was void of treasure,
That, since you had no riches, you might freely take of mine.

'I would have drilled the sunbeams to guard you through the daytime,
I would have caged the nightingale to lull you to your rest;
But love was all you asked for, in waking or in sleeping,
And love I give you, sweetheart, at my side and on my breast.'

Within a year she was dead. She had tried to rally with a winter in the South of France but her heart could take no more. She died in London and Curzon fled to Kedleston to shut himself away. 'I am conscious of no courage,' he wrote to a friend a year later, 'only a sort of mute endurance.'

Victoria Woodhull and Tennessee Claflin could not provide more of a contrast to Mary Curzon. They were Americans to be sure and made respectable, if not glittering, English marriages, but the dowry of talents they brought with them was a world apart from the selfless and dutiful support that Mary Leiter gave to the Empire's most visible servant.

Victoria and Tennessee Claflin were born in a small town in Ohio, the daughters of a gristmill manager and a woman who was a religious fanatic and indulged in visions. Their childhood has been much written up and even if it did not contain the screams and beatings and hysterics so eagerly chronicled by some of their more blindly biased biographers, it certainly had echoes of the fairground about it. At fourteen Victoria was married off to a drunken doctor some years her senior; she produced a daughter in sensationally deprived and fearful circumstances and then set about rising above her tawdry beginnings, taking her youngest sister, Tennessee, with her.

It was said in contemporary America that nothing since the Civil War had taken up more newspaper column inches than the startling careers of Victoria Woodhull and Tennessee Claflin. They started a magazine, *Woodhull and Claflin's Weekly*, as an organ for their strident views on women's suffrage. Despite the outrage that caused and the fact that women had no vote, Victoria Woodhull managed to become the first woman candidate for the Presidency of the United States. Hardly surprisingly, her attempt came to nothing, but undaunted she plunged on to open, with Tennessee, the first female-run brokerage house on Wall Street. It was a great success and netted almost a million dollars a year.

By this time her celebrity had become notoriety. A passionate advocate of free love – one wonders how she had time – she collected lovers who remained astonishingly constant to her. One even wrote an impassioned biography of both sisters in order to vilify their family and celebrate their remarkable achievements after such appalling beginnings. Middle age brought the women a yearning for calmer waters and both sisters – Victoria now termed Mrs Satan by most Americans – set sail for England and respectability.

They found it. Tennessee discovered a lonely baronet and became Lady Cook and Victoria, all lovers now behind her, married John Biddulph Martin of Martin's Bank. Late in life, after a colourful and batty career, Victoria Woodhull put her shoulder to the wheel of Empire. She disowned the sexual adventuring and spiritualism of her youth, poured money into English institutions at home and abroad and became frantic in her urgings that America should join with England and Empire when war broke out in 1914. Three years previously, in 1911, she had even had King Edward VII to lunch.

THE PRAYER

Almighty God our Heavenly Father, we praise Thee for the blessings of our homes; for the fulness of life and opportunity in this Dominion; and for the ties which bind us together within our Empire. We beseech Thee to bless our Queen and Royal Family, and to guide and direct all who sit in authority over us. Grant that peace and the spirit of Brotherhood may prevail throughout the world. Pardon our sins and accept our thanksgiving. Give to each member of our Order grace to serve Thee faithfully and to labour loyally for the welfare of our country; for the sake of Jesus Christ our Lord. Amen.

In 1900 an order was founded which would never have admitted the Claflin sisters, however much reformed. The Imperial Order of the Daughters of the Empire was born in Canada at the instigation of Margaret Polson Murray, who had emigrated as a young woman with her professor husband. The foundation of the order called for 'Patriotism, Loyalty and Service', three qualities it was proud to own to at its golden jubilee:

The IODE is proud to have had a share in the National Life and Progress of This Dominion; proud also to have had the opportunity to gather into the Order's fold thousands of women and children whose chief objectives are to promote loyalty to King and Country and to forward every good work for the betterment of their country and people.

Canada was at the head of the Order but national chapters sprang up at once in Bermuda and the Bahamas, followed by one in Bombay in 1902 which set up a domestic-science school in an attempt to break down the barriers created by the caste system in India. The foundation of the national chapters led to close links with branches of the Victoria League in New Zealand, Australia and South Africa, so that in two years the Empire was fairly well covered with patriotic Daughters, most of whom had actually been born out of England.

The first function of the Order was to raise money, which it did with extraordinary success. Ten thousand dollars sent a hospital ship out to South Africa during the Boer War – within weeks almost of the Order's birth – and enough money was raised within the first few years of the Order's life to build a science block for St Helena's School at Poona and to supply all the equipment and pay the staff for the Canadian Hospital at Nasik. These 'pieces of Empire Welding' occasioned the Order much pride – so much so that sometimes it spent its money in slightly curious ways to demonstrate the fervour of its imperial loyalty. When the dukes and duchesses of Cornwall and York visited Canada in October of 1901, the Order paid for the erection at the north end of Queen's Park in Toronto of the Alexandra Gates, two vast stone pillars bearing ten large iron lamps apiece and supporting a massive pair of iron grille gates. This was acclaimed by the Order in reverent tones as 'a striking demonstration of the Order's patriotism'.

More truly striking was the consistency with which the Order remembered the Empire's soldiers. 'Comfort parcels' went out regularly to the men fighting in the Boer War – and subsequently to those involved in the Great War – and when the hostilities in South Africa were over, it was the Daughters who tended the war graves. An annual report was published, featuring accounts of the prominent part played by the Order all over the world at the celebrations for Empire Day, as well as accounts of countless hospitals, schools, and homes for disabled soldiers assisted by money raised throughout the year. It was, however, doomed to a short life and when the Empire went, its Daughters went with it, taking with them their imperial aims:

To promote in the Motherland and in the Colonies the study of the history of the Empire and of current Imperial questions; to celebrate patriotic anniversaries; to cherish the memory of brave and heroic deeds and last resting places of our heroes and heroines, especially such as are in distant and solitary places; to erect memorial stones on spots that have become sacred to the Nation, either through great struggles for freedom, battles against ignorance, or events of heroic and patriotic self-sacrifice.

Quite apart from those women born outside England who banded together in associations to help the Empire, there are instances of many individuals who were netted in, either by inclination or by marriage.

The most romantic case of the latter must be Juanita Smith – wife of Sir Harry Smith, made Governor of Cape Town in 1843 – who was the inspiration for the naming of Ladysmith. They had married in storybook circumstances when Juanita was only fourteen, after her sister, the widow of a Spaniard killed at the siege of Badajoz in 1811, had cast herself and Juanita upon the mercy of British officers. The first tent they came upon contained Johnny Kincaid and Harry Smith. Johnny Kincaid, ever given to flamboyance, declared of Juanita that 'to look at her was to love her' which Harry Smith, then one of Wellington's subalterns, promptly did.

He taught her to ride and she exhibited a daring and gaiety which endeared her to everyone as she followed him through Waterloo, Nova Scotia, Jamaica, India and Africa. Her portraits show her plump and animated, no conventional beauty but clearly attractive with long glossy front ringlets. She called her husband Enrique and her pug, patriotically, Victoria; she was beloved everywhere she went. Her memorial is, rather inappropriately for someone who was clearly such fun, Ladysmith in Natal but at least she has the consolation of Enrique's twin town, Harrismith, being not much more than an hour's drive to the west.

Melina da Fonseca was less of a fairytale figure but equally resourceful. She was born of Portuguese stock in South Africa and at fourteen – clearly an age at which many nineteenth-century girls could expect something dramatic to happen – she ran away from the Convent School in Wynberg to marry Frederick Yorke, the captain of a visiting English football team. She gives a lively account of shinning down a wall to freedom and dismaying her English lover by confessing to him how young she really was. Marriage had its problems – and the wedding night, euphemistically skated over, clearly did – but it was fun on the whole. They were much in love and happily silly together, so it was a horrible shock to be widowed within months, after Frederick had been kicked on the head in the football field.

Melina, aged fifteen, went home. She stayed a few months but then the attractions of the brief period of freedom and independence she had known in marriage reasserted their pull and she went off to nurse. This was during the first grumblings of the second Boer War and she was much needed, indeed she displayed such competence. that she became known as the Florence Nightingale of the Boer War. She worked, both as a nurse and as an administrator, in hospitals in Mochudi, Gaberones, Lobatsi and Mafeking. On the day that the siege of Mafeking ended, 17 May 1900, Baden-Powell put her in charge of the Victoria Hospital there.

When the war was over, she was presented with an ornamental testimonial from the British South Africa Police, the South Rhodesian Volunteers and from the Rhodesia Regiment, none of whose men had survived to sign their gratitude. In 1902 she was summoned to England and received from the hands of King Edward VII the Order of the Royal Red Cross.

In 1911 the Maharani of Baroda wrote a book entitled *The Position of Women in Indian Life*. It was prompted by the money the Dufferin Fund had made available for the medical tuition of women in India and bears a frontispiece of the Maharani, plump and pretty in a chiffon sari, with her bare brown toes covered with rings.

Her aim in writing was to urge Indian women to imitate the best deeds of women of the West. In so doing she was helping on the process of independence which had worked so well in Australasia and Canada and which might solve some of the awful difficulties of India. She was not alone. The English female pioneers in India had left a legacy that Indian women were eagerly taking up even, in some instances, abetted by authority. Girls' schools, said the Indian Education Commission in a report of 1883, should, because they were still so neglected, receive not only the same funds as boys' schools but 'even something more than that might appear to be a strictly impartial share of encouragement'.

Of all the beginners in the field, three women from Bombay stand out most clearly. Francina Sorabji, quite apart from a lifetime of social and welfare work, was the founder of St Helena's School in Poona, which owed its science block to funds from the Imperial Order of the Daughters of the Empire. Ramabai Ranade, who took a lifelong interest in female education, also turned her considerable energies towards the destitute and the wretched widows of the Hindu system, visiting prisons and founding an Industrial Home of Service, also in Poona, which provided impoverished women with some means of supporting themselves.

The third of this redoubtable trio was Pundita Ramabai, the child of a wandering Hindu pilgrim, who was born in the forest of Gangamula during one of her father's spiritual wanderings. In 1877 when she was twenty-four, she lost both parents and a sister from starvation during a famine. She was herself widowed five years later, and these experiences brought to her notice not only the plight of widows but of Indian women in general. She plunged into social work, in 1889 founding in Bombay the Sarda Sadan (Home of Wisdom), an institution which educated women and sent them out to teach their still-confined sisters. When Bombay became too expensive, she moved the Sadan to Poona and within ten years of the project's starting, two thousand women a year were passing through her Sadans.

These three are examples of what the IODE had so hoped to achieve when it set out to 'foster a bond of union amongst the daughters and children of the Empire'. It was not only loyalty to the crown they sought, but also a unity among 'sister colonies', and, in each colony's case, 'to forward every good work for the betterment of their country and people'. At the turn of the century there was little indication that these noble hopes might not be fulfilled for ever. 'They may cry upon the housetops of Northampton,' Curzon had declaimed in a speech at Kingston in 1895, 'but the twitterings of sparrows have never yet interfered with the stability of an Empire.'

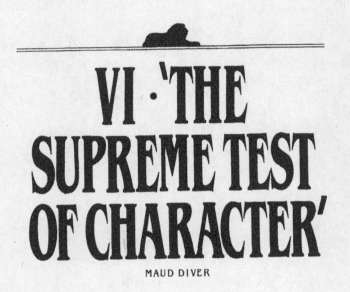

VI · 'THE SUPREME TEST OF CHARACTER'

MAUD DIVER

VI

Call me not false, beloved,
If, from thy scarce known breast
So little time removed
In other arms I rest.

For this more ancient Bride
Whom coldly I embrace,
Was constant at my side
Before I saw thy face.

The ancient bride of this portentous poem of Kipling's was, of course, Duty. 'Duty' was a word which ranked with honour, peace and justice in the imperial vocabulary and with 'propriety' in the social one. It is difficult to appreciate the absolute devotion with which the Victorians regarded the idea of service – it was a personal need in the servants and soldiers of the Empire as well as a requirement of their government that they should regard the giving of themselves in the service of their country and her beliefs as the consummate achievement of a lifetime. Doubtless an enormous amount of personal ambition was gratified in the process, but the sacrifice of time and health and a full life was real enough. From the men who made nations such as Frederick Lugard in Nigeria, to the humblest district officer in the Indian mofussil, hundreds of thousands of men gave their lives, quite literally, to serve the Empire.

And most of them expected their women to serve it too. Henry Polehampton, Chaplain to the East India Company's troops stationed at Lucknow, wrote to his mother in 1856 of his twenty-two-year-old bride, 'Emmie takes it very quietly. I have no manner of doubt she will go where I do.' 'It' was the prospect of India. To go out to India because your husband's calling demanded it was, in the 1850s, to build up a tradition rather than follow it; not many women had preceded Emily Polehampton to that land of 'Dirt and Dastur'. The situation was similar all over the Empire; until the huge and complex system of imperial administration had been built up in the second half of the century, the dutiful wife was not often called upon to support her husband in remote and uncomfortable parts of the globe. Africa, and particularly West Africa, remained almost without white women until the turn of the century, for the climate was known to be a killer. A male administrator might choose to take his own chance in a 'white man's grave' but few Victorians would have contemplated taking the woman of their choice with them.

India, for all the ferocity of its own climate, was where the women camp followers of duty were first to be seen. They were few but articulate, and of course in a land where servants abounded to a suffocating degree – Emily Eden complained that a mildly expressed wish for a vase in her fish pond at Barrackpore resulted in the civil engineer instantly installing two – they had plenty of time to record the pattern of their lives. None has left a record of loving India, though many were intrigued and moved, but all expressed a powerful love for the man who brought them there and his sense of service – which both he and she would have expected to revere without question. Honoria Lawrence wrote to her husband Henry, a revenue surveyor in the north-west of India, '. . . it would be my pride and delight to think you were an even better soldier since you had a wife and son. God forbid that I should throw any obstacle in your road.'

She had married her cousin after a patient wait while he established his career and it was a blissful union. It needed to be, since it brought with it all the sickness and anxiety of late pregnancies and involved trekking about India in a wearisome way in pursuit of Henry's working obligations:

People at home can scarcely picture the small vexations of this roving life; buying things dear because we must have them, selling them cheap because we must get rid of them. Trying to carry about a few household goods; the vexation of their arriving smashed, cracked, drenched. . . . At first I could have cried . . . but every year in India my list of necessities decreased.

She resented her new life only when she and Henry were separated, and otherwise she accepted their peculiarly uncomfortable situation without complaint, able to treasure their moments together as well as the fascinating oddness of life in India. In contrast to later memsahibs, it was no effort for her to like Indians.

Not so Emily Eden, who came for six years with her sister Fanny as company for their brother Lord Auckland, perhaps one of the least successful governors general India had to endure. Emily was highly civilized, irreverent, witty and superior. India was impossible but it provided marvellous ammunition for her letters and journals – she would not have been half as waspishly delightful to read if she had really enjoyed herself. She complained from the moment she arrived, about the pointless formality of their lives, about all the people she did not want to see whom she had to see, about the second-rate-ness of all other women in Calcutta ('Everything is melted down to the purely local'), about the climate (' . . . awful. It is so very HOT, I do not know how to spell it large enough.') 'It is all very magnificent,' she wrote of their existence in Calcutta, 'but I cannot endure our life there.' What she and Fanny liked was Barrackpore, the Governor's dilapidated old weekend house sixteen miles outside the city, where they could re-create, as far as possible, their happy and much-missed life in England.

She had come, like so many women were to come, determined not to succumb to the indolence that gradually crept up on almost every newcomer to India and also to avoid adopting the usual overbearing manner with servants. But it was well-nigh impossible to resist. Houses for people like the Aucklands, and even for less exalted beings, were sumptuous and, as the century wore on, they were immediately equipped with each new Western luxury. But India had the upper hand and the steady, decaying influence of dirt, steaming damp and insects reduced everyday life to a profoundly uncomfortable affair. Servants simply swarmed; the caste system, which demanded that servants should in turn be served by their own servants, resulted in a rigid social pyramid within each establishment, with each layer shouting imperiously at the layer below. At the apex of this sat the memsahib, almost as much a prisoner of the climate and of lack of occupation as her Indian sisters were of the zenana, with nothing to do but write letters, read, fiddle on the piano and yawn. Perhaps it was better to endure the interminable dak journeys of Honoria Lawrence; certainly Emily Eden's best-known journal, *Up The Country*, was written – with a most lively spirit – when she and Fanny and George set off in an 'imperial cavalcade' 12,000 strong, to tour northern India, a journey taken at a pace of 20 miles a day with the ladies safely buttoned up in dhoolies.

Of course not all the women in those early years spent their lives yawning. Sarah Terry, who arrived in Bombay in 1845, must have come with enormous apprehensions. Her husband Sidney had preceded her and had helpfully written to tell her how much she would loathe it; it was, he said, expensive, hot, dusty, snobbish and lonely. But she loved it. She buckled to at once, much encouraged to find familiar home delicacies such as Scotch salmon and Irish butter in tins; she baked and made chutneys, grew fruit, raised hens and ducks in her back garden and drove Sidney to making himself useful by inventing a shoe polish for the family. When he died – remembered as a man of remarkable dullness – she grieved bitterly. It must have been bleak having no one left to drive forcefully onwards.

Sarah Terry had clearly no taste for indolence. Emily Metcalfe did, and could indulge it, later remembering a delightfully happy time spent with her father, Crown agent in Delhi, in the fifties. She had social life and as much freedom as a Victorian girl could have expected, the only restrictions being that her father could not bear to see women eat cheese and also insisted that if she must eat mangoes, she should do so in the bath. Ordinary life in India, the life outside that airy, luxurious house in Delhi, seems not to have touched her at all. On the other hand, Helen Mackenzie, the wife of a brigadier, not only kept all her husband's regimental accounts and copied his despatches, but was keenly distressed at the condition of the men in the 'lines'.

Every Indian town and city had its lines: row upon row of tiny rooms built of brick and plaster in which soldier and sepoy could be cooped up for days on end in conditions of unbelievable heat and boredom. They drank, somewhat understandably, and their plight was exacerbated rather than relieved by the presence amongst them of a few wives, who led an awful life and behaved accordingly. Kipling might write,

> What did the colonel's lady think?
> Nobody ever knew.
> Somebody asked the sergeant's wife
> And she told them true.

When you get to the man in the case,
They're as like as a row of pins
For the colonel's lady and Judy O'Grady
Are sisters under their skins.

but that was wishful thinking. White-skinned they might both be, at the mercy of their husband's job they might both be, but sisters they absolutely were not. The soldier's wife, used at home to camping in the corner of some barrack room behind a piece of sacking that divided every intimacy of her life from up to eighty men, was a toughened animal. She had to be. At best she might be a regimental washerwoman at a halfpenny a day per customer, at worst she scrambled along in the teeming barrack life, cooking in rough communal kitchens, growing vegetables illicitly behind buildings, giving birth, getting drunk, and tumbling her children up anyhow in a life crowded with men and coarse habits, devoid of sanitation and rife with tuberculosis and typhoid.

The brutality of this existence was given an extra menace by the ballots drawn at the time of each foreign regimental posting to see which wives should accompany the men. These ballots persisted into the 1850s. The dreaded papers were marked 'To go' and 'Not to go'. Not to go meant a separation which could last up to ten or fifteen years and no financial support whatsoever, so it is hardly surprising that women would go to great lengths to avoid being left paupers on a parish. Even if they went, they were unpaid – although they received half-rations – and were expected to work hard nursing, cooking and washing. Under such circumstances, morality scarcely existed among soldiers' wives: they were accomplished pickpockets, frequently more addicted to the bottle than the men, and anybody's for a few pence. They even wore oversized boots and uniforms stripped from the dead. The women struggled behind the regiments with their children as best they might since no concessions were made for them at all, sleeping in tents with the men and their families, head to the wall, feet to the central pole. They gave birth unattended, often had to search battlefields alone for their dead, and frequently died pathetically neglected and exhausted in a regiment's wake – and were vilified by everyone.

After the Crimean War the wives stopped going to battlefields. But conditions in the lines of all those barrack towns of the Empire, from the West Indies to the East were, if less taxing physically, psychologically even more so. Hot, bored, diseased and poor, the wives struggled onwards to become indescribably hardened, treated, as Helen Mackenzie said, 'more as an animal than a woman'. Utter destitution remained the most savage threat, so young girls and new widows were married off as quickly as possible.

For officers' wives things were very different, and deliberately kept so. The screaming, leather-faced hoyden of the lines bore no kinship at all – except in her country of origin – to the colonel's lady whose life, for three generations, remained almost unchanged. In Bermuda and Mauritius, Ceylon and China, Canada and India, the officers' families moved in a world of bungalows, servants, outlandish pets, ponies and picnics. Fanny Duberly, unsung heroine (in her own opinion) of the Crimea felt that the officer's wife led a life of singular folly. Having watched the ladies of the regiment dancing and partying for a while, she said sharply that 'people in India naturally become idiotic'. She, of course, had known an old-style campaign. She and her husband – a regimental paymaster of great dullness who came a poor runner-up to her passion for horses and other men – had watched all the major battles of the Crimea, a campaign which had seen the last, she felt, of the real soldier's wife. Had not Lady Errol, wife of Lord Errol of the Rifles, slept uncomplainingly on the floor of their tent at Scutari since there was but one camp bed and her husband, the soldier, must naturally have it?

There is no record that she met Lady Florentina Sale, but any meeting they had would, despite their common view of the duty of a soldier's wife, have been an acrimonious occasion. Lady Sale, wife of 'Fighting Bob' Sale, was perhaps the archetypal general's wife of the mid-century. Overbearing, forthright and extremely conscious of her status, she was exceptionally brave and calm, and the rallying point for all the luckless women and children kidnapped by the Afghans after the disastrous siege of Kabul in 1842. She uncompromisingly called the soldiers' wives 'the women' and when relief parcels filtered through to their prison in an old fort at Budeabad, insisted that she should, as premier wife, have first pick. But she was not afraid of Akbar, their Afghan captor, nor of the cold or the misery. It was rumoured that when the Afghans threatened her husband that they would tie her to a cannon's mouth and blow her to kingdom come, Bob Sale took some time before protesting.

This small and eccentric scattering of wives was altered for ever by the Sepoy Revolt, the Indian Mutiny. Trouble had been brewing quietly for some time among the Indians themselves, since they had an uneasy suspicion that the British, with their ever-tightening administrative grip on the sub-continent, meant to overthrow the Hindu religion and its vital caste system with it. It was a straw stack that only needed a match. The match was struck on 10 May 1857 in Meerut, when hundreds of sepoys – those decent, orderly, quiet sepoys in whom everyone had such absolute confidence – broke out in an orgy of slaughter and burning. The reason given was the issue of cartridges for the Enfield rifle whose ends had to be greased and then bitten off; the grease, it was rumoured, was a pork–beef compound, unclean to both Hindu and Mohammedan.

India erupted. The English fled from Delhi – one officer's wife, Harriet Tytler, was too pregnant to scale her elephant escort, and gave birth to a son in an ammunition wagon – and attempted to flee from all other Indian cities. In several places they were besieged in hideous conditions, notably at Cawnpore, where women and children starved for three weeks. At the end of this time, a free pardon was granted to the emaciated wretches, who were herded on to boats on the river and then fallen upon by maddened sepoys. The doomed 125 survivors were then shut up in unspeakable conditions in a building known as the Bibighur and after eighteen terrible days were slaughtered by butchers brought in expressly for the purpose from the Cawnpore bazaar.

It was a horror story such as England had never known. The Highland regiments who eventually got to Cawnpore and found the well of the Bibighur choked with the hacked-up bodies of English women and children went insane in their revenge. All captured sepoys before their execution were kicked into the Bibighur and forced to kneel in the room where the atrocity had been committed and lick part of the floor or walls clean of blood. The only light note in the whole beastly episode was the story of Bridget Widdowson, whose husband was a private in the Thirty-second. She was a great, hefty woman who in the early stages of the siege was given eleven mutineers to guard, there being no one else available. She made them sit in a row on the ground and marched up and down before them for hours, brandishing a drawn sword while they cowered docilely at her tramping feet. Eventually a regular soldier came to relieve her, at which point the mutineers found no problem at all in slipping away.

The siege of Lucknow, though less sensationally horrible, was not much better. Journals tell of the same overcrowding and dirt and thirst and hunger, the same rollcall of sick children, the same boils and sores on everyone, the same stench and racket and heat. Most of the diary-writers did not expect to survive each day, but waited hourly for their children's deaths, their own, or news that their husbands were no more.

After such a nightmare as the mutiny, India could never be the same again. The calm confidence that Honoria Lawrence had felt bundling alone with her baby around the India of the forties sank to distrust and fear. It was not, as has often been suggested, the memsahib's presence that contributed to the Sepoy Revolt in the first place: there were simply too few of her kind to exert such an influence. But, conversely, the revolt led to the memsahibs taking India by storm. Post-mutiny was the colonel's lady's heyday. Alarmed to their depths by the mutiny, the military administration sought to safeguard its men by distancing them from India. Women and children were sent for and came out in great numbers after 1860. They created established English communities, which in turn distanced white from brown. Military life, in the last third of the century, became self-supporting; there was no need even to countenance the life of the Indian. Small-station days – those stations built in a style only half-affectionately known as 'disappointed Gothic' – were spent in gossip, scandal and, in the hot weather, making a mountain out of every molehill in sight. The memsahib, that caricature of entrenched racial and social prejudice, had come to stay.

She had, even then, her champions. One does not have to go far to find how unbelievably, painfully boring life could be, especially out in the country districts, the mofussil. 'A good many yawns yawned,' Florence Marryat wrote despairingly of Bangalore. How could it be otherwise, with bearers to be had for 10 rupees (about 80 pence) a month and cooks for 14, not to mention the climate, which overpowered all efforts at energy and self-discipline? Maud Diver, one of a handful of remarkable lady novelists whose books were concerned with India and the English in India, understood very sympathetically the demoralizing effects of being the slave to someone else's duty in such as place as the East. She knew the memsahib was derided by her sisters at home and she knew that nothing she could say could give a precise image of what life in India was like:

For no pen – not even the magic pen of a Kipling or a Mrs Steele – can convey to a mind unacquainted with the East the subtle atmosphere of India, the awful lifelessness of her vast dun-coloured Plains, the smells and sounds of her swarming cities, the majesty of her incomparable mountains, and the mystery that hangs over the lives and thoughts of her many peoples; and since environment is one of the strongest and subtlest forces that make for character-development, it is unfair to pass judgement upon any man or woman without giving due weight to this great factor in their lives.

Many of the women, she admitted, were indeed 'idle, frivolous and luxury loving', but that was in large measure India's fault rather than their own:

Yes, those who live for any length of time in India have to reckon with that insidious tendency to fatalism – to accept men and things as they find them, without enthusiasm, and without criticism – which lurks in the very air they breathe. The large tolerance, bred of intimate contact with many-sided aspects of life, slips, all too easily, into a certain laxity – mental, moral, and physical – which is in itself accountable for much that appears incomprehensible to those who have never felt its subtle influence, its compelling power.

The Anglo-Indian woman cannot – in social sense – live unto herself alone. Whether she will or no, her life is blended inextricably with those about her. Be her mental and moral landmarks – on arrival – never so definitely laid down, be her prejudices and her insular aloofness never so deeply ingrained, yet slowly – imperceptibly almost – she will find her outlook on life widened, her heart softened, her nervous system more or less undermined; in a word, she will be called upon to face life's problems and perplexities under conditions wholly different to those under which she faced them 'at Home'.

'Indian life is real,' she wrote with understandable earnestness, 'and you live it desperately from start to finish.' As with everything, that was easier for some than for others. For Flora Annie Steele, author of a dramatically successful novel partly set during the mutiny, India was a perfect place to exercise her enormous, if sometimes controversial, enthusiasms. Married to an Indian civil servant who appears to have been mercifully immune to embarrassment, she flung herself into public life in the Punjab in the 1860s and was eventually made Inspector of Schools. It was her proud boast that she had never been in love – whether that was true or not is immaterial, but there was certainly plenty of imaginative emotion in her which found its outlet in her second major career, as a novelist of India. Although she was enormously popular, it is not for the novels that she is chiefly remembered but for being India's Mrs Beeton. *Complete Indian Housekeeper and Cook*, which she wrote in 1887, became the bible of every Anglo-Indian household until the 1940s. It left absolutely no domestic stone unturned and even included a recipe for making a cement strong enough to hold pieces of steel together.

Perhaps mercifully, there was only one Flora Annie Steele. For the most part, a woman had twelve 'red hot interminable months' in the plains if she elected to stay with her husband during the hot weather, or seven marginally cooler ones followed by a heady respite in the hills.

> Jack's own Jill goes up the hill
> To Murree or Chakrata,
> Jack remains or dies in the plains
> And Jill remarries soon after.

Hill station life was a legend of bad behaviour. Wives on their own, husband-hunters, bachelor soldiers and civil servants on leave, everyone on holiday in climates that brought nostalgia for England and Scotland, with mountain days to fill with nothing but pleasure – it is small surprise that scandal should have been the order of the day. The atmosphere was 'irresistibly infectious'. It was the one place where the tyrant duty could be forgotten, where the sacrifice of health and interest were not demanded, high up there in the fairytale never-never land of Simla and Naini-Tal. Opinion in England was vociferous in condemning the low 'tone of social morality' but Maud Diver claimed that those who voiced such views only behaved well because they had no chance to do otherwise: '. . . it does not follow that the sheltered wives of England are justified in assuming the role of Pharisee. They will do better to consider, instead, whether the saving grace of circumstances may not be, in part, responsible for their own integrity.'

In retrospect, it is difficult to condemn the Mrs Hawksbees – except when one considers the cuckolded husbands toiling away in their districts in the plains. India always meant a great deal of heartbreak, and without the sense of service to sustain them in the certainty of doing right, the women suffered acutely. It wasn't simply the loneliness, or the heat, or the boredom, or the dirt, or the sense of always taking second place, but the fact that nothing in India could belong to them for long, not even their children.

Most Victorian women had no alternative to becoming pregnant, even if they did see their husband's life and family life as incompatible. Soldiers' wives complained that a new posting inevitably meant an unwanted pregnancy, a condition which they could endeavour to do something about by riding hard to hounds or crawling backwards upstairs, methods favoured by officers' wives. For all classes there was the old standby of gin and quinine, a mixture much relied upon even if it did make one's eyesight hazy and induce humming in the ears. But for most women, wives of the hundreds of thousands of civil servants, there was nothing to do but have babies – an undertaking fraught with danger in the filth of India – and once you had them, life was almost as empty as before and a great deal more complicated. The employment of Indian ayahs was initially discouraged as they tended to form a 'promiscuous intimacy' with children, particularly little boys, and were prone to revere their charges, addressing tyrannical toddlers as 'Lord Protector of the Poor' and abasing themselves on the floor. English nurses were preferred, but of course were prone to all the debilitating effects of India from which the *burra* memsahib herself suffered.

Childhood had hardly begun – and a happy thing it was for most of the babies of Anglo-Indian households, in an atmosphere of sunshine and love – when the great and awful choice presented itself. Was the future to be given to the woman's husband or to the children? Should she stay sweltering in Ootacamund, loyal and wretched, at the side of a man working all hours, or should she take the children home to health and education and run the very real risk that her marriage would never pick up again? Most wives chose the former option and it was goodbye to children, often for years. Maud Diver recommended three or four years as the maximum period for which any woman should abandon either husband or children, in a tone that suggests such a time as inconsiderable and shorter than the norm.

With the children gone, the days stretched uninvitingly into the heat-blurred distances. Some women made their own clothes, but if their husband's posting was to India or China, there was little incentive to bother since dresses and shoes could be so cheaply copied. There was always entertaining to do, of course, but there was a dreadful sameness to it, particularly in remote places. The menu remained virtually unchanged for half a century and more – soup, fish, cutlets, pudding and then a savoury or a dessert. Always, at the back of your mind, was the thought of Home. Home was the place that had shaped you, but to which you would never quite belong again, changed as you were by living so differently. Following a man about the Empire was an enormous challenge, leaving you often exhausted, uncertain of the point of your existence, frequently ill and bored, expecting pleasure and service all your life and feeling, as one soldier's wife put it, 'always a little homesick for places that have forgotten you'.

Grandeur could, for the very privileged few, provide insulation from the difficulties of India. For the ladies of the Governors General and the Viceroy, particularly those with a taste for public life and spectacular dress, duty came in a very palatable form. Lady Lytton was one such, wife of the Viceroy in the late seventies and a woman described by Marianne North, the botanical painter, as 'gorgeous and lovely'. She was reputed to have enormous charm and grace, two qualities which are not immediately evident in her letters and her diary. These contain some truly magnificent sartorial descriptions:

. . . a lovely gown of purple blue silk and velvet stamped with blue velvet brocade – the bonnet was a sort of wreath of feathers with rim of pearls making it a Marie Stewart shape which was so becoming and I wore my pearl and diamond bracelet round my neck – the body and skirt fit quite beautifully and made me look so slim. It was handsome and picturesque without being too gaudy.

There are also happy accounts of moments of pomp and circumstance, such as the ceremony at which Queen Victoria was proclaimed Empress of India in 1877:

The troops struck us so much as we approached the Assemblage place, though the plain is so vast it is very difficult for anything to make a show on it. Just outside the circle of the seats of the Assemblage there was a tent for R. to robe. The robe (of the Grand Master of the Star of India) was beautiful blue velvet embroidered with gold flowers and an ermine cape. He looked very well with uniform, Star of India Order and two pages holding his robe (son of the Maharaja of Kashmir, such a pretty boy, and Mr Grimstone, Midshipman, in a Charles II blue and white dress). I walked

'Oh, the heat! The heat! I am getting more used to
it but dressing in it is simply awful.' Mary Curzon
in her famous peacock dress, Delhi 1903

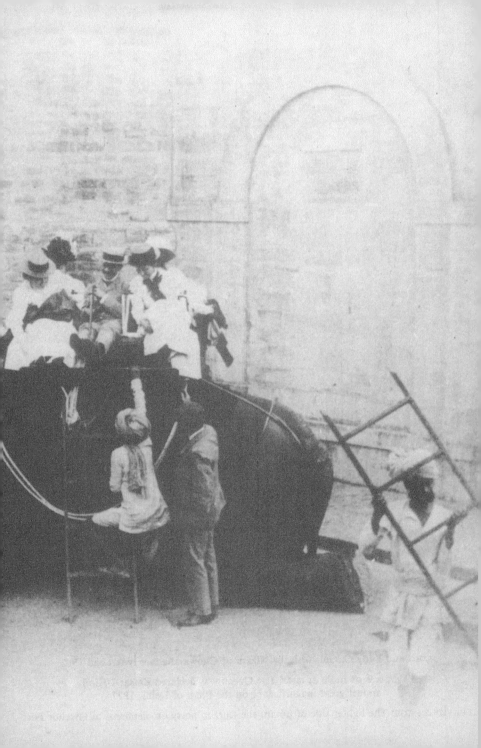

Lord and Lady Curzon with the Nizam of Chowmahalia, Hyderabad 1902

'Empress of India at last.' The Queen was declared Kaisar-I-Hind
amidst great magnificence on the Plain of Delhi, 1877

PREVIOUS PAGE: The lighter side of pomp: the Curzon party on elephants at Gwalior Fort

Transporting the memsahibs. English ladies on
elephant-back with their Indian hosts late in the
century

Flora Shaw, later Lady Lugard, as a young woman. She habitually wore black until her marriage, whereupon she changed to white (see pp.133–41)

RIGHT: Maintaining law and order in Hong Kong. A group of customs officials and armed guards on the British-Chinese boundary, 1898

Stanhopia martiana from *The Orchidaceae of Mexico and Guatemala* by Augustus Innes Withers, known, on account of its size, as The Librarian's Nightmare (see p. 158)

LEFT: 'A valuable and remarkable Bint!' Marianne North sketching in the tropics (see pp. 156 – 8)

Mormyrus Kingsleyae

Ctenopoma Kingsleyae

Mary Kingsley's scientific enthusiasm was for the
collection of tropical fish, her
anthropological one for the cannibal Fans. 'I do
not want to arrive at Rembwé in a smoked
condition, even should my fragments be neat'
(see p. 152)

Margaret Fountaine, butterfly-hunting with Hal Newcomb
at Palm Springs (see pp. 148 – 50)

LEFT: *Ericaceae,* from *The Chief Natural Orders of Plants* by Elizabeth
Twining, a copy of which was presented to Queen Victoria (see p. 158)

Grandmother Extraordinary, Mary de la Beche
Nicholl, whose travels encompassed
butterfly-hunting in the Balkans, an expedition to
the Lebanon and trail-blazing in British Columbia

LEFT: Dorothy Hilton-Simpson, photographed by her
husband among the Berbers in 1914. She wears
Ouled Ziane headdress and jewellery and
presumably her own cardigan

The convict reformed. Sarah Ann Hunt, transported to
Van Dieman's Land in 1843 for receiving a lace shawl, died as
Mrs Gifford, owner of a drapery shop in Hobart, which specialized
in being 'a deposit for family mourning and childbed linen'

after him with a little girl on each side, and the staff, a very brilliant one, fell in after us, and so we walked solemnly up to the dais. Having never walked except in a funeral procession and being rather shy I am afraid I felt very serious but the whole thing was most properly solemn. R.'s chair was, of course, put rather forward and mine at his right and the children's at his left just behind. The Chiefs were all in front in a semi-circular covered stand, and their new banners, gold umbrellas and dress made it a splendid sight, but the British uniforms pervaded very much amongst these. (There had been a hundred elephant processions of the princes to reach the stand.) Our Governors, Lieutenant-Governors and Members of Council were all facing the throne also. The bands placed on the left all played the Tannhauser march which was very effective.

Lytton was not the most popular of Viceroys. He was criticized for his indolence and eccentric love of finery, his egotism and his failure to improve the tone of Anglo-Indian life as he had been relied upon to do. He bore personal criticism quite easily, perhaps encouraged by the praise of his wife who, despite the slight fatuousness of her tone, was evidently staunchly loyal: 'Dear R. was so cheered by my praise after we came to bed, he is so curiously susceptible to being appreciated even by me who always admires him so, and cares for what everyone says of him (though luckily he don't care much for what these papers say).'

So she writes on, copiously and with satisfaction, revealing an endless vista of elephants and peacocks and men bowing over her hand – 'the dear Commander in Chief, to whom I am devoted' – of native princes and receptions and Worth ball gowns. It was some distance, this life where 1700 coolies could be set to work on Peterhof, the Lyttons' house in Simla, from 'that stratum of humanity which lies at the root of all lives, and makes the wide world one'.

Africa presents quite a different picture, not only by virtue of the place itself but also of the comparative lateness of its administrative development and the scarcity of white people, even at the outbreak of the Great War. And if white people were scarce, white women – with the exception of missionaries – were in some places almost unknown. The early district officers either took a *bibi*, a native mistress, or – and the proportion was huge – simply abstained from sexual relations altogether if they were in remote places. The threat of disease was too great to subject women and children to the tropical extremes of Africa, and, besides that, pay levels would have made it difficult to maintain a conventional establishment. Even the Sudan Political Service, the best paid of all the African services, only offered a new recruit fresh from Oxford a little over £400 a year at the turn of the century.

Judging by a list for her trousseau prepared by Edith Hardy in 1912 before she married Donald Duncan in Bulawayo, a wife's wardrobe might have made quite a dent in such a sum:

Underwear	£7. 0.0.	Boots 3 pairs	£2.13.6.
Coat and skirt	5. 5.0.	Ninon tunic	2.10.0.
Silk dress	4. 0.0.	White hat and veil	1. 1.0.
Lace robe	4. 4.0.	Underwear, lace etc.	3.10.0.
Satin slip	2. 2.0.	Khaki skirt and boots	1.18.6.
Gloves, hosiery etc.	4. 5.0.	Blouses etc.	1. 5.0.
Muslin dress	1. 8.0.	Bonnet	1. 6.0.
Motor bonnet	1. 1.0.	Chiffon for tunic	2. 5.0.

It was really not until the 1890s that the wives and daughters of administrators were to be seen in Africa. The first arrivals came to a raw if fascinating country with none of the Victorian comforts that Indian colonizers had become so accustomed to. In 1896 Lord Grey was appointed Administrator of Southern Rhodesia, and took his wife and daughter from Mafeking to Bulawayo in an ox cart, a journey of some thousand miles. His grandson Harry Grenfell recalled that his mother and her parents found themselves in 'government House in Bulawayo, a simple building on the site of the kraal, formerly occupied by Lobengula, King of the Matabele before Rhodes entered Rhodesia'.

Government House may have been primitive in its appointments, but there were chances to participate in the great events that go to making a new country. 1896 was also the year of the Matabele uprising, and Harry Grenfell's mother, then only seventeen, remembered riding into the Malopo Hills with Cecil Rhodes to attend one of the meetings that led to peace with the Matabele. Fifteen years later there was still that pleasurable sense of sharing in new beginnings. Kate Jameson, a bride in Bulawayo in 1911, wrote in old age of her delight in seeing the city grow:

. . . when we were transferred to Bulawayo we lived in Pauling Road, at that time the last street before the bush began. There were street names, on posts, of future streets right out in the bush! I used to go for three-mile walks in the bush with my bull-terrier. My husband said I must always carry a gun. It weighed down my jersey pocket, but neither wild animal nor human molested me. There were herds of sable, and, I suppose, lions – but I never saw any lions.

From the beginning, there is an air of pleased excitement about those first journals and letters written from Africa. Very few women even disliked it, most loved it, and arriving as they did towards the end of the century, there were fewer social restrictions upon their activities. The oppressive pyramid of hierarchy and precedence that had come to make life in India at its worst so stultified did not apply to Africa, either east or west. Neither was the army such an influence, which removed the dominating figure of the colonel's lady. Those early pioneers of Africa, the Nellie Grants and Eleanor Coles, certainly dressed for dinner and furnished their isolated houses in much the way they would have done at home, but they rode and shot and dug gardens and dosed natives and animals in a free and self-satisfying way that was denied to their sisters of forty years before.

Africa seemed, unlike enervating India, to fill the women with energy. Gertrude Coghlan, wife of Sir Charles, the first Premier of Rhodesia, was a delightful woman by all accounts, beautiful, charming and a marvellous hostess. She founded the Women's Institute movement in Bulawayo, and was ceaselessly active in charity and church work despite being extremely frail physically. In India she would have languished and pined, in Africa she showed a most indomitable spirit. After a mild stroke in old age, her doctor said of her despairingly, '. . . the way she sits up in bed is enough to kill her. She *bounces* up, she doesn't sit up slowly and carefully.'

Lady Eleanor Cole, a niece of Lutyens, reacted similarly to Africa. She married a man some years her senior who had already established a sheep farm at Gilgil, Kenya, and sailed with him to Mombasa in a ship 'more like an inferno than anything I ever want to experience again'. There were rats, cockroaches and a plague of ants, the food was revolting, the ship stank and almost everyone was seasick. But when they reached East Africa, it was, in her own words, 'a home-coming':

We arrived at the station here about 4.30. Rain was threatening, and we had to bustle off in the Ford car, which was waiting for us, in order to get down the very bad hill there is, before the road got too slippery. The car refused to start, of course, and the whole station crowd had to give us a push off. We got down just as the rain started and we both felt quite ill from excitement, and I still feel so dazed I can't really write about it. I was freshly impressed with the extraordinary beauty of this part of the country with its lakes and hills. It is looking quite its best in fresh green as the rains have just started. The colours, morning and evening, are truly wonderful. Delicious flowering shrubs, and wild lilies, and birds and beasts of every sort.

She never looked back. She had two sons – writing with relief of the first that she had managed to obtain an English nanny for him which enabled her to be free to help her husband on the farm – to whom she bequeathed her devotion to British East Africa.

Across the other side of the continent an even smaller, slower trickle of white women was succumbing to the charms of Africa, whatever the hazards. Sylvia Leith-Ross, wife of a Captain in Lugard's West Africa Frontier Force, sailed to Northern Nigeria in 1907 as one of only three English wives in the country. She sailed, as most people then did, on a ship of the Elder Dempster Line, with a luggage allowance of eighty 56-pound loads. That was the weight manageable by a native carrier. Everything required for eighteen months had to be taken: food (in 'chop' boxes), drink, clothing, furniture, kerosene lamps and the vital mosquito nets. At Lagos the passengers were transferred to sternwheelers to go up the Niger, leaving behind those who were to serve in Southern Nigeria and who were regarded by the northerners as soft and decadent.

Once up the Niger, her first married house was a standard government bungalow shipped out in pieces from England and put up by the public works department. It had three rooms, a verandah and a punkah and was otherwise empty and extremely ugly. Like India it was dirty, like India there were insects everywhere but, unlike India, servants did not swarm. Africans did not always care to work for a white woman, and if they did, they did not do so in such huge numbers. A boy – a steward – was in charge and beneath him was a small boy, a small-small boy, a gardener and a string of local prisoners to carry water. From the beginning, Africa required female ingenuity and participation.

It also required fortitude. Arthur Leith-Ross was dead of black-water fever within a year, and even though she went home to mourn him, his widow had been bitten by Africa. She returned to Nigeria to become of inestimable benefit to that country, throwing herself into anthropological studies of the Ibo and schemes to set up some form of education. These efforts were so successful that she became Nigeria's first lady superintendent of education. She also found time to continue her studies on the Ibo and to compile a comprehensive catalogue of Nigerian pottery, whose 'wonderful jars and dye-pots of springing curves and absolute symmetry' she felt would soon vanish under the seductively easy onslaught of 'enamel basins and kerosene tins'. She travelled widely and mostly alone and in later life recalled the privilege of being able to do so unafraid:

Years ago, when I first came out, a white man and I were riding up the road to Kano, the only road which had yet been built in the North. We overtook a file of women and girls walking along the edge of the road, singing, their loads on their heads. They walked lightly along the grassy track in and out of shadow and sunlight. Miles from anywhere, all alone, these women and girls walked lightly, securely, singing softly. The white man stopped his pony, looked at them, and said: 'Pax Britannica'. Even after, when annoyed by all the ugly things called progress and all the harm done by civilization, I would think of those women who, because of England, could walk safely through the bush, singing.

Among all these women who gave, willingly or unwillingly, such dutiful service to the Empire, there is one so remarkable that she must be placed in a category quite her own. Flora Shaw was born in 1852 on her grandfather's estate, Kimmage, outside Dublin. Her grandfather, Sir Frederick Shaw, a man of distinction in Irish politics, was to be a major influence on her development, instilling in her the enormous sense of responsibility and duty that was to characterize her life, and reminding her constantly that it is 'the privilege of a gentleman to get the worst of any bargain throughout life'. Her father, while serving as a soldier in Mauritius, had carried off the youngest and best-looking of the Governor's daughters, who bequeathed to her daughter, Flora – the third of fourteen children – her looks and her vivacity. Flora was, said Miss Moberly Bell in her biography of Flora Shaw, 'vivid in every inch of her small person'.

Flora had a comfortable and conventional Victorian upbringing, divided between Kimmage and Woolwich, where her father was commandant. Her mother, never strong and weakened by the inevitable annual Victorian baby, needed a good deal of attention, but there was still time for Flora to spend in the soldiers' library – but not too much, as is shown by a tribute paid to her during her coming-out year which admired her as a girl of vivacity and good looks who was 'intelligent without a trace of bluestocking'. Thank heavens. Flora's mother died when she was eighteen, leaving her with the responsibility of the house and her younger siblings, but she was sustained by her own energetic personality and by some interesting friendships, notably one with John Ruskin who came to Woolwich to lecture. He helped her with the education of her younger brothers and sisters, and with doses of 'stimulating conversation', for which she amply repaid him by listening sympathetically to the endless difficulties of his love affair with Rose de la Touche.

When she was twenty, her father remarried. His relations with Flora had never been very close, and this was the parting of the ways. She took to going to France – anything rather than remain at home – but was frustrated in her wider ambitions by lack of money, that great crippler of Victorian female enterprise. She wrote a children's book set at Kimmage, *Castle Blair*, which Ruskin greatly admired. But it made no money even though, as a result, she was asked to write for a children's paper, and she took up the management of a family connection's household in a true Victorian way, teaching the children until they went away to school. That happened in 1881, when Flora Shaw was already twenty-nine, with a lifetime's knowledge of domestic skills behind her, no formal education and no money.

It was then that the first movements of her future career began. Through the households in which she had lived she had always known public men, but she had had very little direct contact with the outside world. She made a new friend, a Miss Steer, a social worker in east London, and through her Flora came to know a world of human beastliness that she had never suspected. 'It's a dreadful life,' she wrote in her diary, despairing of a degree of poverty that could drive children into prostitution:

It is not possible to look round this part of London without a numbing sensation of despair. . . . The beauty of many of the children, the brightness of the young people, only seems in one mood to make it worse. Notwithstanding the natural human charm, they are to be drawn into the whirlpool of sin, they are to become inhuman and degraded, and the laws which make this so are too strong for us. Private charity, while I admire it, seems to me utterly insufficient. It is like baling out the sea with a teacup.

From her wretchedly unhappy contemplation of the life of the very poor grew the first stirrings of what was to be a powerful imperial impulse in Flora Shaw. Standing one day by the Thames tunnel pier with one of the missioners from the Rescue Home in Wapping, watching Russian ships bringing wool from the Baltic up the river, she was led to think of 'the highway of the world' and to speculate whether ' . . . here perhaps was some part of the answer to the problems of overcrowding and insufficient opportunity – a way of escape, a road inviting them to pass from sin and dirt and misery to space'.

She was not a Christian and therefore – and most unusually for her times – did not see herself as an instrument of kindly, divine philanthropic purpose. She determined to write, to use her pen to alleviate the plight of the poor, and to this end rented a room in a cottage at Abinger in Surrey. Local literary society snapped her up at once. George Meredith, who lived nearby on Box Hill, wrote excitedly to Admiral Maxse that he must ' . . . come and see Flora Shaw, to know whom is to look through an eyelet into the promised land. In matters of abstract thought as well as in warm feelings for the poor muddy fry of this world, you will find her unmatched. She is Irish and French – that's why. Quite as delightful to talk with as to look at.'

She started to write a history of England but as she thought deeply about the project she realized that it was the development of the colonies that absorbed her most, as she believed that ' . . . the life of those younger and more virile communities might renew the heart of the Empire and that a cure for the congestion of population at home lay in migration overseas'.

Her imperial enthusiasm was growing. In 1886 and 1887 she began to travel with friends of former employers, mostly in Gibraltar and Morocco. Enterprisingly she sent back to *The Times* and the *Pall Mall Gazette* articles of such excellence on the political situation after the death of the Sultan that the *Gazette* gave her increasing amounts of work, sending her books for review and begging for more reports. She had left England a penniless lady travelling companion and she returned home a journalist, financially self-sufficient for the first time in her thirty-five years.

The next year she was off again, this time to Egypt, the accredited correspondent of the *Pall Mall Gazette* with an added commission to write regular reports for the *Manchester Guardian*. She wrote home of the dreary and tawdry reality of harem life: ' . . . plain women, dressed in vulgar adaptations of European clothes, sat about listlessly hour after hour, with neither work nor entertainment to enliven the long days'. But her great and growing passion was for politics, in which she was enormously helped by Sir Evelyn Baring, who administered Egyptian affairs. She gained a reputation for 'the informal and intimate atmosphere' of her interviews with government officials, who were impressed by the extent to which she prepared herself before meeting them. Her influence was growing and so too was her circle of friends, which now included Moberly Bell, the celebrated correspondent and later editor of *The Times*, who took care to introduce her to anyone of any significance.

She went home to England in 1889 to nurse a dying friend – her life seems always an attractive mixture of the intensely domestic and the impressively public – and to write and write and write. She wrote on Persia 'in the train between Gomshall and Charing Cross', on the army after War Office interviews – including one with Lord Wolseley who told her that princes and peers would always stand in the way of army reform – on the Mediterranean area and on Australia and its growing problems of immigration. She was more and more becoming a recognized authority on whatever subject she touched and it was perhaps inevitable that she should that summer meet Cecil Rhodes, who was in England to persuade the Government to entrust the opening up and administration of the African interior to a chartered company. He impressed her enormously as a man who made 'other men . . . interested in the same subject [appear] like thread paper beside him' despite his tendency to walk 'like a caged lion all the time through two rooms, answering my questions at times from the depths of the second room in which I was not'.

When she questioned him as to how he could contemplate spending vast sums of money so speculatively, he answered airily, 'Some men collect butterflies. I do this. It interests me.' Rhodes interested Flora and introduced her to Africa, which in turn introduced her to Sir George Goldie, 'Empire Builder Extraordinary'. He was a brilliant man, violent, sensitive, ruthless, wildly attractive to women and by his own declaration 'absolutely germ-proof' to all the recognized forms of ambition. He was also married. Flora admired him, disagreed with him on a number of important issues, and fell deeply in love with him.

She fortunately had plenty of work to distract her from a hopeless passion. In Brussels she attended, as the only woman journalist, the international congress on the suppression of the slave trade, and upon her return found that her friend Moberly Bell was now assistant manager of *The Times*. He begged her to write for him. 'Let me know where you are and when I may see you and I will fly with all the alacrity of sixteen stones.' She wanted *The Times* to become the great imperial organ and even though Moberly Bell was doubtful of this ambition ('I am not so good a John Bull as you') he urged that she should be made colonial editor of the paper. Her sex was against such an appointment but she wrote regular articles on colonial affairs, one of which was so remarkably good that the proprietor of *The Times*, John Walter, declared that 'whoever wrote it [is] the sort of fellow we ought to get on *The Times*'.

When she was forty she suffered a bad bout of influenza and *The Times* sent her to South Africa to 'visit the colonies about which she wrote with so much perspicacity'. To the society of Cape Town she was that alarming phenomenon, the new woman:

Flora at 40 looked very much younger than her age. She was very slim and graceful, undeniably beautiful, with a very fine profile and striking eyes. She always wore black and was very simply dressed, but in perfect taste. Her manner was gentle and unassuming; she had a clear and rather low-pitched voice and her enunciation, like her vocabulary, was always precise. Her face was very expressive and, as she listened, understanding, sympathy, humour were revealed in it. She was so much more interested in the thing she was discussing than in herself, that men discussing politics with her forgot she was a woman and talked to her as freely as to another man.

She was fascinated by the farms and the mines and disgusted by Johannesburg. 'It is hideous and detestable, luxury without order, sensual enjoyment without art, riches without refinement, display without dignity....'

The Times was so struck by her reports that she was sent on to Australia, where she discussed the serious financial situation caused by falling exports, roused everyone's admiration and was appalled by the remote isolation of bush life. 'Everybody separated by twenty or thirty miles from everybody else, nothing wherever you look but grass and trees and sky, and though you may know the station you are on carries half a million sheep, you will perhaps see none in the course of a whole day's drive.'

She had every sympathy for the striking sheep-shearers – one said to her that his life 'would make the Archbishop of Canterbury himself a bit radical' – but, true imperialist as she was, much regretted the pockets of separatist feelings she found, particularly in New South Wales. She left Australia for New Zealand, which she much preferred, presumably because it reminded her, as she said, of Surrey, and then on to Canada whose inhabitants disappointed her, lacking 'the democratic self-reliance of Australia and the executive High Toryism of South Africa'.

She came home to be made colonial editor of *The Times*. Earning enough now to support herself and three of her sisters, she delighted, as she was to do all her life, in making a comfortable home. It was a wonderfully full and satisfying period of her life, in which she entertained frequently, often worked until the small hours at Printing House Square and had the power to appoint all colonial correspondents for the newspaper. Small wonder that in 1894 and 1895, when Rhodes and Dr Jameson were in London negotiating for the 'pulling together' of South Africa into a great imperial whole – a plan which repelled many members of the Government – it was Flora Shaw whom Rhodes relied upon to help plead his cause. She wrote copious letters on his behalf, explaining him to Captain Lugard, a man who had done sterling work for West Africa, as someone who 'cares neither for money, nor place, nor power, except in so far as they are a necessity for the accomplishment of the national ideal for which he lives'.

When the Jameson Raid blew up in everyone's face just before the New Year of 1896 dawned, Flora found herself in a very compromising public position, and a remarkable one, if only because she was the only woman of her time ever to be in such a dilemma. The fundamental grievance behind the raid had lain with the Uitlanders of the Transvaal, the foreigners to whom Kruger's government denied a vote and whose cause Flora had warmly supported in the columns of *The Times*. Things were made worse when, just after the raid, she permitted the publication of a letter, subsequently proved to be a fake, which asked Jameson to ride on Johannesburg at once 'to save helpless women and children'. In truth Jameson had not only raided unasked but absolutely against the express orders of Cecil Rhodes.

There was inevitably a parliamentary inquiry and in May 1897 Flora was called before it. The press were startled but entranced to have a woman speak in such august company, particularly as she made an excellent impression and was also very easy on the eye. 'I observe with some amusement,' Sir Herbert Stephen wrote to her from the Colonial Office, 'the mild astonishment of the ingenuous reporters at discovering you were not a frump.' The inquiry committee wished to prove that she had been involved in a Colonial Office 'plot' to engineer the raid but she insisted, with great success, that she was a journalist not a politician and that her involvement had been entirely innocent. She withdrew at last, worn out but victorious, to a flood of congratulation. Hers was 'the only evidence that has given a clear explanation ...', she was '... the most credible, straightforward and satisfactory witness ...'

Within a year she was off again, to the goldfields of the Klondyke where she stayed at Dawson City ('not a pretty sight'). She was much moved by the squalor of the miners' lives and outraged at the public corruption. She went on to tour the Yukon and the prairies and then travelled to Canada to study the lumber and fishing industries and interview men working for the Hudson Bay Company. She was remembered by everyone as a woman of 'unusual pluck and nerve' and her revelations of corruption resulted in a public inquiry.

At some point during this same year of 1898 a curious emotional episode took place in Flora's life. Sir George Goldie, married for almost thirty years to a governess from his family home whom he had carried off to Paris in 1870, was suddenly widowed. He was stricken, writing wretchedly to friends that even the great panacea of overwork seemed to do him no good at all. Very soon after Lady Goldie's death he was proposed to by Flora Shaw, who had by now been in love with him for six or seven years. Bizarre and brave her behaviour might have been; his was understandable but at best discourteous. He refused her.

However dignified and successful Flora might have been, she was, as *The Times* said in her obituary, 'a thoroughly womanly woman'. She resigned at once from *The Times* and suffered a bitter nervous

breakdown which prostrated her for two years, making her intro-
spective and a prey to moods. It also made her deeply sympathetic to
the man who was to become the founder of modern Nigeria,
Captain, by now Sir Frederick, Lugard, younger than she by some
seven years and also scarred by a profound and passionate trauma
in his life. He was to become the third great imperialist in her life,
after Rhodes and Goldie, and also her husband. 'You once said you
would win my love,' she wrote to him. 'I, too, hope to win yours. We
cannot force it. Let us not try on either side, but let us be content to
marry as friends.'

Which is what they did, the new Lady Lugard being fifty-one at
the time and still prone to nervous prostrations. They were married
quietly in Madeira, Sir Frederick having to nurse her as an invalid,
and they relieved their feelings and frustrations in a splendidly
period manner by taking each evening 'an hour's violent walk to the
top of some hill'. It was Sir George Goldie who had set Lugard on
the road to success in Nigeria by securing his appointment to the
Frontier Force, from which he rose steadily to become High Commissioner, and in that position he took Flora to West Africa.

In the two years of Lugard's administration, Nigeria had ex-
panded from a military cantonment and two trading posts on the
Niger to an enormous dependency ruled by British justice and
almost entirely free of the slave trade. Hardly surprisingly, there
were not enough hours in the day for the work that had to be done.
So Flora found herself, after twenty years of consumingly interesting public life, marooned in a bungalow at Zungeru with absolutely
nothing to do. She admired Lugard's work beyond anything and she
liked the 'big airy bungalow' and the garden where everything grew
so rapaciously, but she had no role to play. Nigeria was too
unsophisticated for her tastes, there were no politics, no civilized
and cultivated people. Inevitably she became depressed and succumbed to malaria. Within a year she was back at Abinger, protesting unhappily to her husband that her weakness and need for
human intercourse 'must perforce teach both of us to live alone and
that is not what we meant to learn when we married'. It was four
years before he resigned his commission and followed her home.

The rest of her life – she lived until she was seventy-six – was
interesting, but it lacks the extraordinary achievements of her
journalistic career. She finally became a member of that galaxy of

distinguished wives of distinguished men, the women who served the Empire as their husband's helpmeets. Sir Frederick was made Governor of Hong Kong in 1907 and Lady Lugard was a triumphant success at his side, entirely refurbishing the official residences, entertaining wonderfully and imaginatively, dealing with great flair with 'this red carpet business'. Government House was 'a plethora of princes' and even though her health was now always poor, she pronounced her life 'delightful'. It was to go on as such, divided after 1912 between London and Surrey, and between writing, gardening and entertaining.

But Lady Lugard could never, inevitably, recapture Miss Flora Shaw. 'We were entertaining at Osterley,' Lady Jersey wrote after Lady Lugard's death, 'a number of representatives of foreign colonial dependencies in addition to certain English friends, among whom were Sir Frederick and Lady Lugard, who had recently married. After dinner the Belgian and the Dutch representatives, between whom Lady Lugard had been seated, came up and asked me in some agitation, "Qui était cette dame qui était si forte?" i.e. in her knowledge of African and Congo politics. "Lady Lugard," I replied. "She was Miss Flora Shaw." "Quoi, la grande Miss Shaw!" exclaimed our friends, throwing up their hands as an indication that there was no more to be said.'

VII
'NO PLACE TO
TAKE A MAN'

ISABELLA BIRD BISHOP

A lady an explorer? A traveller in skirts?
The notion's just a trifle too seraphic;
Let them stay and mind the babies, or hem our
   ragged shirts;
But they mustn't, can't and shan't be geographic!

The Royal Geographical Society, that body whose membership was an essential badge of success for Victorian travellers, agreed with *Punch*. It took over sixty years to acknowledge lady travellers, even after the wealth of botanical and anthropological information brought home had proved these intrepid voyagers to be perfectly serious about their wanderings. They were not the kind of women to be deterred by male prejudice, however; nor were they prepared to waste much travelling time in efforts to have their claims acknowledged. Through China and Japan, Africa and America, the Middle East and Egypt, the mountains of the Himalayas and the islands of the West Indies, across Europe and India and even the frost-bleached wastes of Siberia moved, in the last forty years of the century, an astonishing band of lady travellers, collecting and noting, painting and drawing, photographing and writing poetry.

Mountaineers, it is said, climb mountains because they are there. The nineteenth-century world was undoubtedly there, as well as mostly untrodden, but the impulses that drove Isabella Bird and Margaret Fountaine and Louisa Jebb were infinitely more varied and complex than the simple call of a challenge. Isabella Bird comes closest to admitting a passion for travel for travel's sake – her husband declared, 'I have only one formidable rival in Isabella's affections and that is the high tableland of Central Asia' – in that life was intolerable for her without the prospect of a journey ahead. When she died in Edinburgh in 1904, it was more than appropriate that her boxes and trunks should be standing ready packed, corded and labelled for China, even though she was seventy-three and had never been strong. After all, she had declared roundly that 'the quietest life in London' was too much of a strain on her frail physique, but she had always been able to ride 30 miles a day when abroad, sleeping rough and blithely confronting, quite alone, enraged grizzly bears and howling Chinese mobs.

Another lady – and the Eden sisters in their exalted position in Government House would not admit that she was one – who travelled for the sheer joy of it, was Fanny Parkes. She jollied about India in the forties with a huge cheerful appetite for anything out of the way. She loathed to be still: 'How weary and heavy is life in India when stationary! Travelling about the country is very amusing; but during the heat of the rains, shut up in the house, one's mind and body feel equally enervated.'

She wrote a huge book entitled *Wanderings of a Pilgrim in Search of the Picturesque* and mostly her search was successful, whether hog-hunting or even scaling an elephant by its tail in order to reach the howdah. The Edens thought she was awful – 'She will certainly be the death of us all' – but she was blithely impervious to them and enraptured by travel:

How much there is to delight the eye in this bright, this beautiful world! Roaming about with a good tent and a good arab, one might be happy for ever in India. A man might possibly enjoy this sort of life more than a woman; he has his dog, his gun and his beaters, with an open country to shoot over.... I have a pencil instead of a gun, and believe it affords me satisfaction equal, if not greater, than the sportsman derives from his Manton.

For almost all the others, the ostensible reasons were different, although travel got to them all and gripped them in an addictive vice in the end. Mary Kingsley wrote of a night in a West African mangrove swamp, surely one of life's more alarming experiences:

To my taste there is nothing so fascinating as spending a night out in an African forest or plantation; but I beg you to note I do not advise anyone to follow the practice. Unless you are interested in it and fall under its charm it is the most awful life in death imaginable. It is like being shut up in a library whose books you cannot read, all the while tormented, terrified and bored. And if you do fall under its spell it takes all the colour out of other kinds of living.

She had gone, by her own admission, to West Africa to die. The most intellectually original, the most truly interested in the native and in politics, and by far the funniest of all the lady travellers, Mary Kingsley left England because her life was over at thirty-one. 'My life had been a comic one,' she wrote to a friend later. 'Dead tired and feeling no one had need of me any more. When my Mother and Father died within six weeks of each other in '92 and my brother went off to the East, I went down to West Africa to die. West Africa amused me and was kind to me and scientifically interesting – and did not want to kill me just then.'

Louisa Jebb set off for precisely the opposite reason, to find health for herself and a friend, very much as Isabella Bird had first gone to Australia. So did Charlotte Riddell, writing of a 'mad tour' through central Europe on foot in search of relief from 'a pain which, so far as I know, is scarcely common property'. Central Europe was quite a tame choice; Louisa Jebb and her friend had chosen Baghdad for reasons hardly compatible with physical frailty. 'We were fully agreed on one fundamental point – that we should choose a country which could be reached otherwise than by sea; and that having reached it, its nature should be such that we could travel indefinitely in it without reaching the sea.'

The suggestion that the physical delicacy so many of these travellers mention was really the effects of the nervous strain of being a woman in stifling Victorian England gains credence when one observes how astoundingly enduring all these invalids became when let loose in the world's wild places. Isabella Bird, hurled from a half-broken pony in the Rockies, wrote to her sister, 'The flesh of my left arm looks crushed into a jelly, but cold water dressings will soon bring it right; and a cut on my back bled profusely but . . . I really think that the rents in my riding dress will prove the most important part of the accident.'

Escape was everything, escape from ill health, an ailing mamma, a life emptied by the death of a beloved parent or sister. With sufficient money but never an abundance – Mary Kingsley had to eke out her savings by trading – a keen intelligence, a powerful sense of their untouchability as English ladies and a formidable conscientiousness in documenting their observations, they fled decades of domestic submissiveness. Some were also looking, explicitly or not, for passion, sometimes simply the wild exhilaration of freedom and sometimes a sexual gratification quite unthinkable at home.

Louisa Jebb found the former and wrote of it with lovely candour. She and her woman companion – referred to as X – had ridden like people possessed through Turkey and Iraq, visiting mosques and villages, hitching themselves to passing mule- and camel-caravans, riding at dawn into Babylon, narrowly missing being hacked to death by fanatics at Samarah and coming at last to Sheveh, a mountain village where X was swept in a screaming circle of dancing, stamping men. Louise wrote:

'X,' I said to myself, 'You are mad and I poor sane fool, can only remember that I once did crochet work in drawing rooms.'
A feeling of wild rebellion took hold of me; I sprang into the circle.
'Make me mad!' I cried out, 'I want to be mad too!'
The men seized me and on we went, on and on with the hopping and turning and stamping. And soon I too was a savage, a glorious free savage under the white moon.

Even Isabella Bird, prosaic enough in most things, found the one truly romantic episode of her life on her travels, in the shape of Rocky Mountain Jim, her 'dear desperado', who was exciting evidence of 'how nearly a man can become a devil'. He was wild, scarred and handsome, and a lost soul to boot, and he fell in love with the 'solid and substantial little person' (Marianne North's description) of Miss Bird. She for her part, perceiving a 'good and kind heart' in him, was almost lost for ever to the ranks of travellers and to sister Henrietta waiting patiently in Tobermory for letters. But her excellent sense rallied her and she rode resolutely away from the Rockies and high romance.

Margaret Fountaine, on the other hand, said she was looking for butterflies, but she was looking for something else besides. From her girlhood she had been wayward and determined, with an absorption in men that led her to make gods of most undistinguished admirers and a perfect fool of a chorister at Norwich Cathedral, one Septimus Hewson, who was absolutely bemused by her relentless hounding of him. In 1890, when in her late twenties, fortified by a small income she began upon her travels in pursuit of butterflies and men across Europe, and her diaries are liberally sprinkled with accounts of hungry attempts to clasp her waist, seize her hand and snatch a kiss in shadowed corners. All of which, though lovingly recorded, were rejected because ' . . . I believe there is a direct and special protection over a pure and high-minded woman which no man, however base, can break through.'

Base or not, they kept trying, and if they did not fling themselves upon her at once, she certainly observed their tardiness, complaining at Lake Maggiore of a 'big Italian' who seemed 'at last to have discovered that I was not wholly unattractive'. Yet an American woman she met, also travelling alone but without the alibi of butterflies, who flirted 'desperately', was sighed over as a pitiably lost soul – 'such is the vanity of woman!'

Margaret Fountaine was to find what she was looking for, in the person, romantically enough, of a Syrian dragoman. He was young and fair, 'though his eyebrows and lashes and moustaches were dark', he had a 'boyish face' and offered himself as a guide through Damascus. But initially he had drawbacks:

... while I sat upon his knee with his arms around me, I would feel it nice to be so loved and cared for; another time the whole thing would appeal only to my sense of humour and I would see the absurdity of my situation. . . . I could often have wished that he was not quite so coarse in his words and actions – one thing he would always say was, 'I love very much your legs.' However, I did my best to raise the tone of his mind; though it seemed difficult to make him see that the animal side of human nature was not all we had to live for, but there was a lot of good in the man and I felt it would very much depend upon me what he was eventually.

It was 1901 and Miss Fountaine was thirty-nine. For the next twenty-eight years, she and Khalid Neimy were to roam the world together, amassing an astounding collection of butterflies and displaying a most anachronistic lack of concern for society's startled response to their unorthodox union:

But we were both satisfied as it was, and after all we escaped the cares and worries of matrimony and maybe that satiety which is so often the unwelcome guest to the soft downy pillow of the marriage bed. Ours was a flinty couch, maybe a cavern among the rocks, or some tangled thicket. And we lived for so much besides mere sexual intercourse . . . we worked hard at our pursuit Khalid now being quite as keen as I was. . . .

Miss Fountaine may have had an erotic relationship with her dragoman; Laurence Hope had one with all India. 'O! Life!' she wrote in ecstasy. 'I have taken you for my lover!' She was the daughter of an Indian army colonel and a most lovely Irishwoman, and grew up to marry Malcolm Nicolson, an officer of the Bengal Army in 1889. She began to write extraordinary poetry, a bizarre mixture of sensuous echoes of the Moghul empire and heroic strains of England's own. 'Pale hands I loved beside the Shalimar'; the romance of jasmine and moonlight and ancient dark beginnings stirred both Laurence and her sister to write of Indian male beauty in a way that gave the readers of 1901 a horrified but pleasurable thrill: 'A woman whose eyes had once been opened so that she could see that beauty, one whose senses were captured by it, would never be free, entirely free, until death released her.'

Colonel Nicolson carried his inflammable bride off to the North West Frontier and he would slip away with her on long reconnaissances, with Laurence – and what a double adventure this was, sexual as well as physical – disguised as a Pathan boy:

> 'Tis ice without and flame within
> To gain a kiss at dawn.

She took to painting (one of her works shows the naked body of a murdered native lying in a pool of dark blood) and, between her travels, to receiving visitors, while lolling upon a couch with her feet bare, her hair streaming loose. 'It seemed a pity,' Flora Annie Steele remarked with some restraint, 'with all those dark eyes looking on and British prestige looming in the background.'

The dark eyes were to win the day. Her poems contain ringing phrases about the mountains and a 'hard blue Afghan sky', but she also wrote in 'The Night of Shiva' of a 'wanton' whose 'body lay with hacked off breasts dishonoured in the pass'. In 'Afridi Love', the combination of eroticism and purple passage becomes prize-winning:

> When I have slowly drawn my knife across you
> Taking my pleasure as I see you swoon . . .

Rumours were rife of a love affair with an Indian prince (not, you note, a commoner) and of snatched meetings on marble terraces smothered in roses and drenched in moonlight, but there was no proof. When Malcolm Nicolson died of a maladministered anaesthetic in Madras, Laurence Hope killed herself and prosaically enough at that, with an overdose of perchloride of mercury. It was better perhaps to die dreaming of 'one cold reckless night of Khorasan' than to dwindle into old age and an insupportable conventionality:

> I always feel a sense of loss
> If, at the close of day
> I cannot see the Southern Cross
> Break through the gathered grey.

Mary Kingsley was a self-confessed stranger to love, despite her 'magic personality' which so influenced all lucky enough to know her. She herself admitted, ' . . . humbly, as I would make the confession of being deaf or blind, I know nothing myself of love. I have read about it . . . but I have never been in love, nor has anyone ever been in love with me. It is an imperfection, no doubt. . . .'

It might have been for her, but not for us, because of the emotional energy it left her for her travels and her writings:

> I have always lived in the lives of other people, whose work was heavy for them, and apart from that I have lived a life of my own, strewn about among non-human things. . . . It is the non-human world I belong to myself. My people are mangroves, swamps, rivers and the sea and so on – we understand each other.

Mary understood many things besides. Herself the niece of Charles Kingsley and daughter of a writer and adventurer who found it impossible to stay at home, she took up his work after his death and became an acknowledged authority on most things West African. Her scientific purpose was to collect tropical fish from lakes and rivers, and her work was highly regarded, but her keen interest and observation spilled over into anthropology, tribal behaviour and the colonial administration of that side of Africa which for so long had been in the sole possession of traders and slavers.

The amateur collector of tropical fish, who dressed for the steaming swamps of the Congo just as she would for the pavements of Cambridge, rapidly became a professional. Mary Kingsley was extraordinarily good at boats, declaring that she 'would rather take a two-hundred ton vessel up a creek than write any book' (she was capable of both); she also was on excellent terms with the traders and early officials she found, men whom she considered 'better worth bothering about' than 'people in London drawing rooms', and was quite fearless in a country of terrifying terrain and climate and among tribes known for their penchant for human flesh. She became much attached to the Fans, a tribe notorious for their cannibalism; she reflected as she set off with three of them alone, to traverse uncharted forest, that their habit of killing men in order to 'cut them into neat pieces, eat what they want at the time, and smoke the rest of their bodies for future use' was a slight drawback simply because 'I do not want to arrive at Rembwé in a smoked condition, even should my fragments be neat.'

Mary's humour is irresistible. In the French Congo she obtained permission to go up the Ogowé, where among other things she learned to paddle an Ogowé canoe like a native and also wrote some wonderfully comic sketches:

Going up an inlet of the Ogowé ... with slopes of stinking, stoneless slime ... honeycombed with crab holes and the owners of these – green, blue, red and black – are walking about on the tips of their toes sideways with that comic pomp peculiar to the crab family. I expected only to have to sit in the boat and say 'Horrible' at intervals, but no such thing; my companion, selecting a peculiarly awful looking spot, says he thinks 'that will do', steers the boat up to it and jumps out with a squidge into the black slime. For one awful moment I thought it was suicide, and that before I could even get an address of his relations to break the news to them there would be nothing but a Panama hat lying on the slime before me. ...

She ate hippopotamus and crocodile and the boringly ubiquitous manioc meal. 'As you pass along you are perpetually meeting with a new named food . . . but acquaintance with it demonstrates that it is all the same: manioc. If I meet a tribe that refers to buttered muffins I shall know what to expect and so not get excited.'

She fell into game pits, saved from the twelve-inch spikes at the bottom, she claimed, by her redoubtable skirts, slept in huts where lay the gruesome remains of past meals (she tipped all the ears and toes carefully into her hat to record them), was mostly caked in mud and blood and leeches – and was extraordinarily happy. And yet she only travelled for two years, from 1893 to 1895, even though those two years left her with an abiding longing. 'The charm of West Africa is a painful one. It gives you pleasure to fall under when you are out there, but when you are back here it gives you pain, by calling you.'

Mary Kingsley's *Travels in West Africa* was a huge success and in a sense prevented further travels. She became caught up in a ceaseless round of lecture tours and involved in all the current controversy over the administration of the area. When the Boer War broke out in 1899, Mary went out to South Africa at once and found herself at Simonstown nursing Boer prisoners suffering from enteric fever. She wrote of them with all the easy, humorous objectivity with which she had written of West Africa:

... the Boers are family men and when you rouse one to feed or physic him he asks after his family and then after his trousers because of the money in them. Well, you cannot give a satisfactory account of either. If there is a member of his family in the Hospital, as in very many cases there are – that man is dead or dying. As for his trousers, they are in a heap in the back yard, so you lie both ways. I do, and say 'It's all right,' in both cases which I know it isn't, or that I will find out, which I know I can't, and the patient returns to his oblivion and I to another patient.

Inevitably Mary succumbed to typhoid fever herself and was dead at thirty-eight. At her own request she was buried at sea, mourned by the river pilots and traders who had known her as 'the greatest white woman who ever went to West Africa'.

Whatever other aspects of Mary Kingsley aroused comment, no one could ignore her clothes. She made no concessions to Africa sartorially, at first because she saw nothing incongruous in wearing her skirts, stays and round velvet hat in the jungle, and later probably because it amused her to dress so. She took with her precisely what she wore at home, sometimes finding her wardrobe most useful for trading with the Fans:

A dozen white ladies' blouses sold well. I cannot say they looked well when worn by a brawny warrior in conjunction with nothing else but red paint and a bunch of leopard tails, particularly when the warrior failed to tie the strings at the back. But I did not hint at this, and I *quite* realized that a pair of stockings can be made to go further than we make them by using one at a time and putting the top part over the head and letting the rest of the garment float on the breeze.

Isabella Bird took a more practical view – perhaps with all her leaping on and off horses she had to – and was given to wearing clothes at least convenient for her energetic purposes. *The Times* in its edition of 22 November 1879 stated that she wore 'masculine habilments' but she refuted this stoutly, describing and even sketching her outfit to dispel any suggestion of being improperly clad:

For the benefit of other lady travellers, I wish to explain that my 'Hawaiian riding dress' is the 'American Lady's Mountain Dress', a half-fitting jacket, a skirt reaching to the ankles and full Turkish trousers gathered into frills which fall over the boots – a thoroughly serviceable and feminine costume for mountaineering and other rough travelling in any part of the world.

Photographs show her clad in a number of variations upon this many-layered ensemble; sometimes she crowned it with a small black bonnet and quantities of broad satin ribbon and sometimes with a large white sunhelmet.

Margaret Fountaine's clothes have a decidedly feminine air, graceful garments on a tall and attractive woman; they included a plaid frock and co-respondent shoes for catching butterflies in America and a most becoming high-necked blouse for riding through an Algerian cedar forest with Khalid. She hardly mentions her clothes, beyond remarking on tennis shoes being inadequate for crossing a glacier; she was too preoccupied with her emotions and her health, an aspect Mary Kingsley scarcely mentions apart from the occasional headache.

Charlotte Riddell was dismayed to find that walking through Central Europe was to offer no opportunity for dressing well. She had agreed 'in an insane moment' in 1890 to accompany a young man (relationship unspecified, but her tone throughout is maternal) who permitted her only a knapsack, a waterproof coat and 'a soft tweed hat, the ugliest headgear man or woman ever donned'. Charlotte took, she says, one black dress and a fichu, in which she entrained for Cologne, sailed rapturously down the Rhine and then wore walking in ceaseless rain with great cheerfulness. The one good thing about the rain was, she observed, that it soaked her companion's *Baedecker*, which he read without pause, mostly aloud, instead of looking at the view. 'Had it been left to me,' she wrote, '[the] guide would indeed have proved quite unnecessary.'

Unlike Miss Kingsley and Miss Bird, some lady travellers were acutely conscious of their clothes and the way in which their manner of dressing enhanced for the public the glamour of their voyages. Mrs Alec-Tweedie, the mistress-supreme of the travel-book title – hers included *Tight Corners of My Adventurous Life*, *Danish*

Versus English Buttermaking and *Through Finland in Carts*, not to mention a chapter thrillingly headed 'Painting Alone with a Dozen Nude Blacks (Sudan)' – seems to have been extraordinarily conscious of her image. She was unquestionably good-looking, with regular features and large eyes beneath graceful brows, and her books are full of careful photographs of the author, frequently languishing in oceans of lace and ribbons (presumably not while bear-shooting in Norway or watching a Japanese volcano erupt) or else posed in impeccably tailored divided skirts in Mexico or Jordan with an admiring audience of natives as a backdrop. There is one sketch of her in a corral in Mexico in 1904, glamorously clad in black riding clothes, white ruffles and a sombrero. This costume, she writes, occasioned a 'very grand, rich and lovely Mexican gentleman of Spanish descent' to ask, 'Señora, you are a lady, a real, real lady I mean, who goes to Royal Courts and wears a low dress in the evening, and that sort of thing?'

'I hope so,' she laughed, amused. 'But why do you ask?'

'Because in those breeches and boots you look like a young man, and you ride like a man. I've never seen a lady ride into the wilds (indeed few men do so), or ride astride, or sleep in these strange farm places or under the blue of Heaven before. I don't understand.'

As Mrs Alec-Tweedie said, 'Poor dear.'

All the glory of knickerbockers would slowly gain favour, helped along by the passion for bicycling in the nineties, but for the most part the lady travellers, however intrepid, whatever rivers had to be forded, jungles hacked through or mountains climbed, had to remember the 'high ordeal of womanhood'. As Constance Larymore said in Nigeria in 1902, 'Always wear corsets, even for a tête-à-tête home dinner on the warmest evenings; there is something about their absence almost as demoralizing as hair in curling pins.'

Certainly not for the serious adventurers was *Hints to Lady Travellers* by Lilian Campbell Davidson, published in 1889. Besides emphasizing the obvious necessities such as Keatings powders, for use against fleas, and mosquito nets, her book gave detailed descriptions of how to pack. Ladies who followed her elaborate instructions for wrapping shoes in monogrammed cloths and laying each dress on a separate tray in a truck, every layer rustling with copious tissue paper, were not the serious travellers who, among other things, sought to escape the clutter of Victorian life. Isabella Bird carried what she needed in a roll behind her saddle – except in her later days, when photographic equipment took up much more space – and Mary Kingsley went to Angola with three pieces of luggage, none of them a trunk. For them, space for clothes was limited by the need to take paper, books and other materials, a need even more pressing for those ladies who travelled in search of botanical specimens and whose drawing, collecting and pressing equipment must always have taken precedence over an extra blouse or straw hat.

Botany was a most fashionable Victorian recreation and by the mid-century had taken its place alongside music and the ability to speak French as a required accomplishment. Plants – as long as they were not too grossly tropical – were a safe subject, just sufficiently aesthetic without any danger of being intellectual, and properly sexless. Floriculture periodicals abounded, encouraging the craze, but most of them sentimentalized botany to an often nauseating degree. Mrs Meredith, in her book *Romance of Nature*, exclaims in a rapturous foreword, 'I *love* flowers as forming one of the sweetest lines of the GOD WRITTEN Poetry of Nature.' There was a great deal of wonderfully awful poetry on the subject too, for which Mrs Smith's 'Snowdrop' wins the palm for a first line which runs, 'Like pendant flakes of vegetating snow'.

Mrs Smith and Mrs Meredith aside, there was an enormous and growing band of most serious and accomplished botanists. England had always had its great tradition of gardeners, and a sprinkling of the wives of early administrators, such as Lady Amherst, wife to a governor general of India, had taken their English gardening enthusiasms abroad with them. It was Lady Amherst, painted by Lawrence in a gauzy Empire dress, who brought *Clematis montana* and the spectacular tree *Amherstia nobilis* home to England. But it was not until travelling became such a female passion that many of the serious botanists turned their backs on the woods and water-meadows of England and made for the flora of the world.

Their doyenne without question is Marianne North, born in 1830 and a traveller who equalled Isabella Bird and Mrs Alec-Tweedie in the distance and enterprise of her journeys. Between 1871 and 1884 she visited Jamaica, Brazil, Canada, the United States of America, Singapore, Japan, Borneo, Java, Ceylon, India,

Australia, New Zealand, South Africa, Chile and the Seychelles. The travels were surely something in themselves, but they were also the means of indulging her obsession to find and record 'tropical vegetation in all its natural abundant luxuriance'.

Unlike almost all her fellow travellers, she travelled most of her life with her widowed father. When he died in 1869, leaving her comfortably off but deprived of the one significant emotional tie of her life, her voyaging broadened vastly. Marianne North was a most amiable person by all accounts, friendly, cheerful and lively. Excellent company, she roused a Nile pilot to describe her admiringly as 'A valuable and remarkable Bint!' Marianne's capacity for attracting people comes over again and again in her writings; in numerous places she landed, as she said, 'entirely alone and friendless but soon fell into kind and helpful hands'. Her enthusiasm must have been a great draw to people.

Marianne recounts the high moments of her travels artlessly, such as the time in Singapore in 1877 when 'In the jungle I found real pitcher plants (*Nepenthes*) winding themselves amid the tropical bracken. It was the first time I had seen them growing wild and I screamed with delight.' In Sarawak, 'the forest was a perfect world of wonders'; in Jamaica, 'the Fern Walk . . . almost took my breath away with its lovely fairy tale beauty'; everywhere 'I could not help painting'. She painted furiously and collected huge timber samples in every tropical forest. Her paintings are far from being the fragile watercolours beloved of most Victorian ladies; robustly done in oils, they were as vigorous as their painter even if they have not been consistently admired since for their botanical accuracy. They were, however, accurate enough, and her discoveries startling enough, to attract enormous support in her lifetime, notably from Charles Darwin and from Sir Joseph Hooker, director of the Royal Botanical Gardens at Kew.

It was this connection with Kew that led Marianne North to donate her collection of 800 paintings to the gardens towards the end of her life. In addition she provided funds for a gallery to house the pictures, which was designed under her supervision in the manner of a Greek temple. The gallery still stands just as she left it, complete with clerestory windows and a dado of 250 tropical woods from her collection, with the pictures, hung by her own hand, as close as stamps on a page between friezes she painted herself. In 1893, three years after she died at the age of sixty, the diaries of her travels were published under the title she had so characteristically decided upon herself, *Recollections of a Happy Life*.

Kew, unlike the Royal Geographical Society, early realized the worth of its female enthusiasts. Desmond's *Botanical and Horticultural Dictionary* is stiff with the records of Victorian ladies who collected algae in Australia and lichens in Natal and mosses in the Falkland Islands, the drawings of which invariably came home to Kew. Sir Joseph Hooker must have had a vast correspondence all over the Empire with eager and highly professional collectors, who assisted him to amass catalogues of the plants to be found in places as widely disparate botanically as southern Nigeria and Sikkim. Sometimes, as in the case of Mrs Lugard (sister-in-law of Lord Lugard of Nigeria) in Bechuanaland or Eleanor Vallentin in the Falkland Islands, Kew actually commissioned the collection of plants for the gardens.

The output of books was prodigious, most of them illustrated as well as written by the collector herself. A lady by the sonorous name of Augusta Innes Withers, known as 'Flower Painter to Queen Adelaide', in her youth drew all the plates for what is probably the world's most impressive (in terms of size) botanical book, Bateman's *Orchidaceae of Mexico and Guatemala*. There is a cartoon of it entitled 'The Librarian's Nightmare', which shows an army of Lilliputian figures struggling with the massive tome, directed by a man with a megaphone. Lena Lowis wrote and herself illustrated *Familiar Indian Flowers*, whose preface, dated 'Chota Nagpore 1878' is marvellously expressive of its period. In it she writes, 'Notwithstanding its numerous shortcomings, the Author hopes the book may be valued by old Indians, who have, perhaps, spent many happy hours in the culture of these lovely plants and also by those who delight to hear of the works of the Creator in all regions and all climes.'

Elizabeth Twining, a member of the tea family, presented Queen Victoria with a copy of her *Chief Natural Orders of Plants*, which gave exact details of where each plant could be found all over the globe. Her gift elicited a letter from Victoria Mary of Teck assuring Miss Twining that 'Mamma is very grateful to you and much touched by the kind thought that prompted the gift.' Fanny Elizabeth Mole published her *Wild Flowers of Australia* in 1861, Dorothy Talbot produced a definitive catalogue of Nigerian plants in 1913 and Arabella Roupell travelled for three years in South Africa for the sole purpose of gathering material for her book on the flora of the country.

If they weren't writing books, these women were collecting furiously and having their findings published in the *Kew Bulletin*. Some ladies – such as Lady Edith Blake in Jamaica or Mrs Claud White in Sikkim – turned botanical collectors as a result of being carried off to the farflung outposts of the Empire by administrative husbands. A passion for ferns must have been a prerequisite of marrying Sir Henry Barkly, for both his wives collected avidly, one in Jamaica, one in South Africa, and both had findings published in the *Kew Bulletin*. It was not in the least surprising that Kew should respond so warmly to the efforts of the women botanists when one looks at the quality of the work they produced. The most remarkable thing about it, after its sheer volume, is the accuracy of the drawing and the uniformly high standard of draughtsmanship. All those hours in Victorian schoolrooms peering into the trumpets of foxgloves had not been wasted.

People might be a less decorous study than plants but for some they were more powerfully absorbing. They were always, of course, more entertaining than plants. There was Hassan, the Armenian Turk hired by the ladies of *By Desert Ways to Baghdad*; they taught him to say, 'I am a silly man,' when he was cross so that he got in a worse rage and stamped and shouted 'Silliman *yok*! Silliman *yok*!' (Yok = not.)

Isabella Bird had no direct anthropological purpose, but the peoples of her travels give her books more colour than her descriptions of 'high, frowning, forest-covered mountains' with their 'dazzling summits . . . unprofaned by the foot of man'. She took great pleasure in them, using whenever she could the medicine chest provided by St Mary's Hospital, which was to give her ten-hour 'medical' days in the Bakhtiari hills of Persia:

. . . it was delightful to see the immediate relief of the sufferers. 'God is great,' they all exclaimed, and the bystanders echoed, 'God is Great.' I dressed five neglected bullet wounds, and sewed up a gash of doubtful origin and with a little help from Mirza prepared eye lotions and medicines for seventy-three people. I asked one badly wounded man in what quarrel he had been shot and he replied, he didn't know, his Khan had told him to go and fight.

Such hard work was a small price to pay for the interest and delight the people she encountered gave her, from the natives of Hawaii on an early journey, to the Kurds with their 'kind and jolly women', via the peoples of Korea and Japan and the wild men of the western Chinese border. Of them she wrote:

I was in my chair in the yard when it began, and soon a crowd of men were brandishing their arms . . . in my face, shouting and yelling with a noise and fury not to be imagined by anyone who has not seen an excited Chinese mob. They yelled into my ears and struck my chair with their tools to attract my attention, but I continued to sit facing them, never moving a muscle, as I was quite innocent of the cause of the quarrel, and at last they subsided and let me depart.

Mary Kingsley was equally undismayed by the sudden and uncouth behaviour of the native peoples she encountered, but was also more academically interested in their habits and differences. She was very quick to see that the tribes along a single river could differ as much as 'a Londoner and a Laplander', and was most meticulous in recording those differences, distinctions in habits and customs, the furnishing of huts, and even in the elaborate dressing of hair. She noted that the Igalwa man pursued 'a policy of masterly inactivity', that the M'pongwe and Ajumba were noble peoples given to spurning marriage offers from all inequals, and that the Fans, the most savage tribe to whom she became devoted, existed on a precarious system of individual survival which inevitably toughened them.

She liked the Fans so much partly in defiance of the opprobrium they suffered from everyone else, and partly because they bore a strong resemblance to herself, 'full of fire, temper, intelligence and go; very teachable, rather difficult to manage . . . '. She was a successful anthropologist because she was so free from racial or religious prejudice and because her interest in people was for its own sake:

It is not advisable to play with them [the ideas in men's and women's minds] or to attempt to eradicate them because you regard them as superstitious; and never, never shoot too soon. I have never had to shoot, and hope never to have to; because in such a situation, one white alone with no troops to back him means a clean finish. But this would not discourage me if I had to start, only it makes me more inclined to walk round the obstacle than to become a mere blood splotch against it, if this can be done without losing your self-respect which is the mainspring of your power in West Africa.

Sylvia Leith-Ross was, over and above all her achievements as an educational pioneer, an anthropologist cast in the same mould. In her early years in Nigeria, the Ibo had fascinated her because of the peculiarly lackadaisical structure of their lives that seemed to work so well. They '. . . appeared to have nothing that was cut and dried. Laws, customs, clothing, meal times, crops, buildings, all seemed to exist in a haze of uncertainty. Of course they themselves knew exactly where they were, and just because the rules of their lives were so obvious to them, they were incapable of explaining them to anyone else.'

She was intrigued by the contrasts in the Ibo, that they could be wonderful to their children and yet — victims of dark and ancient custom — be inhumanly cruel to them too, hurling out to die of neglect in the bush any deformed baby, any twin, or any child who cut its top teeth before its lower ones. Writing about these barbarities her tone is almost as objective and humorous as Mary Kingsley's. In this account of visits to Ibo villages she writes:

They often asked me into the 'obi', which is their sort of reception room. It is generally opposite the door of the compound, and is just a mud-floored, three-walled shelter with a low roof of palm-leaf thatch, and there they would offer me a kola nut which is a sign of friendship, and, to show it was not poisoned, they would lick it first and then pass it to me. I would then break it into small pieces and give a piece to all the older people and eat one myself. I tried to keep the unlicked side for myself, but by that time I usually could not remember which it was, and had to hope for the best. I generally got out of drinking palm wine by saying it went to my head, and all the company would make little sounds of commiseration and have an extra pull themselves, glad not to be like the poor weak Europeans.

As time wore on, and the Ibo became more mercenary, she lost her affection for them and became much more attracted to the Fulani and the Hausa; it was a mark of true anthropological interest to feel a decline in fascination with increasing artificial and 'civilized' ways. Margaret Fountaine had wanted to make Khalid Neimy into an imitation Englishman; Mrs Alec-Tweedie only peppered her extensive books with people whose manners (and appreciation of her) approximated to the courtesy she might have expected in London; but the greatest of the lady travellers travelled *because* things were different, the climates and landscapes and, above all, the peoples.

Louisa Jebb, later Mrs Roland Wilkins, speaks for them all. The drawbacks of travelling, such as hunger or fear or being soaking wet, are nothing, she says, because you are, after all,

... brought up face to face with something fundamental ... you are just there, stripped yourself and in the middle of naked realities. And if only you have been wet enough or cold enough or hungry enough, it has been worth while, for you never forget it; and the remembrance of it will come to you over and anon when you are once more tied up in the bonds of conventions and are struggling to keep a true idea of what is a reality and what is not.

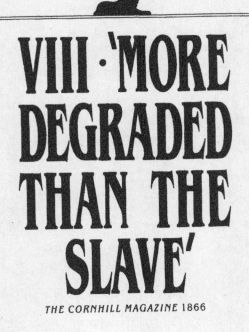

VIII · 'MORE DEGRADED THAN THE SLAVE'

THE CORNHILL MAGAZINE 1866

VIII

'It did seem hard,' one poor girl said to Josephine Butler without particular rancour, 'that the magistrate on the bench who gave the casting vote for my imprisonment had paid me several shillings a day or two before on the street to go with him.'

It was indeed hard but it was not in the least uncommon. The general Victorian attitude to prostitution was at best ambivalent and muddled, at worst hypocritical and plain cruel. The gods of Victorian social behaviour dictated that prostitution was vicious and utterly degrading; the conditions of society itself meant that for both working and upper classes it was inevitable. For the poor it was an understandably easy and independent way of earning money: a girl in the West End might expect a pound a man, and even the shabby streetwalkers of the East End made regular half-crowns and crowns. For the working-class man and the sailor and the soldier, prostitution was as natural as breathing; after all, every Victorian knew that sexual continence should not be required of a man and that homosexuality and masturbation were abhorrent.

For the middle-class man there were these considerations and many more. In the first place, economic pressures usually made early marriage impossible and therefore there might be ten or fifteen years of manhood with no legal bed to go to. In the second place, even when married, they faced the problem that a huge proportion of wives were both enshrined as moral angels at home and also constantly either pregnant or recovering from the last pregnancy. Sexual desire in a wife was not considered compatible with her influential moral position over children and servants – female sexual desire was not thought even to rear its disturbing head until after a girl's initiation – and to help all these pressing needs along, street soliciting was not illegal.

Prostitutes were available in enormous numbers, and there it was. They were not, on the whole, driven on to the street as ruined victims of some rich man's pleasure. It was far more often the case that at about sixteen they had a first sexual encounter with a man of their own class and then drifted voluntarily and gradually into selling themselves for gain. The pickings, in working-class terms, were rich. Rev. G. Merrick, in his resoundingly titled report, *Work Among the Fallen* published in 1890, claimed that of the 16,000 prostitutes interviewed in London prisons, 14,000 said they had been tempted by the prospect of 'havin' nothin' to do', 'plenty of money', 'being a lady' and above all 'perfect liberty' to 'be your own mistress'.

That was the attraction of it, the promise of independence, particularly for the huge numbers of orphaned girls who had inevitably grown up assertive survivors in a harsh world. With a wonderfully simple asset to sell, you could please yourself:

I was a servant gal away down in Birmingham. I got tired of workin' and slavin' to make a living and getting a bad one at that; what o' five pun a year and yer grub, I'd sooner starve, I would. After a bit I went to Coventry, cut brummagem as we calls it in those parts, and took up with soldiers as was quartered there. I soon got tired of them. Soldiers is good, soldiers is, to walk with and that, but they don't pay 'cos they ain't got no money; so I says to myself, I'll go to Lunnon and I did. I soon found my level there.

Even after half a dozen years on the streets – most prostitutes were between sixteen and twenty-two – the future was not so black. Unwanted children were not as common as contemporary and subsequent novels indicate, largely because working-class teenage girls, undernourished from birth, reached a comparatively late age before first menstruating. The same lack of robustness led to miscarriage, while venereal disease resulted in sterility. By their mid-twenties, most girls were married, since their way of life was accepted among their own class as an expedient way of getting through tough times. Of course the working class had its own rigorous standards of respectability – a lodging-house keeper who let rooms to prostitutes would be most assiduous in segregating her family from their influence – but it was tolerant of practical necessity.

Selling her body was the only kind of rebellion open to a poor girl, whereas her brother could and often did run away to sea. That the rebelliousness was important is very plain. It was quite as important as financial gain, which could prove illusory. James Greenwood, in his *Notebook of a Roving Correspondent* of 1873, declares how pathetically ragged most prostitutes were in truth. Money lured them, of course, but so did the vitality of the only kind of self-expression open to them. If it had not been so, there would have been far more brothels, but the number was surprisingly small (only 410 in London in 1857, half the number known sixteen years earlier) and for the simplest reason. Prostitution gave a girl her freedom. She could go on the streets for a few weeks or months, extricate herself from debt, save a little and return to more orthodox employment until need pressed again. In a brothel she was not her own mistress.

Certainly prostitutes lived together, often in conditions of deep suspicion, sleeping with their hats on to avoid theft, but that was also practical. They also had a system of great mutual generosity, clubbing together to provide medical services or, more important to them, a 'decent' funeral. Frederick Rodgers remembered a funeral at Mile End during his childhood in the 1860s, at which the prostitute's coffin was followed by her 'comrades', all dressed in 'old hideous black hoods and scarves', while 'a guard of men, of the kind who were called "bullies", walked on either side of the women to prevent, it was said, any hooting or stone throwing on the part of the virtuous matrons of the neighbourhood through which the procession passed'.

Unreliable these women might be on the whole, but loyalty to each other was not the only strand of dependability that ran through the life of the Victorian prostitute. Many of them, particularly those in garrison towns or ports or the East End of London, formed quite settled connections with men and provided a whole array of social services besides the obvious sexual one. They would live with a man while on leave, often housing him, and then in his absence would look after his money, draw his half-pay and keep it safe from unscrupulous hands. It was a system which worked most comfortably for everyone, as a prostitute in Stepney explained to Bracebridge Hemyng: 'I know very many sailors – six, eight, ten oh! more than that. They are my husbands. I am not married, of course not, but they think me their wife while they are on shore.'

From a higher social perspective, of course, the whole situation was deplorable. The working classes were, in the words of William

Tait, an evangelical physician reformer who for all his enlightenment thought chiefly in the manner of his times, hopelessly susceptible to '. . . licentiousness, irritability of temper, pride, love of dress, dishonesty, love of property and indolence'. All such qualities, said the reformers, drove a girl out in '. . . a gaudy hat and feather, a fashionably made skirt of some cheap and flashy material and nothing besides in the way of undergarments but a few tattered rags that a professional beggar would despise', in order to lure middle-class men to their beds. The men themselves were not so much despised because women were, after all, a perpetual temptation. The cumbrously titled Royal Commission on the Administration and Operation of the Contagious Diseases Acts clarified contemporary morality on male promiscuity:

We may at once dispose of any recommendation founded on the principle of putting both parties to the sin of fornication on the same footing, by the obvious but no less conclusive reply that there is no comparison to be made between prostitutes and the men who consort with them. With the one sex the offence is committed as a matter of gain; with the other it is an irregular indulgence of a natural impulse.

The use of prostitutes was also, for men with hopelessly spreading families, a method of birth control. It was more respectable to frequent a prostitute than to contemplate the 'French' method of family limitation with one's own wife.

Morally the situation was intolerable; practically, beyond the inevitable link between prostitution and crime, it seemed to work. But there was a gigantic drawback, a drawback so terrifying in its consequences that it pulled prostitution out into the daylight as a problem and made it the subject of one of the greatest reforming campaigns of the period of Empire. The drawback was disease. A prostitute of eighteen or nineteen had commonly been on the streets for a year and by then, in almost every case, had contracted syphilis, chancroid (a local ulceration) or gonorrhoea. As the century wore on the incidence of venereal disease rose until by 1864 one out of every three sick soldiers in the army was diseased. Hospitals throughout the country, in London, Newcastle, Manchester and Birmingham, reported that almost half the surgical outpatients were similarly afflicted. For civilians, the only statistics readily available were of deaths from syphilis. Babies died from hereditary syphilis: thirty out of fifty-three reported syphilitic deaths in London in the first six months of 1846 were of children under a year old. Children were hospitalized because of it and eye and ear complaints were rife on account of it. It was so widespread that it has been frequently described as being endemic to Victorian and Edwardian England. It caused pain and shame and death; it also, because of its high prevalence in the armed forces, cost innumerable man-hours.

The treatment was brutal, often involving the use of caustics and mercury, and was only partially successful. Doses of mercury large enough to do the job also frequently did for the patient as well. Syphilis could, and often did, go on for years, manifesting itself in secondary and tertiary infections, even if the risk of infecting others diminished as time went on. It was undoubtedly the disease the Victorians dreaded most. Gonorrhoea, on the other hand, had sinister female overtones since it was believed a man could contract it from a seemingly healthy woman, leaving her unscathed and he the victim. Contemporary doctors did not understand that the seat of the disease in women is in the reproductive organs and therefore the agonizing cauterizations were applied to quite the wrong places. Around the facts, both known and misunderstood, grew the myths of female sexuality and a resulting hostility. Women were the pollutants, the reservoirs of infection, symbols of impurity; and at the head of this tide of danger stalked the prostitute. She it was who formed the 'conduit' of infection from the great unwashed of the gutter to the higher ranks of society who in turn exploited her. Men's fear of her and guilt about their need for her led to an impulse to regulate and confine her. This was perfectly possible because, after all, the lives of the poor, intemperate, overcrowded, coarse and illiterate, were rightfully open to the interference and intrusion of anyone who knew better.

The result was the Contagious Diseases Acts. Three of them were passed between 1864 and 1869 and they were introduced as exceptional legislation to control VD among, at first, enlisted men in garrison towns and ports. Under the terms of the acts, a plain-clothes police officer could identify at his discretion a woman as 'a common prostitute'. His powers were very broad indeed. When stopped, a woman was expected to submit voluntarily to regulations which required her to be registered as a prostitute and then to be examined fortnightly for evidence of infection. If she was awkward about such treatment, she was brought to trial before a magistrate and required to prove that she never had sexual encounters with men, whether for money or not, rather on the principle of the witch and the ducking stool. If she was found to be diseased, she was confined in a lock hospital.

Lock hospitals, or lock wards in general hospitals, had been in existence since the 1740s. The name derived not from any notion of locking away some social contagion but from the French '*loques*', meaning rags or bandages; the earliest institutions had most probably been for lepers, outcasts of respectable society just as diseased prostitutes were. In the eighteenth century, lock wards had also been called 'foul' wards but, whatever their name, their purpose was the same. They confined the disease, thus safeguarding the populace (the male middle-class populace in the main); they provided training for medical students in one of the major problems of the age; and they gave a wonderful chance for the expiation of upper-class guilt, as they were run as subscribers' charities. They were also — and most important in Victorian eyes — houses of potential reform. A girl caught young enough to be susceptible to correction might easily learn the deference, personal cleanliness and respectability necessary for employment as a servant or a seamstress. She would also naturally be grateful for such improvement.

Human dignity and self-respect seem not to have come into it. Men, particularly soldiers, would have had to have been regularly examined themselves for the lock-hospital regulations to have had any effect on the problem, but men resisted such attempts so violently that officers feared their objections might lead to some demonstration. Women, on the other hand, could not possibly object to such physical interference. A fallen woman, after all, had no self-respect left to be injured. As the reformer J. B. Talbot wrote, 'Once a woman has fallen from the pedestal of innocence, she is prepared to perpetuate every crime.' The problem was exacerbated by the appalled view of homosexuality taken by every level of society, so that soldiers and sailors who had in truth infected each other in the long days of bachelor confinement, would point to the nearest woman at hand as the culprit rather than admit the truth.

The lock hospitals were in no way pleasant places. The belief that drudgery could redeem the soul of the whore was very prevalent, and the rigidly disciplined days were divided between prayers, reading lessons, mealtimes, instruction in personal hygiene and hospital laundry work, the latter presumably in an effort to wash away sin. Some hospitals, such as the Royal Albert at Devonport, were clean, orderly and reportedly full of inmates anxious to change their ways. Others were quite the reverse and liable to riots and uproar. Sometimes it was necessary to confine women alone, as in the case of Laura Lewis, held at the Royal Portsmouth Hospital in 1873:

As soon as the door opened, I saw lying on the bare floor what seemed a huddled mass of women's clothing; the woman, Laura Lewis, lying with her garments rolled over her head just inside the door; fragments of earthen ware strewed about, and farther back, the floor sloppy and dirty: the cell contained no utensil for personal wants.

There was no shortage of lurid stories from lock hospitals nor of accusations of 'instrumental rape' during examination. The whole system was inevitably brutalizing, as a registered prostitute complained in 1870 in a reforming pamphlet:

It is awful work; the attitude they push us into first is so disgusting and so painful and then these monstrous instruments – often they use several. They seem to tear the passage open with their hands and examine us and then they thrust in instruments and they pull them out and push them in and then they turn and twist them about and if you cry out they stifle you.

Such stories, and such martyrs as Mrs Percy, a music-hall entertainer from Aldershot who committed suicide rather than endure any more police persecution, were wonderful fuel for reformers who sought the repeal of these dreaded acts. There were most distinguished men, many of them physicians, who had done much to alter the moral thinking of their contemporaries, but in an age remarkable for its protection of upper-class women from all that was impure, it was just such women who were to prove the most influential in getting the acts repealed. If this surprises us in retrospect, it absolutely dumbfounded contemporary men. An MP wrote in bewilderment to Josephine Butler, leader of the Ladies' National Association, 'We know how to manage any other opposition in the House or in the country, but this is very awkward for us – this revolt of the women. It is quite a new thing; what are we to do with such an opposition as this?'

Nobody in opposition to Josephine Butler ever quite knew what to do with her. She had family ties with the ruling Whig aristocracy, she was married to an academic who only encouraged her, she was beautiful, extraordinarily attractive to both sexes, eloquent, exquisitely dressed and histrionic. She was also highly influential and possessed of a mystical sense of 'calling' which led her to rescue, personally, destitute and vagrant girls and to nurse them in her own house. She was the brightest star of the sixteen-year campaign that the Ladies' National Association waged against the Contagious Diseases Acts. For all the glamour of her person and her connections, she identified herself always with those less fortunate than herself, championing their right to a political, legal and economic identity outside their own homes. Perhaps her motives were not as egalitarian as they might have been, but she saw a special obligation to the fallen, an obligation expressed by a fellow worker, a Mrs Steward, in 1876:

When I think . . . what we women in easy circumstances owe to working women – that our clothes are made by them, washed by them; our food cooked by them, our children nursed by them, I cannot understand how we can bear not to pay back, to the best of our power, the debt we owe to them. The wages we pay them are but a poor part of the debt we owe! And where is our justice, our gratitude, if we can stand by and see a terrible wrong done . . . to them who cannot speak for themselves, if we do not rise up and speak for them.

That was written in 1876 but there had already been decades of helpless silence for the stigmatized to battle through as best they might. Such solutions to the 'great social evil' as were attempted were hardly a help to the problem and nor was the part the Empire was to play in its useful but unattractive role as a human dustbin.

The Empire had, wherever its soldiers were, its own prostitution problems. Throughout the century the military authorities, who wanted only an untrammelled bachelor force that could be moved about the globe with the minimum of administrative fuss, took a very simple view of the matter. Although they were reluctant to permit soldiers to marry, it was acknowledged that men were men and that their natural appetites must be satisfied. Soldiers in India, the West Indies and the East were provided with native prostitutes – and the need for lock hospitals arose at once. Officers and officials, on the other hand, were discouraged, because the prestige of the ruling race must be safeguarded, from taking Indian mistresses. Brothels were controlled, European barmaids were discouraged, prostitutes were regularly examined. The Indian harlot, a reformer claimed, was in the same category as any of the basic daily services provided for the average Tommy.

India was no place for human refuse; she had too much of her own. Nor was anywhere else with a large military presence. But the problem of getting rid of a nuisance remained and, as G. B. Shaw said later, 'all social problems of all countries can be got rid of by extirpating the inhabitants'. Women criminals were certainly a social problem and because prostitution was so closely bound up with all the trivial crimes a woman could be convicted for, it is very necessary to understand the prevailing attitudes to all lower-class female lapses in order to perceive why the idea of transportation should ever have arisen.

A woman fallen sexually, Victorian morality said, had nowhere else left to fall. Crime came to her then as naturally as to any hardened male, if not more so. Shut them up in hospitals, send them overseas, what did it matter, if it rid society of a dangerous, diseased, contagious element? Jeremy Bentham had pinned this attitude down in the previous century when he invented the speech of an imaginary judge: 'I sentence you, but to what I know not; perhaps to storm and shipwreck; perhaps to infectious disorders, perhaps to famine, perhaps to be massacred by savages, perhaps to be devoured by wild beasts. Away – take your chance; perish or prosper, suffer or enjoy; I rid myself of the sight of you.'

The eighteenth century had dreamed up the idea of emptying gaols into the uninhabited spaces of the world, first in America, and then, after Captain Cook's arrival in Australia, Botany Bay in New South Wales. As the ballads suggest, it took very little to get you sent there:

> For fourteen long years I am sentenced
> For fourteen long years and a day
> For meeting a bloke in the area
> And sneaking his ticker away.

The theft of his ticker or a sixpennyworth of lace or a leg of mutton, all were petty larceny likely to result in a future in Van Dieman's Land. Theft was so tempting, and for the prostitute so easy. 'I have lived entirely by prostitution and plunder,' Ellen Reece told a court in Salford in 1837. 'Seven times as much by robbery as by the hire of prostitution. None of the girls think so much of prostitution but as it furnishes opportunities of robbing men.'

Such cases were commonplace. Girls who were 'on the town' were often accomplished pickpockets, risking Tasmania for the sake of a few shillings or a gold watch. The notorious First Fleet had sailed to Australia in 1787 carrying 192 female convicts; by 1841 9500 women had gone to New South Wales alone. The numbers went on rising steadily until 1852, fifteen years after Victoria's ascent to the throne, when transportation was at last abolished.

> There's the Captain as is our Commander
> There's the bo'sun and all the ship's crew,
> There's the first and the second class passengers
> Knows what we convicts go through.

The voyage was horrific. It started with a journey, often in irons, to some 'collecting house' prison in London such as Millbank or Newgate, where each woman was registered, bathed and – a trial each one found almost unbearable – had their hair cut short. The day of embarkation was never announced in advance, but when it came the women were woken at dawn, shackled in gangs of ten and taken down to a steam tug on the river. In the grey light of early morning this vessel took the convicts down the Thames to the ship waiting for them at Gravesend, the Blue Peter flying from her masthead.

Transport ships did not change in sixty years. The prison quarters were in the 'tween decks, frequently the orlop, with no ventilation to speak of and in caged conditions so cramped that sickness had a field day. An area 6 feet by 6 feet was considered quite adequate for four women, giving each one 18 square inches to sleep in. Sometimes women were put in larger spaces, but if they were, their numbers were put up to compensate: a prison room on the *Pitt* which measured 13 by 8 feet contained twenty-seven women. This confinement was bad enough in calm and temperate weather, but if the sea was rough or, even worse, the ship was becalmed, the conditions in those cages hardly bears thinking of. 'When the ship was becalmed in the tropics,' wrote John Boyle O'Reilly, an Irish convict, 'the suffering of the imprisoned wretches in the steaming and crowded hold was piteous to see. They were so packed that free movement was impossible. . . . The air was stifling and oppressive. There was no draught through the barred hatches. The deck above them was blazing hot. The pitch dropped from the seams and burned their flesh as it fell.'

To set against such a nightmare picture, convict rations by the 1830s were tolerable. They included, for each mess of six prisoners, 20 pounds of bread each week, 16 pounds of beef, raisins, butter, sugar, a minimum of 6 pints of water and a daily allowance of lemon juice and sugar. Clothes provided for women convicts had improved by the beginning of Victoria's reign so that every woman sailed decently clad in a new jacket and gown with three petticoats, three shifts, three pairs of stockings and two pairs of shoes to her name. By the 1840s, women in the tropics were given checked aprons and white jackets and presented, said an observer, 'a picturesque and neat' appearance.

Neatness must have been well-nigh impossible to maintain. The ships were dark and damp and stank. The overcrowding made the smells inevitable even if, as on the ship *Success*, there was a huge wooden construction on deck labelled 'Compulsory Bath' in white letters. If cholera pounced, it stayed. So did all kinds of fevers and stomach disorders, fermenting in that thick air below decks among people debilitated by their confinement. And it was not only the confinement that oppressed them but the boredom, the long, stifling, dimly lit hours with utterly nothing to do but gossip and squabble. It was not until the last years of the transport ships that lady philanthropists managed to travel on board to instruct and organize the convicts into some constructive way of passing those endless and awful weeks.

Promiscuity was inevitable, despite the cages and the public gaze. On the early voyages persistent sexual abuse was rampant. Contemporary writers mostly put the blame on avid female behaviour. 'In some ships,' a surgeon wrote, 'the desire of the women to be with the men was so uncontrollable that neither shame or the form of punishment could deter them from making their way through the bulkhead to the apartments assigned to the seamen.' One accepted punishment was to be put in a barrel, which rendered both sitting down or lying impossible.

Spectators of both promiscuity and these punishments were

frequently the children of convict women, taken along because there was nothing else to do with them. They comprised on average about a quarter of the female convict numbers on a ship, and were provided, by the late 1830s, with government clothing of an infinitely higher standard than anything they had ever possessed before. There is very little record of their life on board, beyond that their mortality rate, particularly among babies, was appallingly high. Like the adults they had to sit and endure, month after month, in a cage without air or light on the endless journey to heaven knew what fate.

Fate after 1820 was often Van Dieman's Land, modern Tasmania. At least there were no iron bars there since the place was in itself a prison, but the early convicts found that there was nothing else either. Most of the women went back to selling their bodies, the only and age-old asset a destitute woman had, and they were handed out among settlers, on a system known as 'assigning', very much in the manner that equipment or food might be distributed. It was to ease this 'enforced whoredom' that the first female factories were built in the early years of the century, great barracks of buildings where women who had not been assigned, those who had been rejected by settlers and those who had committed some second crime since arriving, were accommodated. Like all Victorian penal institutions they were full of discipline and drudgery, with days spent at washtubs or looms. Conditions were grossly overcrowded; in 1842 1203 women were crammed into Parramatta in a space originally designed for 200.

Hardly surprisingly, riots were frequent. The women could not be flogged, but they could be put in solitary confinement, fed only bread and water for up to a fortnight and have their heads shaved. The most difficult inmates bore a large yellow 'C' on the back of their jackets. As in most places of reform where tough treatment made the inmates tougher, an impudence of spirit prevailed in many of the convict factories. In 1843, Governor Franklin of Tasmania visited the female factory at the Cascades and, like the inmates, was subjected to an interminable sermon from the convict chaplain.

These women had had quite enough of Mr Bedford; they were compelled to listen to his long stupid sermons, and knew his character, and that he loved roast turkey and ham with a bottle or two of port wine much better than he loved his Bible, and when he commenced to preach, they with one accord endeavoured to cough him down, and upon the warders proclaiming silence they all with one impulse turned round, raised their clothes and smacked their posteriors with a loud report. The Governor was shocked and the parson was horror struck, and the Aide Camp laughed aloud. . . .

It must be remembered that all women of the poorer classes in the first half of the nineteenth century went without underclothes.

Cascades was even more cramped than Parramatta and was housed in an old Tasmanian distillery which lurked unhealthily in a sunless valley. In the early days there, the women had worn spiked collars of iron weighing about 14 pounds apiece, but when these were abolished in the 1830s, a treadmill was substituted, that barbaric revolving device that caused hideous pain in the internal organs of women and could lead to miscarriage. Each prisoner in the factory received a pound of bread a day, half a pound each of meat and potatoes and two ounces of roasted wheat and sugar (a luxury forbidden to the worst offenders) to make a hot drink mildly reminiscent of coffee. They all wore 'white mob caps and a dress of grey duffle' and their working days were arduous:

One of the great yards of the factory was devoted to laundress work. Squads of women were up to their elbows in suds – carrying on the cruel process of wringing – or displaying their thick ankles as they spread the linen over the drying lines. The townsfolk may have their washing done here at 1s. 6d. per dozen, the money going towards the expenses of the institution. I was pained to see so many young creatures in this yard – delinquents in their earliest teens; debauched ere the pith had hardened in their little bones. We next had a glimpse of a room full of sempstresses, most of them employed in fine work. It was not impossible, the matron stated, that some of the elaborate shirt-fronts we should see at the Government-house ball this evening had been worked in this, and washed and 'got up' in the last ward. A rougher fabric done by the less skilled prisoners is a coarse kind of woollen tweed, only used for prison dresses.

Parramatta was airier and cleaner but the punishments were as brutal, and it possessed the added refinement, undisguisedly, of being both a brothel and a marriage market. Ex-convicts or settlers only had to indicate to the matron that they were in search of a woman for the prisoners to be paraded in front of them so that each might take his pick. If the chosen woman proved troublesome later, she could always be sent back to the factory. Considering the disproportion of the sexes in Australia then, not a great number of convict women – only about a quarter – did manage to get a husband. Their reputations were against it.

Assignment, if it were possible, was always preferred to female factories. The government preferred it because it took a woman 'off government stores' and ended the expense of keeping her in a factory. In order to encourage the system, Brisbane had laid down that a settler must keep one convict for every 100 acres of land granted. The settlers took a dim view of this, complaining loudly that among the women allotted to them 'rarely indeed was a sober and well conducted servant to be got'. Louisa Meredith, writing of Tasmania in the forties, described the problem:

And now began my real experience of colonial housewifery and its attendant troubles, although these did not prove very distressing and nearly all originated in servants. . . . Prisoner women servants are generally of a far lower grade than the men. . . . My first prisoner nursegirl was taken at random by our agent in Hobarton, from among the herd of incorrigibles in the female house of correction, or 'Factory' as it is termed; and was indeed a notable example: – *dirty* beyond all imagining! She drank rum, smoked tobacco, swore awfully, and was in all respects the lowest specimen of womankind I ever had the sorrow to behold. Before I had time to procure another, she drank herself into violent fits, so that four men could not hold her from knocking herself against the walls and floor, then went to the hospital, and, finally, got married!

Respectable families preferred a man or a free emigrant servant of some decency. That left the convict women to what was termed 'the lower description of settlers', by whom they were employed as prostitutes to a large degree. What else could the authorities expect? Confined, abused and brutalized, their only pleasures the easy oblivions of drink and tobacco, how could a convict woman adjust to the constraints and refinements of a middle-class household?

For a female convict there was little alternative to a life of prostitution. Everyone expected her to lead it, and most men assumed a right to exploit it. It was a vicious circle of a problem as described by Lord Molesworth:

At times they are excessively ferocious, and the tendency of assignment is to render them still more profligate; they are all of them, with scarcely an exception, drunken and abandoned prostitutes; and even were any of them inclined to be well-conducted, the disproportion of the sexes in the penal colonies is so great, that they are exposed to irresistible temptations: for instance, in a private family, in the interior of either colony, a convict woman, frequently the only one in the service, perhaps in the neighbourhood, is surrounded by a number of depraved characters, to whom she becomes an object of constant pursuit and solicitation; she is generally obliged to select one as a paramour to defend her from the importunities of the rest; she seldom remains long in the same place; she either commits some offence, for which she is returned to the Government; or she becomes pregnant, in which case she is sent to the factory, to be confined at the expense of the Government; at the expiration of the period of confinement or punishment, she is reassigned and again goes through the same course; such too is generally the career of convict women even in respectable families.

It is evidence of the intense dislike most of the women felt for the assignment system that they were ready in such large numbers to go back to the factories when their employers washed their hands of them. Even prison drudgery and confinement were preferable to the abuse and inhumanity of life at some settler's mercy. In 1837, two pretty girls were imprisoned at Parramatta for the murder of their former employer, and although they confessed themselves sorry for the crime itself, they were adamantly unrepentant that such a man should die.

'As one reads history,' Oscar Wilde wrote, 'one is absolutely sickened not by the crimes the wicked have committed, but by the punishments the good have inflicted.'

'The facts are horrible but they are plain,' said a public pronouncement by the Archbishop of Canterbury in 1910. 'The police and the magistrates are beyond doubt hampered in what they strive to do by the restrictions of the existing laws.' Mrs Bramwell Booth was even more eloquent. 'The thing is truly a monstrous evil. . . . Charnel houses of filth and bondage. . . . Negro slavery is bad enough but this, in all its essential evils, is the worst slavery that has ever been.'

The slavery was that of white girls sold into whoredom abroad. The practice was nothing new. Elizabeth Barrett Browning, the poetess, had known of it, claiming that such atrocities arose 'because pure, prosperous women choose to ignore vice [and thus] miserable women suffer wrong by it everywhere'. Josephine Butler had known of it too. She made a formal declaration before a board of magistrates in Liverpool in 1880:

English, Scots, Welsh and Irish girls were being bought daily for exportation to Brussels and Paris and there detained in horrible slavery, and that large numbers of girls under the age of 21, many as young as 12, had been bought or induced to go abroad and then placed in brothels; that the placeurs had received from £18 to £32 after buying them for as little as £5 each and that these girls and children had no power to escape.

A year later she wrote an open letter to the ladies of Birmingham to tell them that 'this modern slave traffic in young girls is, I am sorry to tell you, worldwide'. When the National Vigilance Association and International Bureau for the Suppression of the White Slave Traffic was founded, twenty-four countries subscribed. The organizations attracted some vigorous support including that of Lord Kitchener, who was an active campaigner during his time in Egypt. He was successful too, so much so that a contemporary report declared of Cairo that '. . . the traffickers are now in the iron grip of the authorities and they need not expect much sympathy from Kitchener of Khartoum'.

Money was what the slavers sought rather than sympathy, and if successful they found it. One English syndicate was reported to have made £40,000 profit in 1909 alone and the National Vigilance Association dealt with 17,000 abductions in the first seven years of this century. On the whole, however, facts and figures are hard to come by. Contemporary books are full of graphic accounts of abduction of 'an unfortunate', with lengthy and often unattractively lip-licking descriptions of the 'purity' and 'whiteness' of the victims, but there is no doubt that London was a great clearing house and that girls did simply vanish. Leman Street police station in Whitechapel alone had a huge stock of missing names and descriptions. Against this must be set the undeniably extravagant mythology that grew up around the whole subject, and the lack of precision as to the sources and subjects of the stories. The more lurid the tale, often the more veiled its exact origin, a quality which enhances the drama but casts a shadow upon the authenticity.

Mrs Archibald MacKirdy in her book *The White Slave Market*, published in 1912, reported a 'first-hand incident' in just such an unspecific manner:

It was only a few days ago that a young lady told me she was followed as she came out of a large London store by a nasty, sleek-looking, well-dressed, well-oiled-looking foreigner who tried to attract her attention and induce her to go with him. Asked why she did not give him in charge of the first policeman, the young lady said the disagreeableness following this course of action was so great to the woman that she did not like to do it.

'A Mother of Girls' wrote to the *Daily Chronicle* on 26 July 1911 to relate how her two young daughters, aged fourteen and fifteen, vanished while on a train journey to London to visit the dentist. As like as not, they ended up in Buenos Aires, where excellent prices could be obtained for English girls, or in the East where they might have been distributed from celebrated collecting houses at Pondicherry or on Malay Street, Singapore. The Bishop of Singapore mentioned the sorry business in a sermon in the cathedral, saying, 'Every boat that comes to Singapore brings its quota of human freight in the form of these unfortunate misled girls, nearly all of whom go into Malay Street and are borne out again only to be buried.'

The most successful pimps plying the trade operated between the city slums and the East, searching for the 'daughters of the poor' to supply the market. Cairo, luckily for them perhaps, did not set its sights as high as English girls. W. N. Willis, the Australian MP, interviewed a madam in Cairo and asked her if American and English girls came to Cairo. 'No, no,' she said. 'The life is too rough; besides it's dangerous here to have much to do with English girls . . . we could not afford to live at all if we employed the better woman.'

'The better woman', as seen by a brothel-keeper in Egypt, had not seen herself so at home. Theatres and concert halls had always been perfect places to find poor and discontented girls ready to clutch at any alternative to the way they presently lived; and tea shops and cafés were equally fruitful. In the eighties and nineties a girl might work as a waitress for over twelve hours a day, forbidden to sit down or receive tips, for this earning between five and eight shillings a week, of which her lodgings could cost her three. A male customer promising her freedom, travel and money did not have to be very persuasive to gain her exhausted attention.

In September 1912, the Female Slave Trade Suppression Bill was introduced into the council of the Government of India:

The Government of India, of Burma, of the Straits Settlements, of the Federated Malay Straits, including Singapore, of Hong Kong and the Eastern Treaty Ports, enforce a strict prohibition against women of ill-fame plying their trade in these Asiatic dependencies; the law is rigidly enforced in Calcutta, Madras, Bombay, Poona, Burma, Penang, Singapore, Hong Kong and British Borneo that no British woman is allowed under law to live a life of infamy either in houses of ill fame or with coloured Asiatics.

The bill seemed, like so much reforming zeal, to have missed the point. Who, after all, was exploiting whom? In England the White Slave Traffic Bill of the same year fared not much better. It passed its first and second readings and then a parliamentary committee weakened it to nothing by amendments. The bill had proposed that a policeman might arrest on suspicion, but the committee amended his powers to require him to possess a warrant before he could make an arrest; such a procedure would allow any pimp plenty of time for escape.

It all came back to the same theme, the theme that echoes dully and sickeningly, down the long Victorian years: that women, even pure women, are morally weak and that the impure are the invention of the devil. As an anonymous contributor to the *Cornhill Magazine* wrote in 1866:

Again, it is notorious that a bad man – we mean one whose evil training had led him into crime – is not so vile as a bad woman. If we take a man and a woman guilty of a similar offence in the eyes of the law, we shall invariably find that there is more hope of influencing the former than the latter. Equally criminal in one sense, in another sense there is a difference. The man's nature may be said to be hardened, the woman's destroyed. Women of this stamp are generally so bold and unblushing in crime, so indifferent to right and wrong, so lost to all sense of shame, so destitute of the instincts of womanhood, that they may be more justly compared to wild beasts than to women. To say the least, the honour of womanhood requires that a new appellation be invented for them.

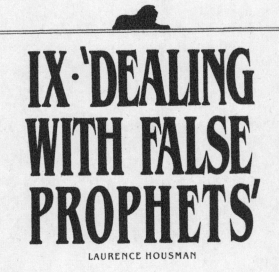

IX · 'DEALING WITH FALSE PROPHETS'

LAURENCE HOUSMAN

IX

In Housman's *Happy and Glorious* there is a scene, set in 1898 in the royal apartments at Windsor, in which Lord Kitchener explains the Sudanese situation to the Queen:

KITCHENER: Christianity is rather thrown away, Ma'am, in dealing with false prophets and people of that sort. It was a bloody tyranny and it had to be put down. . . .

QUEEN VICTORIA: Very satisfactory. And is there any prospect of the natives becoming Christian, now that they see what Christianity really means?

KITCHENER: The missionaries would say yes, Ma'am. They always do, to justify the expense of their missions and their large families, for which they get a capitation grant. . . .

There was certainly plenty of money – the wealth of industrial output – available in Victorian England to foster and encourage missionary zeal, and plenty of evangelizing fervour to provide the spiritual fuel. With the self-confidence that characterized their influence in all other ways, the Victorian Protestants set about a spiritual campaign among the heathen, on the face of it with a blithe disregard of all the work the Catholic Church had been doing in the same field for decades. It was, after all, a way of easing their own consciences, first prodded long before by Wesley and his Methodists, and aggravated by the huge social problems of the nineteenth century. The targets for this urge to convert were provided with generous hand by the Empire itself, whose great routes for free trade opened up bottomless wells of barbarity, millions of pagan souls crying out for Christian rescue.

An absolute need to convert lay in the heart and soul of the Victorian missionary. With a few notable exceptions – particularly that of Mary Slessor – a consideration of the peoples so converted and their native ways of life was so irrelevant to the central purpose as to be almost irreligious. The prospect and, even more, the achievement, of Christian conversion brought a spiritual glory which could hardly be equalled by any other religious experience. 'Oh Mother, will it not gladden your heart if the Lord permits me to enter into His work?' Mary Livingstone's mother wrote in 1818. 'I say, will it not gladden your heart that the Lord made you the mother of at least one child who was so highly honoured as to be an instrument in His hands, however humble, of doing something towards the conversion of the heathen? Oh, mother, were I a mother, I should esteem it the greatest honour which could be conferred on me or my child.'

Baptisms, Sunday schools, Bible classes and simple services from the West Indies to the remotest regions of China, across Africa and India and South-east Asia brought to the vigorous missionaries of Victorian England what one of them, Arthur Saker, called hours of 'hallowed feeling'. Not for them a respectful observance of other people's right to live and worship as they chose, only an evangelizing zeal which it is necessary to acknowledge in order to comprehend the fortitude, the enterprise and the all-too-frequent lack of imagination of the nineteenth-century missionary. 'Quite safe here with Jesus,' Annie Taylor wrote on Christmas Day 1892 from the savage ravines of the Tibetan borderland, accompanied only by treacherous native servants and in weather of appalling cruelty. She meant it.

For women the life of the missionary had particular appeal, not least because there were areas of the mission field open to them alone. The Victorian Church held a special attraction for women, not simply because ardent religious devotion was an acceptable emotional outlet but also because there was a new emphasis upon women's role in church life. There was a great revival of celibate sisterhoods – not unconnected with the huge surplus of women in England – whose charitable work among the fallen and the destitute endowed them with a special grace, and status. By 1850 there were sixteen such sisterhoods in London alone, nursing cholera victims in Stepney, caring for the orphaned, the old, the criminal and the prostitute. The first such community of sisters had been set up in Nash's imaginative Park Village West, in Regent's Park, whence four ladies sallied forth intrepidly to visit 'the hovels off the Euston Road'. It grew to encompass institutions in Bristol and outside

Birmingham, and even though it and all the other sisterhoods remained an eccentric fringe, they filled gaps in the social service and gave religiously minded women with philanthropic gifts a particular and distinctive position.

Married women too were making their presence felt. In 1876 Mary Sumner, wife of the rector of Old Alresford in Hampshire, started the Mothers' Union. Its aim was to arouse parents to a sense of responsibility for the religious upbringing of their children, and in fourteen years its journal grew in circulation from a single parish to 13,000 subscribers. Mary Sumner was remembered as 'a great and gay lady, taking cold baths daily, refusing to have a telephone when they came or a motor car or smoking in her house. She thought herrings were food for cats and was astonished to be offered them at a vicarage.' For all that, when in 1912 a count revealed that the membership of the Mothers' Union was almost 279,000, almost all the mothers were working-class.

As for the middle-class households, hardly one was without its copy of *The Heir of Redcliffe*, Charlotte M. Yonge's novel of clerical life that did as much for the moral idealism of the educated as any book of Victoria's reign. In other books too, in the novels of Trollope and Dickens and Mrs Gaskell, many of the women characters are seen to exert a peculiar and powerful moral influence, almost as if religion were the private and particular province of their sex.

From about 1870 onwards, the proportion of women to men in church congregations was almost two to one. Between 1870 and the outbreak of the Great War, sixty-five out of every hundred Anglicans in church were women. There was a powerful belief, much bolstered by the vastly spreading missionary progress across India, China and Africa, that the Victorians were part of a huge religious revival, a triumphant spiritual progress, expressed by such hymns as this, written in 1894 by A. C. Ainger:

> God is working His purpose out
> As year succeeds to year,
> God is working His purpose out
> And the time is drawing near –
> Nearer and nearer draws the time
> The time that shall surely be
> When the earth shall be filled with the glory of God
> As the waters cover the sea.

The missionaries saw God's purpose with clarity, and, what was more, saw the ways in which it could be worked out. In most of these ways, women were of inestimable value either because they could penetrate where a man might not go, such as into the zenanas of Hindu and Moslem households, or because they provided the irreplaceable support of the helpmeet. Livingstone's father-in-law had paid tribute to the value of having the right woman by one's side in pagan places. 'A missionary without a wife . . . is like a boat with only one oar. A good missionary's wife can be as useful as her husband in the Lord's vineyard.'

Similarly useful were the spinster missionaries, women such as Annie Taylor or Mary Slessor whose sex was in itself a protection since they represented no threat to peoples understandably resentful of such fundamental intrusion as a religious conversion. In a way they were in a position to get even closer to the people they sought to bring to Christ than the missionaries' wives, whose inevitable domestic authority was distancing in itself.

This was a problem encountered all over the Empire as married missionaries set up house together. Other problems were legion and akin to those encountered by all the pioneers. Arthur and Helen Saker, a couple who represented perfectly the ideal of Victorian missionary dedication, arrived in 1844 at the Cameroons mission to a windowless native hut – soon de-roofed by a tornado – constant attacks of fever and plagues of wood ants which devoured all their clothes. They suffered a diet which after a year lacked all butter, flour and sugar and whose only meat was the odd squirrel or fowl. Whatever the privations, they could not help but establish some kind of household, however primitive. That, however, was regarded by the local king, A'kwa, as a rival establishment to his own. He was a man of cruel and unattractive habits to whom human life was of no consequence at all. When he died his tribe went on the rampage, ransacking the mission house and carrying off all Helen Saker's knives and spoons and linen, not to mention the flour that was so vitally precious.

Notwithstanding all these trials (to which were added several births and the death of a little daughter), when Helen Saker was asked to return to the Cameroons after a recuperative spell in England in 1861, she declared herself eager to go back. She and her husband toiled on together, upheld by the conviction of the glory of what they did. 'Truly God is here,' Helen wrote of her endlessly exhausting and debilitating life among people who, even if they could not fully comprehend the spiritual fervour that drove her onward, were grateful for her medicines and interference in the brutal ways of the slave trade. She survived her husband by six years and was buried beside him at Lewisham. 'The man's work,' says her autobiography firmly, 'is the woman's memorial.'

Mary Livingstone was cast in much the same mould. She was 'famous for roughing it in the bush and never a trouble', her husband recalled proudly; she baked bread in ant hills, made candles and soap, endured not only the demands made upon her by Livingstone's religious zeal but also the extra burden of being married to an intrepid and tireless explorer. She was a distinct asset to him on these journeys since her presence, not to mention that of the three Livingstone children, reassured the natives of the interior that the explorer meant them no harm. Their travels were beset with dreadful anxieties, particularly when Mary contracted an unknown ailment which left the right side of her face temporarily paralysed. There were many occasions when the children were almost frantic with thirst and their father felt both his own responsibility and his wife's astounding generosity and trust:

The less there was of water, the more thirsty the little rogues became. The idea of their perishing before our eyes was terrible; it would have been a relief to me to be reproached with being the entire cause of the catastrophe, but not one syllable of upbraiding was uttered by their mother, though the tearful eye told the agony within.

When consideration for the failing health of the children forced Mary to take them home to Scotland, the parent Livingstones found their own separation hard to bear. Mary was rather a labourer in her husband's vineyard in the Lord's name than a toiler in the divine vineyard directly. They were apart for four years, from 1852 to 1856, during which time Livingstone made his celebrated African journey from sea to sea, an achievement about which it must have been extraordinarily difficult for Mary to feel anything except the acutest anxiety, marooned as she was half a world away in Scotland.

Lord Shaftesbury, for all his admiration for her husband, paid understanding tribute to Mary's behaviour under such stress:

... when she reached this country she passed many years with her children in solitude and anxiety, suffering the greatest fears for the welfare of her husband, and yet enduring all with patience and resignation, and even joy, because she had surrendered her best feelings, and sacrificed her own private interests, to the advancement of civilization and the great interests of Christianity.

She died six years later of a fever contracted on the Zambesi. Livingstone was heartbroken. She was 'a right straightforward woman', he said of her, '. . . one whom I felt to be a part of myself'. He buried her beneath a baobab tree at Shupanga, a fitting resting place for a woman whose mother, the wife of Dr Robert Moffat, the great missionary of Bechuanaland, had all but dedicated her at birth to what the century thought of as the Dark Continent.

The quality of endurance in the diaries and letters of a Victorian missionary's wife makes hard reading. One longs for a word of complaint, even a wondering suggestion that the Lord might not need or even ask that such huge sacrifices be made. But these are very few, stray hints scattered in a general and eloquent conviction that a life given up in this way was one fulfilled to its utmost limits. Eliza Field had created a sensation in 1833, not by marrying a missionary in itself but by marrying a missionary who was a North American Indian. He had been born Kahkewaquonaby (attractively meaning Sacred Waving Feathers) of the Ojibwa tribe, but had been converted to Christianity by the Methodists at twenty-one and progressed to become the Reverend Peter Jones, a leading native preacher in Canada. The Methodists sent him – 'a fine looking man, . . . tall, dark, high boned, muscular . . .' – to London to raise money for their mission, and there he met Miss Field, the daughter of a prosperous Lambeth factory- and property-owner. The romance and subsequent marriage of the Indian and a 'little fragile, delicate London lady' sent a pleasurable *frisson* down the spines of respect- able society; the prospect of life on an Indian mission station on the Credit River had a similar effect upon Eliza. She had been sheltered and spoiled since birth; now she had to venture into the kitchen, 'to gain a little information in household concerns', and to exchange her novels for church histories, Bunyan, and Fenimore Cooper's *The Last of the Mohicans*.

For all her earnest preparations, Canada, the Ojibwa, the poverty and the dirt oppressed her terribly. She had confided to her diary on her wedding day a desire and prayer 'to be made very useful' and, like all similar wives of her time, wished for nothing but to be of invaluable help to her husband. At first, she coped with resolute cheerfulness with her one-roomed wooden hut, with the filthy disorganized children in the Indian school, with endless domestic tasks that were new to her. Then the undeniable separateness of herself from her husband's people and their habits was borne slowly in upon her and she showed glimpses of a state of mind many missionaries' wives must have felt but would not own to. After an appalling night of watching Peter's sister-in-law and her new baby die in great pain and high fever, Eliza admitted that she felt '. . . that I was in circumstances different to any I had ever experienced before, now I thought my trials are beginning. . . . When I awoke this morning I felt the most distressing weight on my spirits. I could for a time only sob and try to pray.'

In the end she was to be another wifely success story. Despite two miscarriages and two stillbirths, she gave Peter Jones four sons and a lifetime of staunch support, polishing him socially until he was fit even for an audience with the Queen at Windsor Castle. Victoria found him a pleasant surprise: 'he expressed himself very well', she noted in her diary. Eliza and Peter became prosperous enough to build themselves a substantial redbrick house, called Echo Villa, yet the feeling remains that the gap Eliza had felt between herself and the Indians never closed, but merely became less poignant with time. Her triumphant account of her drawing room in Ojibwa filled with Indians lustily singing the old Methodist hymn 'Let Your Joy be Known' has more than an edge of the ludicrous to it; Miss Field's Lambeth refinements had overcome the Indians' natural inclination to spit on the floor.

Spinster missionaries were another matter altogether. Freed from emotional loyalty to another human being and the encumbrance of setting up house, they were, like the lady travellers, very much their own mistresses. Unlike the travellers, however, they needed no apology, no excuse for what they did since being 'mighty in the scriptures' was more than reason enough for astonishing adventures. They were also free to do what no man could do. All the medical work which so changed the lives of the piteous captives of the zenana was built upon the early achievements of the missionaries who worked their way, with endless patience and armed with nothing but Bibles, into the filthy, illiterate and superstitious labyrinths of the Moslem and Hindu women's quarters. 'If we can give them the power to read and the Book to read, God will bless His word.'

The Zenana Mission Society, a body which continually and ever more pompously changed its name while remaining steadfast to its purpose, sent out a steady stream of spinster missionaries who, even though most were 'Miss Sahibs', lived away from the English cantonments and as much with Indians as they could, in that strange life of barbaric contrasts, a world '. . . of dirt and jewels, of discomforts and finely carved archways and doorways, . . . houses tenanted by the cows and goats in the basement story and by the women in the upper. . . .'

So wrote Miss Hull in Benares, the Sacred City, in the 1870s. She was a powerful woman, appalled at the marriage of children of seven to old men of sixty and the cruel humiliation of Hindu widows, but determined that her own status should never be called in question. 'Every Babu was made fully to understand when inviting me to his house that I should come only as a Christian teacher and with the Bible in my hand.'

She was sure that the work she did was effective if performed by her sex alone and begged the society to send as many more women as they could. 'Do you know of any willing to devote themselves to God's Service?' she wrote. 'If so, tell them of India's perishing souls whom no missionary save a woman can reach.'

Mr Taylor, father of the intrepid Annie, was no sharer of such opinion. He was a traveller himself, a fellow of the Royal Geographic Society, but he was violently opposed to the religious obsession that seized his indulged and wayward daughter, so much so that the argument between them over her missionary calling raged for twelve years.

Annie was born in 1855 with a weak heart. She was spoiled on account of it and took advantage of the spoiling. She did nothing but to extremes and when a lecture given by Dr Moffat, Livingstone's father-in-law, called her to missionary work, she flung herself passionately into religious fervour, visiting the sick in slums, studying medicine and selling her jewellery to move into lodgings when her father, at his wits' end, stopped her allowance. She wore

Mrs Smith in a carrying chair. The mobile
missionary in East Africa at the turn of the century

Three sisters in Christ. Victorian missionaries
in Africa

'Quite safe here with Jesus.' An itinerant
missionary and her flock in East Africa

'A missionary without a wife is like a boat with only one oar.'
Mr and Mrs Wood in Africa with baby and bicycles

'Tell them of India's perishing souls whom no missionary save a woman can reach.'
A group of Zenana missionaries on medical safari in India (see p. 88)

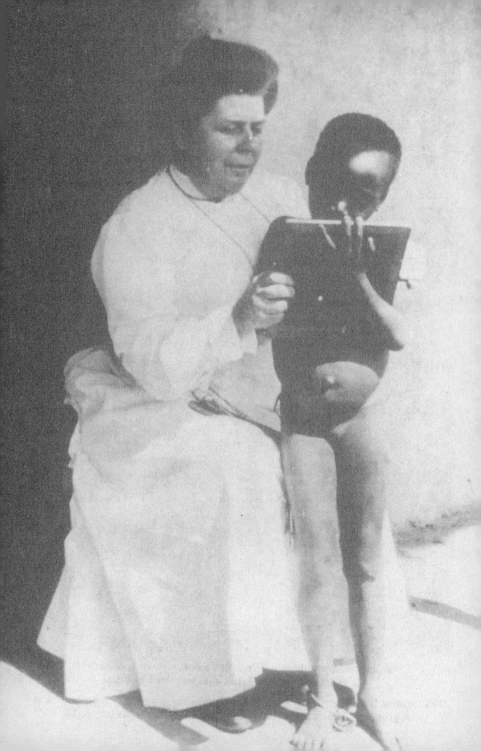

The Archdeaconess. Ellen Mort and her sedan
chair, the China Mission

LEFT: 'As long as I can nurse a motherless bairn I'm to
stick to my post' (Mary Slessor). Miss Pilgrim
teaching a child in Elgon district, in the 1890s

'They shall see his face.' Foochow blind boys
exhibit for Nanking, 1911

'Riding improves the temper, the spirits and the appetite.' Stately hurdling
with the army in India, 1905

'In Simla, a place not noted for its horizontal planes, tennis courts were perched on
every level space large enough to take one' (see p. 209). Tara Devi Hill, 1907

A peaceful pleasure. Women fishing at Riverton,
near Kimberley, South Africa

Enterprising users of Australia's first snowfield: a
ladies' toboggan race at Kiandra

'It is very easy to find every scope for developing
self-control and energy in many a tight corner.'
The Ladies' Bisley at Penang in 1909

'If you don't kill a tiger, he will kill you'

Ladies in the field. Pig-sticking in India in 1920

RIGHT: A trophy for the drawing room. It was a
traditional courtesy to offer any lady in the party
first shot since the beast belonged to the first gun
to hit it even if that shot were not the *coup de
grâce*

'Games aside, there was always amateur theatricals.' The principals in *The Merry Merchant of Venice,* performed in Darjeeling in 1891, photographed al fresco

LEFT: Essie Jenyns, the star of the Holloway touring company, as Juliet, with her mother, Kate Arden, as the nurse. Kate was also the company's business manager, wardrobe mistress and publicity manager (see p. 210)

'There are lots of duchesses but there is only one
Melba' – Nellie Melba (see pp. 213 – 16). Nellie
Melba as Nedda and Fernando de Lucia as Canio
in *I Pagliacci* at Covent Garden

him down in the end and at the age of twenty-nine sailed for Shanghai and the China Inland Mission, her passage and clothes paid for by her father who, with persistent optimism, gave her a return ticket but no money.

The China Inland Mission had been founded by James Hudson Taylor in the sixties and was run on the strangely successful principle of praying for missionaries and funds as and when they were needed. Prayers in 1884 not only produced as missionaries Annie Taylor but also the former captain of the Cambridge cricket eleven and the stroke of the university boat. The mission's watchword naturally was 'Jehovah Jireh!' – 'the Lord will provide'. The mission bred travellers, teams of hymn-singing, unsalaried itinerant preachers who moved relentlessly through the vast Chinese interior.

The women of the mission were of huge importance since they could penetrate into the women's quarters of Chinese households, bearing Bibles and unbinding feet. 'I do thank the Lord for bringing me out to China,' Annie wrote from An-Kang on the Yangtze River. 'He has indeed given me more than a hundredfold and I claim the promise made by God to Abraham when he left his own country: "Thou shalt be a blessing."'

The urge to penetrate Tibet grew as steadily and powerfully in her as had her first religious conviction, and she attended the annual Butter Fair at Kumbum on the China–Tibet border. Her account of it gives a foretaste of what a disappointing chronicler of marvels she was to prove; the Kumbum monastery was one of the strangest, least known and most fascinating places in Central Asia yet of the shrine she has left no description at all, merely a dull account of the texts she distributed in the crowds and the children she dosed. And on her fantastic Tibetan journey five years later, in 1891, Annie Taylor was, as far as posterity is concerned, equally unrewarding.

It was, solely as a journey, an astounding project. God had called her, she felt, to go to Tibet; to this end she learned the language, acquired Tibetan clothes and a Tibetan servant, Pontso, and set off into possibly the most daunting territory on earth. Her aim was to blaze a trail for God from the Chinese border across Tibet to Darjeeling, the trail beginning with a terrifyingly arduous terrain of rivers and ravines in winter weather. Annie was ambushed and robbed, she battled through swamps and over great rivers, her men quarrelled all the time, one died, wolves howled and eagles loomed overhead.

'My eyes are unto Him who made a passage in the Red Sea for the children of Israel,' she wrote staunchly. 'All must be right with the ambassador of the Lord. I am in His charge.' The wind screamed round her, her horse dropped dead beneath her, she was threatened by a servant whenever she ran out of money to bribe him with, and the travellers lost their way constantly. Yet, she wrote imperturbably, 'A nice Christmas Day,' at an altitude too high to boil a pudding, showing the same unruffled absorption in her purpose that seems to have blinded her to the crude magnificence of the Tibetans themselves. For her, they were simply pagans. 'Poor things, they know no better, no one has ever told them of Jesus.'

Just short of Lhasa, Annie was apprehended by a military chief and tried by the provincial governor on charges of spying. She battled to justify herself and to obtain the horses, supplies and escort she needed to get out of Tibet. She then set off on a return journey almost as horrifying as her outward one, beset with slicing winds, waist-high snow and dying ponies. Annie went home to a grand reception and lectured – rather badly – on her evangelizing adventure. In 1894 she returned to Sikkim with the unfortunately named Tibetan Pioneer Band, which disintegrated within a year. She persisted alone among the traders of the border, described by William Carey, a missionary from India, as a 'strange complexity of daring, devotion and diplomacy'. Annie Taylor retired finally to England with broken health in 1909. Even if she had not wrested Buddhism from the Tibetans, she had been the first European to penetrate their intriguing and inaccessible land in almost half a century.

Annie Taylor might be remembered for her enterprise and eccentric courage; Mary Slessor is not forgotten because, almost above all others, she embodied the best aspects of the Victorian missionary. She was born in Aberdeen in 1848, the daughter of a strict Presbyterian mother and a shoemaker with a fondness for the bottle. It was a grim period in Scotland's history, with churches the only public places people could go to on a Sunday – even parks were closed. But the drink trade thrived to such an extent that in most Scottish cities whisky shops were five or six times as plentiful as bakers'.

Mary knew of missionaries almost from her first breath. Mrs Slessor was an ardent supporter of the overseas work of the United Presbyterian Church, and particularly of the new venture at Calabar on the slave coast of West Africa. For Mary, tracts and missionary magazines abounded in a girlhood of hard work, rigid discipline and Calvinist threats of eternal damnation for those who enjoyed 'all the barefoot, grimy, unsupervised freedom of the children of the poor'. Two brothers destined for mission work died young and Mary knew she would follow them abroad as soon as her struggling family could spare her. The moment came when Livingstone died in 1874, leaving a gap for another Scottish missionary to fill. In 1875 Mary Slessor sailed for Calabar.

Calabar had been a prosperous slaving post composed of four towns above the junction of the Calabar and Cross rivers. When the mission started, thirty years before Mary's arrival, the place was decadent and depressed, with great ritual slaughters of slaves to honour the deaths of the local trading chiefs and a consumption of raw local spirit disagreeably reminiscent of Scotland. After 1845 all slaves were technically free, but thousands hung about as dependants in much the same helpless and abused condition they had endured before abolition. Their masters regarded the mission with great wariness, reluctant even to admire the courage of the first white men to set up house on a coast infested with disease and danger. All white men before had lived on board ships, safely anchored some distance out to sea.

The Calabar mission was a remarkable one. Its aim was not to convert the tribes of Africa itself but to raise up a native agency to evangelize its own people. This imaginative approach was frustrated by the local chiefs, who used the mission as a means to teach their children sufficient English to make them successful traders. This meant huge church attendances and a very small church membership. The mission could not stamp out the sickening custom of sacrificial slaughter, or that of the 'fatting house' where young Calabar girls were prepared for marriage in the manner of Strasbourg geese. Mary was appalled. She wrote, 'I never thought that my sense of delicacy would be so far blunted. There are scenes we cannot speak or write of. . . .'

She found mission life stifling and her work among the women and children unprogressive. Photographs of her at this time show a small woman with a square, strong, big-featured face, a slightly Mongolian cast to humorous eyes and uncompromisingly practical short hair. The particular energy the mission rules would not allow her to fuel into her work she disposed of by climbing trees, and claimed to have scaled every sizeable tree between Duke Town and Old Town notwithstanding being almost thirty and hampered by anklelength skirts.

Four years later, she got what she wanted, the independent charge of the decaying old mission hut in Old Town where she could live on native chop – thereby saving money to send home to her mother and sisters – and dispense altogether with 'model housekeeping and gracious entertaining', the tea parties and genteel meetings so dear to most missionary ladies keeping up standards in remote and uncivilized places. She supervised three schools, trudged round local hamlets on Sundays to preach and took in the babies and children brutally abandoned in obedience to local custom, whether on account of being a twin or a girl or of cutting teeth in an unorthodox order.

There was much in Mary Slessor that was also in Mary Kingsley (they met in the early nineties and began a correspondence that was dear to them both). Despite the savage local feuds that made every bush path a menace, Mary.Slessor walked barefoot through the forests, risking leeches, jiggers, snakes, scorpions and human malevolence. She knew the dangers were real enough but 'the Lord promised we could take up serpents so why be afraid of leopards'. She practised rudimentary medicine from a dispensary of Epsom salts, quinine and laudanum. She became immensely successful in settling trading quarrels and preventing the appalling punishments the chiefs were in the habit of doling out to minor wrongdoers. Chief Okon wished to slice off the ears of two of his young wives for visiting the men's quarters, but Mary challenged him, pointing out that the practice of marrying spirited young girls off to old men who possessed more women than they knew what to do with already, was tyrannical, unreasonable and impractical. Whether converted or merely stunned by her impudence, Okon agreed to reduce the sentence to ten lashes.

When news came of the deaths of her mother and remaining sister, she felt, as Mary Kingsley did, an almost unwanted freedom to risk herself entirely as she chose. 'There is no one to write and tell all my stories and troubles and nonsense to,' she wrote. 'Heaven is now nearer to me than Britain and no one will be anxious about me if I go up country.'

Her choice was the Okoyong district, a swampy, forested region upriver from the coast, where the natives waged ceaseless and bloody war against the local government and the ruling Efik tribe of the region, and exhibited every disagreeable savage characteristic. They stole slaves, sacrificed them, practised witchcraft and trial by ordeal (boiling in oil or eating the deadly Calabar bean) and traded with the Calabar merchants in gin, guns and chains. Every Okoyong, young and old, was perpetually drunk; gin was the medium for all inter-village trade. Mary bearded the king of the district when he was alone and obtained permission for a mission, though she had to find her own hut and was ostracized when in it. It was decaying and filthy but she was free, both to work as she wished and of reproving reminders from colleagues that no mission lady *ever* went out without a hat.

Her work was exhausting and largely unrewarded among people whose casual cruelty to each other was enough to dampen the highest spirits. For a year she lived, with five children, in her collapsing hut with its mud floor, crowded on every side by ' . . . men, women, goats, dogs, fowls, cows, rats and cats all coming and going indiscriminately so there is no accommodation for being sick and it is too far to go to Calabar to lie down'.

In the end she built her own house with intermittent local help, her reputation having been enhanced after she had averted blood poisoning in one of Chief Edom's wives. He had bitten her in an excess of drunken amorousness and the story of her healing spread like wildfire. Mary began to be appealed to in local disputes and found people building houses close to her as if she were some touchstone of superstition. She herself knew that her work was only 'seed time', that she must be 'borne along the main stream' of the lives of the Okoyong before she could even contemplate any spiritual change in them. The prevalence of drink left them 'utterly besotted' and the persistent fighting and human sacrifice meant that whole tribes were literally dying out.

One solution, she realized, was to interest them sufficiently in trading with neighbouring tribes to leave little time or energy for their barbaric habits. She insisted upon a meeting between chiefs at which neither weapons nor gin be present, even though the Okoyong chiefs protested that their manhood would be at stake, saying, 'Oh Ma, you want to make women of us. Of a truth you want to make women of us.' Women or not, they went unarmed and at least part sober and came away triumphant with an agreement to trade in palm oil. Mary's reward was a vast increase in her influence and a new mission house, whose windows and doors were made by a carpenter sent from Scotland for the purpose.

He left a brief but vivid portrait of her; he was struck forcibly by her personal courage and the fact that she regarded slapping grown men who were reluctant to take medicine or standing between drunken tribesmen and the casks of gin they craved as no more than routine. She would take no personal credit for her influence, seeing it only as the combination of her familiarity with the people and divine intervention. 'My medicine and the fact that God has blessed it in some instances marvellously has made the whole country mine,' she wrote. 'Every chief more or less, has been under my care, or some of his people have been and they have expressed in various ways their appreciation of my services. No white person need fear to go anywhere now.'

Mary's feelings for the Okoyong amounted to little less than a passion. Her engagement to a young schoolmaster came to nothing as he was too frail for West Africa and she could not leave the tribe who were now the ruling commitment of her life. When on home leave, her time was spent begging for more effective missionaries to be sent out, men who could teach skills and crafts rather than the text distributors who could provide no sufficiently seductive rivals to the charms of drinking and slaughter. She hated the public speaking that was such a highly regarded part of any missionary's home leave and spent much of her time in Scotland begging to be allowed to return. 'If ye dinna send me back, I'll swim back!'

Her achievements are extraordinary for one human being. She had a house to keep and a family of adopted children for whom her feelings were intense; she was vice-consul for the area (saying firmly that Livingstone had done just the same on the grounds that politics never harmed religious purpose as long as they came second); she ran schools and a dispensary, sorted out endless quarrels, struggled with intermittent but savage bouts of malarial fever, repaired her own possessions, from roofs to petticoats – and all without any help or back-up. She was admittedly impossible to work with, being very personal in her methods, but her sense of justice and her courage made her a legend in her own lifetime. As time went on her health deteriorated hideously, leaving her bald, covered in boils and racked with rheumatism, but ever determined not to die in Scotland. 'As long as I can nurse a motherless bairn or help to keep peace in a home or town, or be a mother to my own bairns, I'm to stick to my post,' she wrote, 'and you would be the first to cry shame if I turned tail for a bit of fever or even a bald head.'

She died at last in 1915 and was buried with extravagant pomp and splendour in Calabar. One of the carpenters who had worked with her remarked after the ceremony that 'that was a fine service but it wasna the Miss Slessor I knew, she was nae so holy'. Her tragedy was that the civil war in West Africa after her death reduced all that she had done to rubble – churches, schools and hospitals. Thousands of people starved or were killed and the old brutal tribal systems reared their ugly heads again. Yet glimmers of her light remained in the midst of all:

... wherever along the lower reaches of the Cross River and particularly the Enyong Creek, an African woman earns her own living; where a mother of twins rears her children and her husband stands loyally by her; wherever parties to a quarrel seek the mediation of the courts instead of leaping for their matchets, something endures of the spirit of a slight red-haired woman who in the midst of this region was whirlwind, earthquake, fire and still, small voice.

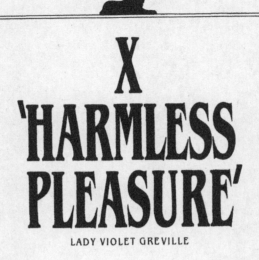

X
'HARMLESS
PLEASURE'

LADY VIOLET GREVILLE

X

'I was, darling Child, rather shocked,' Queen Victoria wrote to her seventeen-year-old granddaughter Victoria in March 1880, 'to hear of you shooting at a mark, but far more so at your idea of going out shooting with dear Papa. To look on is harmless, but it is not ladylike to kill animals and go out shooting and I hope you will never do that. It might do you great harm if that were known as only fast ladies do such things.'

Many a Victorian girl must have sighed in envy of fast ladies and the freedom that accompanied their lost reputations; they themselves, prisoners of propriety, were confined to 'moving from chair to chair, finding comfort in none and tired of every employment'. It was not that exercise was actually discouraged, but rather that its acceptable forms were so limited as to offer little allure to women whose lives were already over-sedentary. Sarah Stickney Ellis, whose handbooks on moral and social conduct were so widely influential in the mid-century, devoted only two paragraphs of her 400-page *The Daughters of England*, written in 1842, to the subject of exercise; the rest of the book consists of relentless moralizing upon economy of time, on love, on gratitude, on accomplishments, on respectable young ladyhood in general.

Her view of exercise was moral too. She advocated walking as a recipe for giving a girl an eager appetite for those tasks she had but an hour before cast aside in listless boredom:

How often have I seen such a being come in from a winter's walk, with the countenance of a perfect Hebe, with the energy of an invigorated mind, beaming forth from eyes as beautiful, as clear and with the benevolence of a young warm heart reflected in the dimpling freshness of a sunny smile. How pleasant is it then to resume the half-finished work – how refreshing the social meal – how inviting the seat beside the glowing hearth – how frank and free the intercourse with those who form the circle there! And if such be the effect of one single walk, how beneficial must be that of habitual exercise, upon the conditions both of mind and body!

A 'brisk and healthy walk' was the antidote to 'all headaches, want of appetite, pains under the shoulders, side-ache, biliousness', but until much later in the century, that was it. What was manly in a brother was wildly improper in his sister, which ruled out for her any really exhilarating physical exercise (except hunting, for the intrepid few) in an age when the women of the leisured classes actually had enough time to indulge in it.

Yet what you could not do in England under the watchful eye of mamma or of society in general, you could very often do abroad. Some of the rigid rules of respectable behaviour were carried to the furthest outposts of the Empire and there adhered to with fervour, as touchstones of familiarity and civilization in the backblocks of Australasia or the prairies of Canada; other rules seemed more adaptable once transplanted to the Indian plains or the Queensland bush. Lady travellers and missionaries clung to hats and corsets in impossible climates; young pioneer couples in the wilds of New Zealand, ten days' journey from their nearest neighbour, would not have countenanced living together, even briefly, before being officially married; but the woman who in England had longed to seize her husband's shotgun or to swing her horse's head wildly away from 'the flat and unprofitable constitutional in Rotten Row' and career madly across Hyde Park, found that in the outposts of the Empire she could ride and shoot to her heart's content.

Punch of course knew that exercise could only be good for girls. A verse published in its edition of 8 March 1884 advised:

> Let the ladies learn gymnastics, if they please, as well as men,
> Alternating feats athletic with the pencil and the pen;
> They'll improve too-pale complexions, and their eyes will shine as stars
> After practice on the ladders and the horizontal bars.

Lady Violet Greville, a passionate horsewoman, declared roundly, 'Women who ride are easy to please and unaffected; in fact what many men describe as a "good sort".' In her book *Ladies in the Field* published in 1894, she advocated that a girl could do no better than to take a riding man for a husband and be out-of-doors as much as possible. Such a life trimmed your figure, brightened your eyes and banished the glooms:

The healthful, exhilarating feeling caused by rapid motion through the air, and the sense of power conveyed by the easy gallop of a good horse, tends greatly to moral and physical well being and satisfaction. Riding improves the temper, the spirits and the appetite; black shadows and morbid fancies disappear from the mental horizon. . . .

Over and above riding's merits as a basic recipe for a sound mind in a sound body, Lady Greville admitted that 'there is a peculiar charm in Indian riding'. She was not by any means the first to perceive its possibilities. Isabel Savory had proclaimed her delight in physical freedom in *A Sportswoman in India*, in which she expressed her pleasure in being able 'to rove about in gypsy fashion', which was 'a complete change for an ordinary English girl . . . it is very easy to find every scope for developing self control and energy in many a tight corner.'

Energy was what the average memsahib in India lacked, though it can have required very little to embark on exercise since servants did everything but actually ride or shoot the beast. Lady Greville makes dawn rides in India sound wonderfully attractive, an intoxicating change from the confines of home. Tea or coffee was brought to your room and then the syce, or groom, led your horse to the door and you were up in a second, in the brief and blessed cool of dawn, to ride as far and as fast across the plain as you wished. You were 'pulled up by no fear of trespassing, no gates nor fences, nor unclosed pastures with carefully guarded sheep and cattle, no flowery cottage gardens'; your galloping progress was only broken by low mud walls and ditches to jump, on and on, reins on the neck, between the occasional mango clump, until both you and your mount were tired.

On a winter morning in northern India there were the 'Bobbery' packs to follow in pursuit of jackals and wolves, before riding home to a bath and 'a lingering toilette', with an excellent appetite for breakfast – 'fish, beefsteaks, cutlets, the most savoury and delicate of curries, fruit and coffee'. The syces swarmed, spending days squatting on the ground beside their charges with bits and buckles held between their toes while they polished furiously. Their numerous and ceaseless presence meant that a woman could ride, quite literally, any time she wished, and even participate in Sunday paperchases in the hours before sunset. Horses known as 'old screws' were kept for this activity, since it entailed thundering recklessly through rolling clouds of dust, through sugar-cane plantations and native villages, over ground baked hard as iron and therefore potentially dangerous to thoroughbred legs. When the chase was over there was the charm of the ride home:

Gloaming there is none, but a lovely starlight and the clear rays of the moon to guide you safely on your way home. Ruddy lights shine out from the native huts, sundry fires shed a wild lustre, the faint sickly odour of tobacco and opium fills the air and the weird beating of the tom-tom is heard in the distance.

Compare that with an hour's walk along English lanes 'with strong boots, waterproof cloak and umbrella'. Few people, Lady Greville declared, 'would exchange the wild daring horsemanship of India with its pigsticking and its wild game hunting, necessitating the utmost degree of nerve and determination for . . . the country ride along a road or even the delights of fox hunting in England'.

It was not simply the physical excitement of participating in these glorious adventures that was so attractive, but also the fact that a woman could do so alongside the men. When the Edens were in India at the beginning of Victoria's reign, the ladies, although taken along on elephants, were usually left sketching decorously on a riverbank while the men plunged off, six rifles apiece, in search of tigers. By the eighties the women were going too, not only service-ably dressed in hunting suits specially made up and dyed jungle green by a native tailor, but also with their own 450 double-express rifles made by such gunsmiths as Alexander Henry and carried in the back of the *howdah* by a *shikari*.

Kate Martelli, whose husband was Political Agent and Superin-tendent at Rewa, Central India, in the eighties, wrote a book unaffectedly entitled *Tigers I Have Shot*, largely to make quite clear to the world which tigers were hers and which her husband's. The rules of hunting were simple and designed to avoid indiscriminate firing which would, among other things, ruin the skin; the tiger belonged to the first gun to hit it, even if that shot were not the *coup de grâce*.

A tiger shoot was an impressive performance. The guns travelled in pairs on elephants, whilst splendid 'lunch–breakfasts' were taken ahead of the party into the jungle and spread out to await their arrival. (Mrs Martelli writes with irritation of a bearer who took fright at the proximity of a tiger and ran away, taking breakfast with him. 'Imagine our disgust.') The hunt began with three or four hundred beaters pressing through the jungle shouting and blowing bugles, 'beating drums and tom-toms ... and firing blank cartridges'. From elephant-back or a convenient rock, the guns waited 'in profound silence', with a great deal to amuse them the while:

As we waited, all sorts of creatures, scared by the beaters, passed us – pig and deer, pea-fowl and jungle fowl, the majestic sambhur and the pretty nilghai, not to mention foxes and jackals, went by within shot, but for today, at any rate, they were safe. At last came the tiger. He advanced like an enormous cat, now crouching upon the ground, now crawling forward, now turning round to try and discover the meaning of the unwanted noise behind him. When he was about eighty yards from us, I fired and hit him on the shoulder; then the others fired and the tiger bolted.

Her husband pursued him on a fresh elephant and finally killed him, but she had fired the first shot and the beast was hers, all nine feet of him. For all her enthusiasm for the sport, she frequently showed a greater regard for her victim. On several occasions she was 'so struck by [the] magnificent appearance' of a tiger that she missed her privileged first shot. One can imagine Colonel Martelli's reaction at such a moment.

Local maharajahs, whatever their true feelings about rifle-toting English ladies, were generous and courteous in their invitations to shoot tigers. These occasions were formal, with huge retinues, specially built shooting-boxes like small stone towers, and *tonjons*, or sedan chairs, to carry the ladies through the jungle. The ladies of course were offered first shot – their hosts tended to be 'much put out' if they missed – and, from most accounts, seem to have acquitted themselves honourably both in terms of skill and of service to Indian villages. Tiger-shooting, as Mrs Martelli makes plain, did not, among the best Victorian sportsmen, have anything to do with blood lust:

If, from the description I have given, anyone should be inclined to say that the tiger does not appear to have much chance of escape, the answer is that it is not intended that he should have any. Tigers are shot in India, not as game is in England for hunting, to give amusement to men, horses and dogs, not as in pheasant or partridge shooting with a remote reference to the demands of the table, but to save the lives of natives and their cattle. If you don't kill a tiger, he will kill you. But although the odds are on the shikari and against the tiger, whether you fire from the back of an elephant, from the top of a rock, or in the branch of a tree, there is always room, unfortunately, for a misadventure, and consequently tiger shooting will always be a useful school for endurance, judgement and self-reliance.

India was a wonderful playground, but it was not the only one. The Empire abounded in space and in strange beasts to be pursued across it, not least of which were the Australian outback and the kangaroo, a challenging and dangerous prey. As in India, it was considered perfectly natural in Australia for women to come hunting too, not only to give themselves pleasure but also, as Beatrice Jenkins pointed out in her description of sport for women in Australia in the early nineties, to increase the happiness of male sportsmen by having 'the weaker sex share [his] propensity with him'.

The formality of Indian hunts and shoots had no place in Australia. A group of friends would gather together on horses that were 'well bred, though many of them not well groomed', with a pack of kangaroo hounds – a cross between a deerhound and a greyhound which hunted on sight rather than scent. The pack commonly belonged to the owner of the sheep station whose land was being hunted; he acted as 'leader', the field simply following him with 'pretty riding . . . and British pluck'. The kangaroos were usually to be found in small groups 'springing along at an amazing pace', led by an 'old man'. They provided splendid sport. A catch was immediately skinned and its tail was cut off to make soup later; but if cornered the kangaroo could prove the most terrifying foe:

The kangaroo stands up to his neck in water, beating about with his legs, and the hounds swim around. A young one, not knowing the danger, makes a snap at his throat, he is instantly seized in the animal's arms and his back broken. Poor Daisy! your hunting days were short and you had yet to learn that discretion was the better part of valour. The older hounds keep swimming round, gradually coming nearer, and several at once make snaps at different parts of the kangaroo. A hand-to-hand fight takes place, the kangaroo ripping and wounding the hounds with his powerful hind claws, but the plucky beasts keep their hold, and amid yelps of rage and pain, the splashing and the reddening of the water, and the shouts of the huntsmen to encourage the hounds, the victim sinks after a vigorous struggle for his life.

Between these bloodthirsty episodes there were some gentler scenes. The landscape was often marvellous, particularly when the wattle trees were in full yellow bloom, and the rivers abounded in platypus and wild duck. And of course there was always food, prepared by the hunters themselves, this being Australia, and eaten, after strenuous exercise, 'under a bright sun and balmy breezes':

A fire is soon lighted; one is told to unpack the basket of good things; another grills some steak, someone else undertakes potatoes, the oldest bushman of the lot says he will regale us with 'Johnnie Cakes'. These are made of flour and water and a little salt, rolled very thin and cooked in the ashes, and very good they prove to be; and last but not least, we make the tea, boiling the water in a tin pot and putting the tea into it.

As well as sport, there were games. Indeed life in Simla and Naini-Tal would have been empty without games, in which ladies were active participants from the beginning. Archery at Annandale was a Simla legend throughout India, followed later by a passion for croquet and, in the 1870s, for lawn tennis. In Simla, a place not noted for its horizontal planes, tennis courts were perched on every level space large enough to take one. Women took to the game with 'vigour and spirit', only taking time off for dog shows, paperchases and a game called 'tilting the ring', which involved a lot of breathless galloping about on horseback and losing one's hat in the process.

No women seemed to have wanted to climb from the Indian hill stations – or at least none has left a record of so doing – but there were notable women climbers elsewhere by the turn of the century, headed by Mrs Aubrey Le Blond, president of the Lyceum Alpine Club. Her book *Adventures on the Roof of the World*, published in 1904, contains photographs of her and her husband skiing; she was dressed in a short tweed skirt, matching jacket with peplum and a neat hat, and he wore knickerbockers and a Norfolk jacket. Both husband and wife are balanced on enormously long skis, whose ends rear up like horns, and clasp purposefully a single and immense ski pole.

Games aside, there was always amateur theatricals. This was a passion which extended all over the Empire, from the Christmas shows in hospitals through the upper-deck revues on board ships taking civil servants to Bombay or soldiers to Cape Town, to the fully fledged amateur productions of Simla's Gaiety Theatre. Farces and burlesques were much favoured, particularly when in-jokes about the relevant community could be included, and everyone fought to take part including, in the late eighties, the Viceroy of India, Lord Dufferin himself.

Running alongside all this amateur drama and eager dressing-up, there was a steady stream of professional entertainers to the colonies, quite literally 'playing the Empire'. Stars of the London stage whose sun was just beginning to set could trade upon their reputations for several seasons more in the theatres of Sydney and Johannesburg, enriching both themselves and the cultural lives of the colonies at the same time. In fact so energetically did the people of Australia and South Africa, in particular, respond to the chance to see *Hamlet* and *Romeo and Juliet* in their local theatres, that several touring companies sprang up for the express purpose of travelling the Empire. These brought Shakespeare to the man in Commissioner Street with dirt from the mine dumps under his nails.

The most celebrated and successful of these wandering troupes was the Holloway Theatre Company, actor–managed by W. J. Holloway and his remarkable wife Kate. Born in Gloucester, niece to the inventor of the Morse code, she was the daughter of a poetry-writing clerk who was also a Unitarian minister. She was the eldest of four, possessed of a contralto voice good enough to make her a soloist with the Gloucester Choral Society and sufficiently pretty to have been proposed to three times before she was eighteen. The fourth suitor was accepted. He was Richard Jennings, the son of a local squire, tall, fair, personable and with a medical degree. His family seemed strangely willing to accept the dowerless Kate for their son, and even more strangely eager for them both to emigrate. On the journey to Australia Kate discovered she was both married to a violent alcoholic and pregnant. For seven months she was confined in a ship to face both these problems and gave birth to a son at sea.

The Jennings's early days in Australia were unsettled and unsettling. The doctor's method of running his practice was to open his surgery for a few days, hand out medicines in return for payment, and, when he had enough money, to shut his surgery and head for the bars of the local mining township. To keep herself and a fragile child alive, Kate, who was pregnant again, would sell medicines and pills during her husband's increasingly prolonged absences, hoping very much that they were appropriate to the malady but having no alternative. When her second confinement was due, she was entirely alone and in the best pioneer tradition she gave birth to a daughter attended by nobody except her small son. She had even had to rise from her bed to find her husband's gun and shoot a deadly black snake that was sliding along the rafters.

After months of solitude, penury and squalid searches through bars and gutters for her husband, Kate gave up. Packing up a bundle and her babies she simply walked out into the bush leaving everything behind. She survived because of the splendid Australian tradition of sundowning, the open, easy hospitality extended to any traveller who asked for food or lodging at sunset. In her absence Dr Jennings gave up the unequal struggle with the bottle, staggered on to South America and was killed in a brawl the very day he landed.

Kate's assets were her looks and her determination. They won her friends and eventually a post as matron of a Sydney orphanage, a job whose status enabled her to enter a social circle she had never known before. Among her new friends was a visiting star actor from England, William Creswick, who, struck by her resourcefulness and her face, asked her to join his company. It was a less startling suggestion then than now. In the Australia of 1870 there were no drama schools; actors learned to act by acting, and when they were not acting they were performing a thousand other functions around the theatre. Creswick's company appears to have accepted the orphanage matron and her children with such ease and warmth that by the end of the first season she was engaged to be married to the company's leading man, William James Holloway.

W.J. had led a life almost as colourful as Kate's. He was born in Seven Dials in 1843, the son of a piano-factory worker who emigrated to Australia when W.J. was thirteen. His formal education had finished at the age of nine, but he had persevered on his own while he served an apprenticeship to a watchmaker in Clerkenwell. The journey to Australia took six weeks less than Kate's awful voyage, but his mother died in childbirth two days out of Cape Town. When Australia was at last reached his father announced that he intended to farm, a prospect that held no attraction for his son at all. As Kate walked out on Richard Jennings, so W.J. at fourteen left his father's farm and went to Sydney and a job as a trainee shipbuilding engineer.

In Sydney the theatre bit him, so much so that he built his own tin-shack theatre on a piece of waste ground, where he put on immensely successful comedies illumined by candles. The call of acting was too strong to resist so he gave up his engineering job to join a Brisbane theatrical company at a quarter of the salary he had previously earned. Learning every theatrical skill the hard way, he performed, as did every actor of his day, in the traditions set by Garrick and Kean. He progressed first to Adelaide and his first role as leading man, then to the city of Sydney, William Creswick and Kate.

With Kate, he started his own company. Whatever her acting abilities, not significant beside those of her husband and children, her true administrative talents now came into their own. She was business manager, wardrobe mistress and such a successful publicity manager that the company played to full houses throughout its first tour of the 1883 season. Australian audiences, the company had been warned, were not to be wooed as English ones were: 'You must not regard our audiences as if they were a West End public – they range from Peckham Rye to Whitechapel. They want strong effects, not fine acting; they want sensation, not style.'

Whatever they wanted, they got it and were prepared to pay for it – takings during the company's most successful five years in the eighties were never less than £500 a week. Costs came to about £400 and no member of the company received less than £4 a week, which was both adequate for the time and about two or three times as much as a governess might expect to earn in England. There were enormous vicissitudes; on one voyage between Melbourne and Sydney, all the scenery and costumes sank uninsured. And on a subsequently celebrated occasion in Ballarat, W.J. sacked a local singer called Mrs Armstrong for incompetence. He was the only manager who ever dared do such a thing to the great Melba, even unknown and untrained as she then was.

Kate's first daughter, Essie, born in such solitary deprivation, rose to be the star of the company, but then abandoned it for an unsuccessful marriage, leaving her stepfather prostrated at the collapse of his professional hopes. Kate, capable and resourceful, bundled the family back to London, where W.J. understudied

Irving's Lear (and actually played the part on alternate nights). But he realized that there was no chance for him in a London ruled by the great actor–managers. Australia was a lost place to him after Essie's desertion but there was always, as Kate pointed out, South Africa. In 1899, with a magnificent new wardrobe contrived by Kate out of material salvaged from shipwrecks and out of the trains of peeresses' robes sold by their owners, the Holloway Theatre Company arrived in Johannesburg, a city hardly remarkable for cultural sensitivity. Their first production, *Othello*, opened inauspiciously three days before the Jameson Raid, but that tour, ragged and unprofitable as it was, was to be the first of several, with the company swelled in talent by the involvement of the Holloways' own children, two daughters and a son.

The couple retired at last to a cottage outside Stowmarket and a life of rural quiet that neither of them much cared for. Once a widow, Kate threw herself into making costumes for her son's tours of South Africa and travelled to Durban to inspect his fiancée and then to Germany to visit a niece. It was only to be expected. Village life in Suffolk after decades of hectic travelling with a theatrical company must have seemed like riding in Rotten Row after pig-sticking all one's life in Rajputana.

The brightest single theatrical star in the Empire's heavens was undoubtedly Nellie Melba. She was born in Australia in 1861, the child of an emigrant Scottish builder named David Mitchell who passed on to his formidable daughter his profound disbelief in the doctrine that the meek shall inherit the earth. He was to achieve success; starting with a single sovereign, he went on to build some of the most distinguished buildings in Melbourne. His daughter was to show much the same gritty drive: although her mother would beg her to stop her childhood humming, she eventually became the world's most celebrated soprano.

Nellie had an extraordinary character, its purposefulness much assisted by a belief stemming from her earliest days that she possessed musical genius. Her mother and two aunts were musical, her sister Belle and her brother Ernest both sang, but her own gift transcended any of theirs and she knew it. From the beginning she displayed an inexhaustible toughness of mind and spirit which manifested itself in sharp business acumen, a steely determination to both be and stay the best, and a readiness to obliterate any rival who constituted the least threat. In addition to these alarming qualities, she possessed great generosity and a huge vitality and appetite for life, as well as a disregard for its sillier conventions. This trait she already displayed in her early teens, when she would rush out of her organ lessons at the Ladies' Presbyterian College in Melbourne to swim naked with the local boys in the Yarra River.

Melbourne was a strange nursery for such a vigorous character; Sydney would have suited her better with its air of cheerful defiance. Melbourne was very proper and proud of it, and Nellie was always glad to escape the city and rampage about on her father's grazing property thirty miles away. From the men and boys on the land she learned the oaths that she used all her life. She would say cheerfully of her supposed resemblance in later life to Queen Victoria, 'Don't say that! I hated the bloody woman.'

If Melbourne's rectitude was ill-suited to Melba's personality, Australia as a whole was hardly an adequate nurturing place for her voice. Musically the country was backward and the few professional teachers resident there were not of significant talent and were forced to patch together a living out of lessons and the occasional theatre and concert appearance. The first really big operatic production by international standards in Australia – Donizetti's *Lucia di Lammermoor* – was staged in the year of Nellie's birth, but that was only the beginning of an invasion of Australia by overseas singers and instrumentalists.

When Melba was nineteen she began singing lessons with Petro Cecchi – 'the most fashionable teacher in Melbourne' – who predicted that her voice would 'enthrall the world'. A year later, in 1881, she was 1400 miles away from Sr Cecchi, near Mackay in North Queensland where her father had taken both her and her sister after their mother's death. But she practised faithfully and was much in demand in local drawing rooms.

By the time she was twenty-one, Nellie had met and married Charles Armstrong, the son of an Irish baronet. His connections were a powerful attraction to Nellie, as were his looks, his horsemanship and his adventurousness. Whatever attracted him to her, it was certainly not her music and the marriage was a disaster from the beginning.

At least it took her south to Melbourne again on her honeymoon and she resumed her lessons. Concert audiences began to acclaim her as the 'Australian Nightingale' (the singing world of the late Victorian and Edwardian periods abounded in nightingales of various nationalities) and the return to a tin-roofed house in Mackay filled her with despondency. The despondency grew to despair and in January 1884 she accepted an invitation from Cecchi, bundled up her baby George, and left Armstrong for what was to prove an astonishing career.

It began with her introduction to John Lemmone, the flautist who was to become a lifelong friend and accompanist at concerts. In the first year, these brought her £750 in £5 fees. Twenty years later, returning to Australia as the 'Queen of Covent Garden', she could command over £2000 for a single concert. London was not initially bowled over by her, as it was inundated with aspiring prima donnas from the colonies; Sir Arthur Sullivan told her kindly that if she studied for another year he might manage to arrange a small part in *The Mikado* for her. What Sir Arthur missed, the great Paris teacher Mathilde Marchesi spotted. She took Nellie on as a pupil and ten years later was able to say with justifiable pride that Melba 'is today without rival on the lyric stage. . . . I am only repeating what the critics of every country in Europe and America have written, when I say that unquestionably, as regards taste, style and vocalization, this pupil of mine is superior to any living singer.'

In the operas of Verdi, Puccini, Donizetti and Gounod, Melba was to reign supreme, chiefly on account of her voice – she really did not possess much dramatic talent – but also because of her 'sharp ear for opportunity's knock'. She was to rule with undisputed though dictatorial sway at Covent Garden from 1888 until 1926, seeing the opera house through its golden period from 1890 until the outbreak of the First World War. For the building contractor's daughter from Melbourne to possess the opera's chief dressing room for her exclusive use, with 'MELBA. Silence! Silence!' painted on the door, was something indeed. She could command £400 a performance and boasted a host of influential friends and patrons.

Melba's handling of money was impressive. For many years she earned about £1000 per week – the Australian opera season of 1911 alone brought her in £46,000 – and although she spent freely, she kept strict accounts and was astutely advised by Alfred de Rothschild. Eventually her Rothschild-guided investments yielded more than her income, which satisfactory state of affairs – coupled with her voice and her way of life – enabled her to say briskly to a duchess who had inquired timidly if she would prefer to be a duchess or Nellie Melba, 'Melba! There are lots of duchesses but there is only one Melba.'

Nellie's emotional life was not quite so well arranged. Its high point was a liaison with the pretender to the French throne, the Duke of Orléans, who was eight years younger than her and was scared away in the end by the threat of being cited as co-respondent in divorce proceedings. A great deal of emotion was certainly channelled into her ruthless maintenance of supremacy both on stage and behind it. Even as eminent a tenor as John McCormack, who admitted that he sang better with her than with any other person, confessed between clenched teeth that he considered her 'an interfering bitch'.

She was, but she achieved great things despite, even partially because of it. For twenty-five years she travelled between England and Australia welcomed by phenomenal crowds and fanfares, discoursing upon music and the indestructibility of the British Empire, singing, teaching and buying and doing up houses. She sailed through on the massive tide of her talent and her personality. For highly favoured admirers she had tiepins made whose heads were in the form of a gold 'M' set with enamel and small diamonds; she made enough gramophone records to bring her £18,000 a year, insisting that each record should cost one shilling more than that made by any other singer and should bear her own distinctive mauve label; and during the First World War she sent soldiers notes pinned to socks exhorting them 'to show the Germans how the Australians can fight'.

She was, as Dr Johnson said of human nature in general, 'a mixture of Vice and Virtue, a contest of passion and reason'. She was also extraordinary, not least because her belief in herself carried her through 'at least twenty-five farewells' to a kind of immortality. 'There is no Anno Domini in art,' she told a newspaper reporter superbly in London in 1919. 'I have the voice of a genius. Then why should I not always sing beautifully as long as I always take care of it and do not forget what I have been taught? Why should I not sing for a thousand years?'

In fact she sang for sixty-five. She died in 1931 in Sydney. Her tombstone bears a few words of Mimi – her most celebrated and best-loved role – '*Addio senza rancore*' ('Farewell, without bitterness').

BIBLIOGRAPHY

ALLEN, Charles (ed.), *Plain Tales from the Raj*, Deutsch, 1975.

ALLEN, Charles, *Tales from the Dark Continent*, Deutsch Futura, n.d.

Articles from *The Bearer*, Summer 1977.

BALFOUR & YOUNG, *The Work of Medical Women in India*, Oxford University Press, 1929.

BARR, Pat, *The Memsahibs*, Secker & Warburg, 1976.

BEDDOE, Deidre, *Welsh Convict Women*, S. Williams, 1979.

BEER, Patricia, *Reader I Married Him*, Macmillan, 1974.

BENSON, A. C. and ESHER, Viscount (ed.), *Queen Victoria's Letters*, 1st series, John Murray, 1907.

BIRD, Isabella, *A Lady's Life in the Rocky Mountains*, University of Oklahoma, 1969.

BLACKWELL, Elizabeth, *Pioneer Work in Opening the Medical Profession for Women*, 1895.

BLANCH, Lesley, *Under a Lilac-Bleeding Star*, John Murray, 1963.

BRONTË, Charlotte, novels.

BROOKE HUNT, Violet, *A Woman's Memories of the War*, J. Nisbet, 1901.

BUTLER, Josephine, *Women's Work and Women's Culture*, Macmillan, 1869.

CALDER, Jenni, *The Victorian Home*, Batsford, 1977.

CARPENTER, Mary, *Our Convicts*, 1864.

CATER, W. F. (ed.), *Love Among the Butterflies*, Penguin, 1982.

CHADWICK, Owen, *The History of the Victorian Church*, Black, Vol. I, 1971; Vol. II, 1972.

CUNNINGHAM, Gail, *The New Woman and the Victorian Novel*, Macmillan, 1978.

DELAMONT, S. and DUFFIN, L. (ed.), *Nineteenth Century Woman*, Croom Helm, 1978.

DESMOND, *Botanical and Horticultural Dictionary*.

DICKENS, Charles, novels.

DIVER, Maud, *The Englishwoman in India*, W. Blackwood & Sons, Edinburgh, 1909.

DRUMMOND, Alison, *Married and Gone to New Zealand*, Oxford University Press, 1960.

ELIOT, George, novels.

ENSOR, *England 1870–1914*, Oxford History of England Vol. 14, Oxford University Press, 1936.

ESHER, Viscount, *The Journals of Queen Victoria*, John Murray, 1909.

GASKELL, Mrs, novels.

GRAND, Sarah, novels.

218

GREVILLE, Lady, *Ladies in the Field*, Ward & Downey, 1894.

GWYNN, Stephen, *The Life of Mary Kingsley*, Macmillan, 1932.

HADFIELD, HARLING, HIGHTON (ed.), *British Gardeners – A Biographical Dictionary*, Conde Nast, n.d.

HEALD, Madeline, *Down Memory Lane with Some Early Rhodesian Pioneer Women*, Books of Rhodesia, 1979.

HETHERINGTON, John, *Nellie Melba*, Faber, 1973.

HIBBERT, Christopher, *The Great Mutiny – India 1857*, Allen Lane, 1978.

HOBHOUSE, Emily, *Letters*.

HOBHOUSE, Emily, *Reports on the Distress Fund for South African Women and Children*, Friars Printing Association Ltd, n.d.

HOLLOWAY, David, *Playing the Empire*, Harrap, 1979.

HOWE, Bea, *A Galaxy of Governesses*, Ver Schoyle, 1954.

JEBB, Louise, *By Desert Ways to Baghdad*, Thomas Nelson & Sons, Edinburgh, n.d.

KAMM, Josephine, *Hope Deferred*, Methuen, 1965.

KINCAID, Dennis, *British Social Life in India 1608–1937*, Routledge & Kegan Paul, n.d.

KINGSLEY, Mary, *Travels in West Africa*, Frank Cass, 1965.

KISNER, Arlene, *Woodhull Claflin's Lives and Writings of Notorious Victoria Woodhull and Tennessee Claflin*, Time Change Press, Washington, New Jersey, 1972.

LAURENCE, E. C., RRC, *A Nurse's Life in War and Peace*, Smith, Elder & Co., 1912.

LEITH ROSS, Sylvia, *Beyond the Niger*, Lutterworth Press, 1951.

Letters from Charlotte Godley 1821–1907, Christchurch, New Zealand, 1951.

Letters of John Stuart Mill.

LONGFORD, Elizabeth, *Victoria RI*, Weidenfeld & Nicolson, 1964.

LUTYENS, Mary, *The Lyttons in India*, John Murray, 1979.

MACGREGOR, Miriam, *North Island Women of the Colonial Era*, Vols I & II, A. H. & A. W. Reed, Vol. I, 1973; Vol. II, 1975.

MADGEWICK, R. B., *Immigration into Eastern Australia*, 1937.

MARTINEAU, Harriet, *Home Duties*, Warne, 1869.

MARTINEAU, Harriet, *The Young Lady's Book of Advice and Instruction*, n.d.

MIDDLETON, Dorothy, *Victorian Lady Travellers*, Routledge & Kegan Paul, 1965.

MOBERLY BELL, E., *Flora Shaw*, Constable, 1947.

MOBERLY BELL, E., *Storming the Citadel*, Hyperion Press, 1982.

MOSLEY, Leonard, *Curzon*, Longman, 1960.

MUFFETT, D. J. M., *Sir George Goldie, Empire Builder Extraordinary*, Shearwater, 1978.

NATRISH, Sheila, *On the Edge of the Bush*, Craig Printing Co., Invercargill, New Zealand, n.d.

New Horizons, Her Majesty's Stationery Office, 1963.

NICOLSON, Nigel, *Mary Curzon*, Weidenfeld & Nicolson, 1978.

NORTH, Marianne, *Recollections of a Happy Life*, Macmillan, 1892.

POLLOCK, J. C., *The Shadows Fall Apart – The Story of the Zenana Bible & Medical Mission*, Hodder & Stoughton, 1958.

POWER, Frances, *The Duties of Women*, Cobbe, 1881.

PURDY, R. L., *The Journals of George Eliot*, Yale University Gazette, n.d.

QUAYLE INNIS, Mary (ed.), *The Clear Spirit – Twenty Canadian Women and Their Times*, University of Toronto Press, 1966.

RATTRAY, J., *Great Days in New Zealand Nursing*, A. H. & A. W. Reed, 1961.

RAVEN, S. and WEIR, A., *Women in History*, Weidenfeld & Nicolson, 1981.

RIDDELL, Charlotte Elizabeth, *A Mad Tour*, Richard Bentley, 1891.

ROBINSON, GALLAGHER & DENNY, *Africa and the Victorians*, Macmillan, 1965.

ROVE, Constance, *The Punch Book of Women's Rights*, Hutchinson, 1967.

SEARLE, Charlotte, *History of the Development of Nursing in South Africa*, Struik, Cape Town, 1965.

STENTON, D. M., *The English Woman in History*, George Allen & Unwin, 1957.

STICKNEY ELLIS, Sarah, *The Daughters of England*, London, 1845.

TEALE, Ruth, *Colonial Eve*, Oxford University Press, Melbourne, 1978.

TELFORD, J. C., *Women in the Mission Field*, W. Kelly, 1895.

TERROT, Charles, *The Maiden Tribute*, Frederick Muller, 1959.

THOMAS, P., *Indian Women Through the Ages*, Asia Publishing House, 1964.

TOOLEY, S. A., *The History of Nursing in the British Empire*, Bansfield, 1906.

TREVELYAN, G. M., *Illustrated English Social History*, Vol. IV, Penguin, 1964.

TROLLOPE, Anthony, novels.

VAN KIRK, Sylvia, *Many Tender Ties – Women in Fur Trade Society*, Watson & Dwyer, 1980.

VICINUS, Martha (ed.), *Suffer and Be Still*, Indiana University Press, 1972.

VICINUS, Martha (ed.), *The Widening Sphere*, Indiana University Press, 1977.

WALKOWITZ, Judith, *Women, Class & The State*, Cambridge University Press, 1980.

WATT, Margaret, *The Parson's Wife*, Faber, 1943.

WILLIS, W. N., *The White Slaves of London*, Stanley Paul, 1912.

WOODWARD, *The Age of Reform 1815–1870*, Oxford University Press, 1962.

YONGE, Charlotte, novels.

YOUNG, G. M., *Portrait of an Age: Victorian England*, Oxford University Press, 1977.

INDEX